W9-ABL-175

THE AUTOBIOGRAPHY OF A YAQUI POET

Refugio Savala, 1955

THE AUTOBIOGRAPHY OF A YAQUI POET

by Refugio Savala

Edited with
Background and Interpretations
by KATHLEEN M. SANDS

The University of Arizona Press
Tucson, Arizona

About the Editor...

KATHLEEN M. SANDS has worked personally with Refugio Savala since 1976. A specialist in American Indian literature and folklore, she joined the English faculty at Arizona State University in 1977. Sands holds a Ph.D. in literature from the University of Arizona. She has published articles in journals of American Indian studies and American literature.

Photographs courtesy of: Arizona Historical Society, pp. 72, 81, 94; George Dante Iacono and the Arizona State Museum, cover and frontispiece; David J. Jones, Jr., p. 184; Rosamond B. Spicer, pp. 4, 17, 24, 26, 56, 144, 170.

THE UNIVERSITY OF ARIZONA PRESS

Copyright © 1980
The Arizona Board of Regents
All Rights Reserved
Manufactured in the U.S.A.

Library of Congress Cataloging in Publication Data

Savala, Refugio.
      The autobiography of a Yaqui poet.

      Bibliography: p.
      Includes index.
      1. Savala, Refugio. 2. Yaqui Indians—Biography.
I. Sands, Katheen M. II. Title.
E99.Y3S28   970'.004'97   79-19817
ISBN 0-8165-0698-1
ISBN 0-8165-0628-0 pbk.

CONTENTS

PREFACE

The Man and His Work

Refugio Savala is a person of poetic sensibilities, a man of words. His autobiography is a detailed and comprehensive portrait of the growth of a man and artist in a period that parallels the growth of the Yaqui culture in Arizona.

In his youth, Refugio felt a strong urge to preserve in written form the Yaqui stories he had heard, and as he matured and came to broader and more complete knowledge of his unique cultural heritage, his desire to become a man of letters intensified. His driving interest in language and in Yaqui perception and way of life inspired him to attempt literary forms familiar to the non-Yaqui world in order to communicate his personal and cultural vision to those who might otherwise never know of it. In the course of his lifetime, he has translated oral tales, written his versions of Yaqui legends, described Yaqui personalities and occupations in character sketches, recorded and analyzed ceremonial songs and sermons, composed original ballads, created a body of personal poems, and set down his own and his family's history in his autobiography.

More than in any other aspect of his literary accomplishments, Savala demonstrates in his autobiography both his growing comprehension of the culture which bred him and his expanding facility with literary forms. Though it is his most ambitious written work, Refugio himself would probably never have considered setting down the story of his own life; he is a modest man. It was his long-time friend, Muriel Thayer Painter, with whom he had worked in translating a Yaqui Easter sermon and other traditional works, who suggested that his life might be of interest to the general public.

In 1964, while Refugio was in poor health and living in a Tucson nursing home, he showed Mrs. Painter some pages of a manuscript on which he had been working. They contained fragments of the story of his life, written in English and testifying to Refugio's ever-present urge to put his experiences and impressions into writing. These vignettes, however, were rather impersonal accounts of events.

Mrs. Painter suggested that Refugio try to personalize more fully what were essentially descriptions of various aspects of life in Yaqui communities. She told him to write about what he knew best, Yaqui culture, but to explain it in terms of his family's participation in it. She explained carefully that he should tell the story of his family in detail, as he had heard it and taken part in it.

Writing as Mrs. Painter suggested, Refugio slowly conceived the present form of the autobiography. Over a period of five years he set each incident down separately in a careful English longhand, then turned it over to Mrs. Painter, who typed it just as he had written.

The narrative which follows is essentially what Refugio wrote for Mrs. Painter. Some deletions and changes have been made to make it read smoothly, and the structure of separate parts has been reformed into logical chapters.

Refugio finished his autobiography in the late 1960s, and though both he and Mrs. Painter intended that it be presented to a general readership, it instead was consigned to the archives of the Arizona State Museum in Tucson, along with the other manuscript materials used in this volume. The project was not given any further attention until the spring of 1974, when I was told about it by Dr. Edward H. Spicer.

Only one reading convinced me that Refugio's narrative was significant for both its cultural and literary merit. Here was one of less than twenty existing written autobiographies of Indian men—an original piece of work, not an "as told to" narrative that was in any way affected by an intrusive recorder/editor.

I became determined to achieve Refugio's goal of giving his story to a non-Yaqui world. With continuing support and advice from Dr. Spicer, I began to edit the manuscript for publication.

After a year of work on the project, Refugio's location became known. When I finally met him, I found he fulfilled every expectation I had formed of him through my familiarity with his life story. The hours I spent with him increased my admiration, and I was honored by the acceptance, trust, and friendship he subtly and kindly offered me.

Refugio did not tell all in his autobiography; he is a rather private man. Hence I compiled a series of interpretive chapters to supply additional information and commentary on the events of the autobiography. These chapters were placed after the narrative, not before, for I wanted to avoid editorial intrusion in Refugio's very personal story.

Throughout the interpretive section, the emphasis is on the development of Refugio the writer, on the refinement of his poetic vision and his skill in expression. This is fitting, for Refugio, despite all his travels and all his occupations, is essentially a man of words.

KATHLEEN M. SANDS

ACKNOWLEDGMENTS

I am very grateful to Dr. Spicer for his confidence, advice, and support during my work on this narrative, and to the University of Arizona Foundation which, on his recommendation, granted funds for the research and translation necessary for the completion of the work. To Dr. Spicer and the Arizona State Museum, I am also grateful for the collection of Refugio's literary works and the character sketches in unpublished manuscripts. Without these resources, a full portrait of Savala would have been impossible.

I am also indebted to Western historian David Myrick, who made possible much of the clarification of railroad terminology and practice contained in the notes. His personal and professional enthusiasm for the project was invaluable.

For information concerning railroad policy and history in the Tucson area, I wish to acknowledge Charles McKissick and members of the Tucson Southern Pacific Engineering Department, who took time to educate me.

I also extend my thanks to my friend and colleague Rebecca Lee for the hours she spent criticizing the manuscript, especially for her thoughtful comments and suggestions. The University of Arizona Press deserves special credit for the sensitive and careful handling of the manuscript in all stages of editing and production.

For photographs, great appreciation goes to Rosamond B. Spicer, who not only provided pictures taken contemporaneously with Savala's young manhood, but who also, with the invaluable aid of Donald Bufkin of the Arizona Historical Society, did the research for the map of Tucson included in this book.

Finally, I extend my deepest appreciation to Refugio Savala for the strength of his narrative, the power of his style, and the resonance of his character.

K. M. S.

INTRODUCTION

Refugio Savala,
Cross-cultural Interpreter

By Edward H. Spicer

Refugio Savala's family, one among many groups of refugee Yaquis in about 1900, plodded behind their donkey cart northward through Sonora. All along the unpatrolled border mothers with babies, kinless old people, orphaned boys and girls cared for by compassionate friends, and occasional fortunate families who had somehow managed to hold together—Yaquis by the hundreds walked the desert trails. They searched for freedom from the daily fear of being shot, hanged, or herded together and shipped by boat from Guaymas southward into permanent exile. Refugio, tiny refugee with his loving family, lay in the cart unaware that he was one of the many suffering the most desperate crisis of their history.

Refugio Savala's life spans that phase in the experience of the Yaqui people during which they faced the threat of extinction, held fast, and went on to survive. In Sonora during the later nineteenth century, fertile Yaqui land was coveted by the landlords who ruled the state. Yaquis fought to keep their land from being absorbed into feudal estates on which, if the governors of Sonora had their way, they would have become landless peons. Yaqui resistance to this fate was so determined and so effective that federal troops had to be sent to back up the Sonoran soldiers whom the Yaquis had come to despise. In the face of Mexico's full military strength, Yaquis were forced out of their ancient towns along the Yaqui River. Nevertheless from mountain strongholds they continued to wage guerrilla warfare with such telling effect that President Porfirio Díaz declared a policy of deportation of all Yaquis to the henequen and sugar plantations of Yucatán and Oaxaca. Colonel Emilio Kosterlitzky, commanding the Federal Rural Police, relentlessly rounded up Yaquis wherever they could be found in Sonora. By 1908 he had picked up thousands and either killed them or shipped them southward. What had been a population of at least 20,000 was rapidly reduced to less than 5000. Many not picked up in the net of the Rural Police escaped into Arizona. If President Díaz's government had not fallen in 1910, only the few hundred Yaquis who had fled to the United States would have lived to carry on the proud Yaqui tradition.

It was in the new Yaqui settlements in Arizona that Refugio Savala lived the major portion of his life. We glimpse in his autobiography something of the tribulations suffered by the early Yaqui pioneers. We see their beginnings as penniless immigrants, forced to squat on land and build makeshift houses. We see them start at the bottom in the lowest paid jobs as railroad workers and cotton-pickers. We get some feel for early twentieth century Tucson viewed from this particular level of society.

However, it is characteristic of Refugio Savala that he tells his story without the slightest tinge of self-pity. He does not look upward to compare his boyhood with that of people better off. Rather he looks steadily at everything immediately around him and describes his enjoyment in it, as a boy in a good family coming into contact with warm and friendly teachers. There is no doubt about the poverty of the squatter communities or the people's desperate uncertainties; they never knew if they could remain where they had settled from month to month. These were the realities, and Refugio recounts them. But his emphasis is on the delights of family life and boyhood in a freer and, as he saw it, happier era in Tucson.

For Yaquis in this period the contrast with what they had left behind was tremendous. For the first time within the lifetime of most there was no sudden crack of rifles, no constant fear that Rural Police would ride up and demand whether they were Yaqui or not. There was still the hope that the desperate guerrilla fighters in the Bacatete Mountains would somehow, against impossible odds, keep the Mexican soldiers from taking every inch of the sacred homeland. In fact there were Yaquis here and there among the refugee population of Tucson and the Salt River Valley who urged that Yaquis in Arizona smuggle ammunition and guns to the Yaqui River, where a few guerrillas held out through the first decade of the twentieth century. But all this was further and further behind, and days began to be full of new satisfactions as jobs became steady, families regrouped, and children were all around.

At first Yaquis in Arizona had no understanding of their legal position. They had been accustomed to hiding their identity in Sonora and even had been forced to abandon their distinctive ceremonies, because such observances would reveal they were Yaquis, and neighbors might tell the Rural Police. Yaqui refugees had in fact been given political asylum in the United States and were not regarded by immigration officials as subject to deportation. This, however, was nowhere stated in any official document until 1931, and so the situation was still doubtful as Yaquis saw it. Nevertheless they did begin to revive their most characteristic and important religious ceremonies—in 1906 at Guadalupe Village near Tempe and in 1909 at Tierra Floja Ranch near Tucson. At the ranch the Yaqui laborers brought the whole complex organization of the traditional Easter ceremony into operation. From this time on the Yaquis may be regarded as having laid their new foundations in the United States. In Sonora, however, the Díaz government had not yet collapsed, and deportation and massacre continued until the Revolution in 1910.

The revival of the religious life of the Yaqui towns made it once more possible for Yaqui children to learn the traditional ways in which the heart of their culture was expressed. As a boy Refugio Savala became ill, and his mother made a vow to the Virgin Mary that he would dance with the Matachin dancers for three years, a vow which he fulfilled. Other than this, Refugio did not participate formally in the developing communities; he stood aside from the various political crosscurrents in the villages, but maintained a deep and continuous interest in all that took pace, especially in his home community of Pascua Village. Such interest, without holding office or participating in the political conflicts that evolved around such men as Juan Pistola, seems wholly consistent with Refugio's basic approach to life—a blend of loving appreciation combined with personal detachment, which is in fact the mark of the literary person.

It may come as something of a surprise to find that a railroad track laborer saw beauty in iron spikes and rail clamps, in the tongs of the gandy dancers, in the tamping of the rocks between the ties, and in the heaving up and carrying of the rails by the eight-man gangs. But Refugio finds as much to make poetry about in railroad tools, routine daily jobs, and proud accomplishments like bridges and smooth trackbeds, as he does in the desert trees of Cañada del Oro or in the pine forests of the Mount Shasta country. There have been others who have expressed something of railroad work and workers; but in Refugio's songs we find much more than the delight and pride expressed in such American folk traditions as the saga of John Henry, the steel-driving man. Refugio's joy in track labor and its accoutrements is a different thing from the lore of John Henry; it is the product of an authentic poet seeing and feeling beauty without the need to shout tall tales at the top of the voice.

The breadth of Refugio's humanity is apparent as he moves from steel tools to the natural world. There is quiet savor to be found in both his prose and poetry as he writes of the desert trees, plants, and flowers, a pleasure rooted in close observation. This is apparent in the account of his summers as a "walking cowboy" with his boyhood companion at the western end of the Santa Catalina Mountains near Oracle, Arizona. The feeling is deeper in his later account of how the Oregon forest moved him as he viewed it for hours on end while on military guard duty.

It is hard not to connect Refugio's delight in natural things with his awareness of Yaqui traditional poetry in the deer songs. Nearly all of these sing of the *seya aniya*, the "flower world" in which the supernatural deer lives "under the dawn." Most give some vignette of this "magical" world, as he calls it, from which the deer and his music come: the "flower fawn" among the trees, the deer rubbing his velvet-covered antlers on the tree branches, a cloud towering up and coming down as rain. The special feeling that Refugio has for nature seems somehow connected with his capacity for immersion in the traditional ancient flower world, which he has interpreted for non-Yaquis.

The personal qualities which appear in Refugio's writing are important for understanding his human quality as a poet and as a man, quite apart from the particular culture and language which have given him his chief nourishment. However, these remarkable personal qualities also have contributed to an exceptional kind of culture contact in the Arizona-Sonora milieu. Refugio has been a figure of some importance in the cultural life of Tucson, and hence in the whole region of Sonora-southern Arizona. More than any other Yaqui he has brought about significant cross-cultural understanding between the native Yaqui and the Anglo cultures. His contribution here, stemming in part out of his poetic and literary quality of mind, is unusual in any situation of contact between very different cultures.

Of course, there is no such thing as "cultural contact." There is contact rather between individuals participating in different cultural traditions. Refugio has throughout his life been very much a participant in Yaqui tradition. In contast with a political and leadership involvement, Refugio's immersion in Yaqui society has been intellectual and emotional—a wellspring of his interest in life from his sensitive youth through his later years in a hospital room. His depth of feeling for the core values of Yaqui tradition and concern for shades of meaning have made him an exceptional interpreter of Yaqui culture. Moreover his interest in the role, deepening through the period of his maturity, has been successfully coupled with his intense concern to master the intricacies of three languages. Apparently on his own initiative in the first burst of his youthful talents, Refugio tried to write about Yaqui life in the homeland as it had been told to him by his uncle Loreto Hiami. Coming somewhat mysteriously out of what was for the Arizona-bred child the legendary land of his parents, Don Loreto was a force in Refugio's life that left its permanent mark. The boy had felt a great compulsion to listen and then a similar need to repeat the *etehoi* (tellings) to his companions; the result was indelible formulations of how people had lived in the old country, as well as what were to the Arizona youths the mysteries of Yaqui ceremony, ritual, and belief.

For Refugio literary expression was also a necessary part of learning Spanish and English. When a retired Kansas schoolteacher, Miss Thamar Richey, became deeply involved in Yaqui affairs and suggested that Refugio write out in English what he knew of Yaqui tradition, he had Don Loreto's accounts ready in his mind. The enterprise received further impetus when Professor John H. Provinse of the University of Arizona came to see Refugio in 1934–35. The young Yaqui man produced a sheaf of sketches (some of which appear in this book) in imperfect English but with honest feeling for Yaqui life in Sonora. They carry some of the character of the "rural" life that his parents had lived, and the mountain Yaqui life, as Refugio calls it, which is to say, the life of those Yaquis who took refuge in the Bacatete Mountains during their almost continuous fighting with the Mexican soldiers.

The next phase in this aspect of Refugio's life as cross-cultural interpreter was for him a period of profound new experience which he remembers both as a discipline and an exciting creation. In the spring of 1939 the great anthropologist Bronislaw Malinowski came to Tucson for a brief stay. During the visit he became interested in the Yaqui Easter ceremony and inspired a Tucson woman, Muriel Thayer Painter, to begin what became a lifetime study of that complex and beautiful ritual. Refugio was not in Tucson during Malinowski's residence, but in 1947 I introduced him to Muriel Painter in what was the first meeting of a long and fruitful association. Their first period of work together involved the translation into English of a long sermon in Yaqui, which a Maestro of Pascua Village had allowed to be recorded on discs in 1941, before tape recordings had come into use. The process of making a really satisfactory translation required first a careful transcription of the long discourse. It was in making this transcription that a new phase of Refugio's life began.

University of Arizona scholars had developed a way of writing Yaqui which Refugio immediately recognized as much more exact and understandable than the rough and ready orthography which he already knew and which Yaquis had used for centuries in writing letters to one another. He has said that learning to use this system of writing marked a new understanding for him not only of Yaqui, but also of the other two languages which he had been using all his life. He worked regularly for months under the direction of Mrs. Painter until a complete and carefully checked transcription had been produced.

The next step in the translation made it clear that Refugio possessed a genius for the work on which he had embarked. It involved the closest possible contact with the Maestro Ignacio Alvarez, in an effort to become aware of every shade of meaning which he had intended. The necessary discussion between Refugio and Don Ignacio was carried on, of course, in Yaqui. In the course of it, it became apparent that Refugio was thoroughly capable of listening and learning and not imposing his own understanding of Yaqui words and phrases on the older, experienced ritual specialist. Long periods of discussion were required before Refugio was ready to try the translation into English. Discussion was also often necessary between Refugio and Don Ignacio on the one hand and Muriel Painter and myself on the other.

Ultimately there emerged a translation which was essentially Refugio's, and we had no doubt that it was a rendering into English of what the old Maestro thought and originally intended his sermon to mean. Passages of the translation seem often not fully clear in English; this is more a result of the fact that there are many concepts, especially in the realm of ritual, which are not readily expressed in English, rather than of inadequacies in Refugio's English. It was during the months of group work in seeking and putting into English Don Ignacio's ideas that Refugio learned, as it were, a new trade—the interpretation of one culture for full understanding by participants in another culture. It is clear from what he said in later years that he has always regarded this professional calling with high seriousness.

The sermon is concerned, primarily, although not exclusively, with ideas and rituals which stem most clearly from Christian sources, that is, from the teachings of the original Jesuit missionaries who first converted Yaquis, beginning in 1617, and from subsequent Christian influences. All these Christian features have acquired their own shades of meaning for Yaquis, who for more than 100 years during the nineteenth century were not in close contact with representatives of the Catholic church. It was these special Yaqui interpretations, which had grown up through the centuries, that Don Ignacio was deeply concerned to have made clear in the translation and which resulted in Refugio ultimately realizing that he was getting a new education in Yaqui traditions. But there was much more in the Easter ceremony besides these obviously Christian-derived elements, and there was something more even in the sermon.

The next phase of Refugio's work with Muriel Painter involved the interpretation of this aspect of Yaqui religion. Ultimately the greater part of ten years was devoted intermittently to Refugio's dictating texts in Yaqui and translating short texts which Mrs. Painter recorded from fifty or sixty other Yaquis. These had to do with the performance and meaning of the Deer Dancer and the Pascolas, the songs to which the Deer Dancer dances, and the stories which the Pascolas tell, as well as with a dozen other aspects of the rich and intricate Yaqui ceremonial activities. In this work Refugio achieved what certainly no other Yaqui has in the careful, conscientious interpretation of Yaqui cultural values in language that can be understood by non-Yaquis. The volume of the work thus accomplished is tremendous and appears as a part of Muriel Painter's thirty-year study of the Easter ceremony at Pascua Village, *With Good Heart* (Tucson: University of Arizona Press, in press).

It seems to me that Refugio is justly spoken of as a poet. If his specific use of words in English or Spanish seems often to fall short of truly affective language, it is still apparent that his imagination is no ordinary one and that its tendency is consistently toward the poetic transmutation of experience. There is no doubt in my view that Refugio is truly a man of letters, as a newspaper reporter of the 1940s so surprised Refugio by calling him. In this respect he is not wholly unique, for he once had a contemporary who was also a poet and a Yaqui. Well known in the Yaqui towns of southern Sonora during the 1930s and 1940s was a resident of Esperanza named Ambrosio Castro. Castro was, like Refugio, a many-sided man of letters, but limited to two languages since he knew no English. He wrote poems in Yaqui, popular ballads called *corridos* in Spanish, and told them to others who recorded them in a considerable volume of tales, legends, myths, and creative prose of his own composition. Some of these pieces were published in a 1940 book in Spanish by Alfonso Fabila, *Las Tribus Yaquis de Sonora, su Cultura y Anhelada Autodeterminación*. Others appear in a 1959 volume in English edited by Ruth Warner Giddings, *Yaqui Myths and Legends*.

The literary interests of Castro and Savala suggest that they represent a not uncommon type of Yaqui intellectual. How many have there been in the Yaqui past? We may expect others, I believe, others who will continue to develop the Yaqui tradition in the future.

I first met Refugio in November of 1936. He had come back to Pascua Village after a year of wandering in California and other western states. He had returned, characteristically, to fulfill his kinship obligations as a relative of a man who had been killed on the Southern Pacific Railroad tracks.

When Refugio's duties at the funeral and after were over, he dropped in to visit my wife and me where we lived that year in a crumbling adobe house in the village. He made a most vivid impression on me as he sat through the afternoon and shared a supper cooked hastily on our old kerosene stove. It was a cold night, but cozy inside. Refugio was in a mood to talk and went over in a thoughtful way his recent varied experiences in hobo jungles and in railroad work.

Our guest was in a deeply melancholy mood. His talk ran to death, first long, detailed speculation regarding the several alternative causes of the death of his relative on the railroad tracks, speculation in which careful rationality was dominant. Then he suddenly changed mood to tell us of the death of his mother and how he himself now wished for death. He described death as an angel whose attraction for him was almost irresistible and told us that in his dreams he found himself having to follow her. Later I learned that some of the phrases Refugio used were actually verses from a poem he had written when in the same melancholy mood.

This mingling of his poetry with his life was still characteristic of Refugio much later, when he wrote and talked from his bed in the Tucson Veterans Administration Hospital. When I visited him there in 1976 I found that he frequently used in his talk whole lines and stanzas which I had recorded thirty years before. He also broke occasionally into corridos, which he sang softly there in the hospital, corridos which he had composed and his fellow Yaqui laborers had liked and sung to one another in Yaqui. The songs were not irrelevant to what we were speaking of, but on the contrary illuminated our conversation about the old days on the railroad track gangs. From the November night of our first meeting there had been no question in my mind about the remarkable qualities of Refugio Savala as man and poet.

In the spring of 1941 I had asked Refugio to teach me Yaqui preparatory to going to Sonora to work among Yaquis on their cultural history and town organization. For a couple of months he demonstrated that he loved teaching. I still have a very thick folder of his many paradigms of Yaqui verbs illustrating the use of the great number of verbal suffixes and pronouns as prefixes. He gave me pages of lessons ringing all the possible variations on a single verb form. Painstakingly written out in the transcription form used for Don Ignacio's sermon, these lessons were homework which I had to perform and have ready the next day. For hours then we discussed the daily lessons. When I finally left for Sonora, Refugio's voice speaking Yaqui was ringing in my ears. It served me in good stead when I took up my research in the Yaqui towns and found myself immediately challenged to demonstrate what command of Yaqui I had.

Refugio Savala was still vigorous, despite a disabling stroke, when this autobiography was published in 1980. He was devoted, as always, to hard work. He maintained a daily routine, sitting on his hospital bed, translating the Old Testament into Yaqui. He had been converted in 1967 to an evangelical Protestant sect and felt that he had been called by God to make the translation, as the "best thing that I could do for my people." He said that he never really wanted for a Yaqui word, that he got divine help always in his search for the Yaqui equivalents of the words that he found in the Spanish version of the Bible from which he worked. Often he looked up Spanish words in English; then he worked from the English into Yaqui. He was using the Yaqui transcription which he first learned for the Easter sermon of Don Ignacio Alvarez.

We may be sure that Refugio's translation has been as careful and exact as he can make it, and also that his rendering in Yaqui very probably has something like the picturesque and poetic qualities which have moved and charmed readers of the King James Bible for centuries. Of course, only native speakers of Yaqui will be able fully to appreciate his work. Who among the 25,000 Yaquis in Sonora and the 6000 in Arizona will be Refugio's audience? The translator has not been concerned with the practical outcome of his divinely inspired task. Between visits of relatives and friends, he has remained occupied almost wholly with the exacting duty of producing a precise and deeply meaningful translation. He began by putting Yaqui thought into English; in the end he was putting Spanish and English versions of Hebrew into Yaqui.

THE AUTOBIOGRAPHY

by

Refugio Savala

The Yaquis in Sonora in 1904

An Autobiographical Poem by Refugio Savala

Where my Indian parents had a home
Just awhile ago I was born.
The sun circled the celestial dome
And began my task; I am outworn.

A home it was by them called,
A mere hut built of clay and stone.
It once my mother recalled
In her words of most pleasant tone.

Out of the hand of Izábal,
Through miracles of St. Francis,
My father Martín Savala
Left us in desperate frenzy.

For Indians of my native race
All were persecuted, young and old.
The wolf was on every trace
To away with every Indian household.

These things happened in the days
When I was a baby in the cradle,
The time mother in town delays.
She was caught, but she was prayerful.

Still a feeble child, my dear sister
In agony spent the whole night
Alone with me in sinister fear
All night long crying to clear daylight.

Desperately she made a rag doll
Soaked in milk to me was given
Till the bell in capilla *did toll.*
It was morning in Magdalena.

My mother was allowed to speak to Barrón
in broken español,
"Ne ca mutiam veje tua matchi.
Tengo niño que mama."

[2]

"Lady thou art not criminal
To pay the fine and depart from here."
Thus Barrón spoke. It was final,
And mother returned to sister dear.

Mother saw women and children;
Because they were Yaqui Indians,
They were tortured and stricken,
Were made guilty as barbarians.

From the great haciendas all over,
The innocent workers were taken,
Peons who were all peace lovers,
But were Indians, thus forsaken.

Some kind masters saved their men
Before their great misfortune came.
The unmerciful only kept them
To betray them as preserved game.

Those who were caught were cast in jail.
"Las embarcaciones ya se van"
Was then made a song and tale,
Yaquis taken to Yucatán.

While the wild ones in the jungle
Were not then even mentioned,
The drum continued its rumble,
and the hostile warriors cautioned.

For this reason men to this date
Forever hopeful God worship
As the last to mark their awful fate,
Bear the scars of their master's whip.

A great man among many was risen
To free in Mexico her people
For whom many songs enliven,
When joy he brought to the feeble.

[3]

1. RELOCATION

The Search for Freedom and Security

It's springtime again in Pascua.
We are all together again.
Happiness crowns the little village.
Laughter replaces the thought of pain.
$\qquad$—Refugio Savala

In the beginning of 1900, the federal government of Mexico sent out a decree to get rid of all the Yaquis in the state of Sonora. By reason of this order, the governor of the state started persecution and execution of the race, and in many cases even Yoris [Mexicans] were taken just because they spoke Yaqui.

In this tribulation, I was born in August of 1904 in the little town of Magdalena south of the U.S. border. The persecution going on, my father, to avoid being taken, drifted to Arizona to work on the Benson-Nogales branch of the Southern Pacific Railroad. My mother, though, remained at home in Magdalena, making tortillas to sell among Mexican *comadres* [friends]. When my mother made a trip to town with my brother Agustín,* the raiders came and they were both taken

---

*Throughout the narrative Savala refers to this brother by the name Fernando.

[5]

to jail. When this occurred, I was still a child at the breast, and my older sister Agustina was left at home to care for me alone. At night, when I started crying, she found some milk in a container and made a fire to warm it, but then she found it hard to feed me with a spoon. In her predicament, she conceived an idea to make a little rag doll, and dipping the head of the little doll in the milk, she managed to feed me until I stopped crying. This performance she continued until morning. This part of the story my sister told me years later when she was a grown-up and married.

Meanwhile, all during the night my mother had been prayerful in jail. When morning came, she asked a guard if she could talk to the chief of the jail. He arranged for her to see the judge. My mother was determined to say whatever she could in her broken Spanish, and when she stood before the fierce-looking person they called Barrón, she said, "*¿Señor, no puedo pagar la multa para ir con mi hijo chiquito?*" [Can I not pay the fine in order to go with my little boy?] Here God answered her prayers because Barrón answered her, saying, "*Señora, tu no eres criminal si vas a salir para ir con tu hijo ahorita.*" [You are no criminal if you should leave in order to go right away with your little son.]

When Barrón released her, he sent two guards to protect her from being taken again. Thus released, my mother came home to me and my dear sister. In later times she told me this story to instruct me in the power of prayer.

Soon my father got enough money and came back home from Arizona to take us out of Sonora. He brought good news to our people about himself and other Yaquis who had accompanied him on his first trip and about the opportunities to work freely for a good wage. Many Yaquis, learning of this, started drifting on their way north.

The Yaquis did not go to Arizona because of ambition or to seek riches, but went in search of peace and freedom and to escape from heartless killers.* We hail the Southern Pacific

---

*By 1900 the conflict between Yaquis and Mexicans had become so intense that the military came to occupy the eight pueblos of the Yaqui people which stretched east along the Río Yaqui from near Guaymas, Sonora. The occupation led most families to leave their native villages, for they would not accept

for having provided all these Yaqui refugees shelter, wage work, and food.

During this time, when all the jails in the state of Sonora were loaded, the government started the embarcation to take Yaquis to Yucatán. The good masters saved their peons by informing them before the raiders came so they could escape to the mountains. Among those who got away were my grandparents, so when my father came, they were with us at home.

My grandfather had four good pack burros, and these were used to move us to Arizona, carrying all our belongings. I was brought in my parents' arms, being a baby refugee— therefore Refugio.

The railroad company gave accommodations in camp cars to all the workers. The camp we moved to was equipped with stoves inside, a water car, and a commissary car loaded with food.

The foreman of the extra gang was Palmer Gauch, called "palma gacha" by his men, which means stooped-down palm tree. Memories of this good man have stayed in the minds of all the Yaquis of Tucson. Talking with men who actually were in the camp we came to from Sonora confirms my parents' story concerning these first days in Arizona. The camp was mobile, moving as jobs required. Soon we moved from Patagonia on the Benson-Nogales branch to the yard in Benson. Our camp was placed at the west end of the bridge crossing the San Pedro River. Here I started seeing things as grown-up people saw them.

Then my father was given a transfer to Sahuarita on the Tucson Nogales branch, and we got acquainted with some Mexican nationals. My brother and I enjoyed hearing stories

---

confiscation of their lands and domination by the Mexicans. Some fled north to the rugged Bacatete Mountains from which they carried on an intense guerrilla war with federal troops. Others dispersed to the haciendas of northwest Mexico, seeking refuge by blending in with the peon population.

Many Yaquis crossed the border into Arizona, where they found work on the railroads and in the cottonfields or manufactured adobe blocks for sale. In Sonora, those who did not escape were arrested, jailed, and deported to the sugarcane fields of Oaxaca or the henequen plantations of Yucatán, where they were worked brutally. Families were scattered, the children often being distributed as servants to households throughout Sonora.

[7]

that our Mexican friends told us under the pleasant shade of the huge water tank. Our friends told us about their country, praising it in a simple way for little children to comprehend. These two men were educated, I perceived, for the way they accented their words showed their refinement. This planted in my mind a strong desire to speak Spanish like they did, a skill which, by grace, I later acquired.

In those days my father was getting only one dollar a day, a section laborer's pay, but my mother, being thrifty, soon got enough money for the next move. She was anxious to join her sister who had separated from us at Benson, moving with all her family to Tucson, so my father asked for a transfer to come to work in the Tucson section yard gang. The road master arranged this transfer for him, but transportation was not provided. This move would have been much easier with pack burros, if we had still had them, but they had been sold away to a trader. Nonetheless there was money to pay the fares for all of us. Tickets were not bought, but the conductor was to charge the fares from each of us, and all our belongings went on the baggage car. The bedding was all made up in two large rolls, wrapped with heavy canvas tarps kept together with ropes. The only up-to-date item in our belongings was a trunk that was the family wardrobe.

Then the hour came when I had to leave my Mexican friends, "Cele," my baby-talk name for Celedonio, and "Mon," for Ramón. I was really crying and Cele, the oldest of the two, obviously knew why. He started comforting me with the words, "*No llores, Kuquito. Dios te lleva en tu camino.*" [Don't cry, little Kuko. God takes you on your road.] Kuko is short for Refugio. He gave us the last blessing, "*Dios sea vuestra salud*" [God be your health]. Shaking hands, I said, "Adios, Cele! Adios, Mon!"

They both said, "When you come to the city, you will have many children to play with, Kukito." "City" was a charming word, so I was happy after all. (My father reminded our friends to come downtown to see us, giving them directions to the section workers' quarters in the Tucson yard.)

The train loomed into view. My father stood in the center of the track, and with a white handkerchief, he started swing-

SAVALA FAMILY GENEALOGY

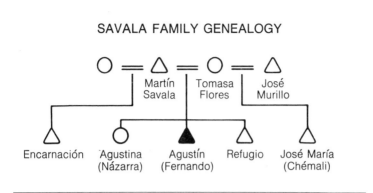

ing his right hand below his waist to stop the train. The engineer answered with two short blasts of the whistle, and the train stopped. The engine was of the type we later saw near the University of Arizona campus. We climbed aboard with all our things.

Our compartment on the train was half chair and half baggage car. All the members of my family were snugly in place. It was afternoon, and I was on the sunny side, so I could see the San Xavier mountains.

This trip was the most exciting of my whole life. All the landscape seemed to me like it was turning around in circles, but somehow I controlled myself from going dizzy. We spent the afternoon on the trip, almost at sundown arriving at the Twin Buttes depot in Tucson. There were horse-drawn taxis waiting for the train. Obviously my parents knew what to do, so they hired a taxi to take us to my aunt's place. The taximan was a generous person to take all of us for two dollars to the south edge of the city. I later learned that a man named Valencia was the owner of the taxi buggies and that they were called *berlinas*. It was sundown when we finally arrived, and there were tears of joy shed in this family reunion of my mother and aunt.

That evening my father gave me the greatest surprise of my whole life, playing the harp while my uncle played the

[9]

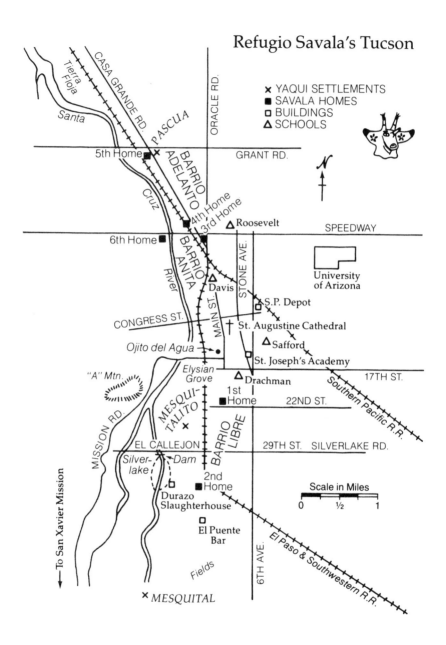

Refugio Savala's Tucson

× YAQUI SETTLEMENTS
■ SAVALA HOMES
□ BUILDINGS
△ SCHOOLS

Drawn by Nora Voutas
from information compiled by Rosamond B. Spicer
with the assistance of Don Bufkin.

violin. My uncle brought the harp inside, and he sat down to tune his violin. The pitch was set in *campanilla*, which is regular tuning for Mexican tunes, the *contradanza* and *mariachis*. These two men were both artists, for they displayed the most beautiful melody in Yaqui Pascola music.

Working in the SP yard, my father saw that the scrap lumber which came from the repair shop was put to good use. He asked for scrap and was given permission to take it all. We hauled it from the yard to a location not far from my aunt and uncle's home.* When enough lumber was brought to the place, the house was started. The posts to hold the beams and rafters were made of whole and split track ties. The house was a long boxcar shape at first; then it was divided to make two big rooms which later served a good purpose and proved the foresight of both my parents. The east end room was for us to live in.

When we were settled, my father started digging a well. Within a week water was reached and from then on all went right.

The next important step my parents took was to put us in school at St. Joseph's Convent.† It happened that all three of us were put with the same teacher, Sister Catalina, a Mexican expatriate of Sonora, who had the class of *parbulos*, the baby class. In class, I was always falling asleep, so the sister would pick me up in her arms to take me to the convent. I think I was still a *tutu' uli ili usi goochia* [pretty little boy baby, or grasshopper] when she was carrying me. I would look on her face, enjoying a most glorious sensation, thinking she was a

---

*During the first decade of the twentieth century, Yaqui households grew up in small clusters on unoccupied land at the edges of new agricultural areas or in urban barrios on the outskirts of cities. Like Refugio's family, the refugees were often squatters on land not yet seen as desirable by others. Refugio's aunt lived at the north end of Barrio Libre, a small settlement of Yaquis, Mexicans, and Papago Indians on the south side of Tucson. Tucson was at that time an active community of 13,000, a tiny fraction of its 1978 estimated population of 460,000.

†That Refugio should be enrolled in the nearby Catholic school is not surprising, since the Yaqui people were Christianized by the Jesuits in their original eight pueblos in the seventeenth century. Though Yaqui religious beliefs and rituals have taken on such highly distinctive characteristics as the well-known Easter ceremony, the people's affiliation to the Catholic church has remained basically consistent.

[11]

saint of my dreams. *"Tutu' uli ili usi goochi."* [Cute little boy baby.] This was in the morning. In the afternoon she would take me to the convent and give me a warm glass of milk and cookies and put me to bed until time to go home at two o'clock. I was blessed in the time of my childhood—many children to play with, my brother Fernando always my guardian. I was always having a pleasant time.

With the abundance of water available from the well, my mother started a miniature farm to teach us children to plant and cultivate all sorts of edible plants that bear fruit. These were corn, beans, chilis, watermelons, cantaloupes, tomatoes, and pumpkins. The corn was planted in rows, and all the vines were sown in basins separate from the row plants. Here we were also in school, and my own mother our teacher, but there was no falling asleep in class for me.

When all the plants were well started, we came from school just to water our little farm. This we did by drawing water from the well by a pulley and rope. My brother drew the water, while my sister and I carried it in pails to the basin plants. The row plants we irrigated by pouring the water on one end of the row.

My mother planted the chili and tomato seeds in a box until they came up in little sprouts, and when they were ready, she transplanted them in between the corn in the rows. We had started planting in May and the harvest began in July. By August we had green corn, fresh string beans, green chilis, watermelons, cantaloupes, and tender pumpkins to eat. We did wonderfully well for a first season, but unfortunately the city claimed all the land along the arroyo where we lived, though they informed us to remain at our location until next year.

Since we did not have to relocate right away, my father started to build a ramada on the north side of the house. There was an ancient willow tree due west down the arroyo, so when the structure was up, my father started carrying shoulder-loads of green willow branches. My brother and I made *tercies* [bundles] to carry on our shoulders too, and soon there was enough to cover the top. Presently, there was a fresh green ramada. My father walked a distance and looked back at the finished work, well satisfied. He sent my mother and us to look. We went, and facing it, we all shouted in one voice, "*Tutu'uli, tutu'uli, tutu'uli!*" [very pretty!] thrice for emphasis. When we came back to Father, there was no need to speak. He saw our pleasure in our expressions. Others did not see the ramada as we saw it, but to us it was truly enchanting.

My mother already visualized an olla under it and arranged to have one brought to her. To put it up, my father went to the woods to cut a three-pronged branch. When he brought it, he dug a deep hole in the ground, planting the bottom part of the post deep so that the olla's rim would be within the children's reach. Then he stripped the green bark from it and changed it white. When the post was set in the right place and the bark peeled, my mother gave the last touch to the olla to bring out the color, and then it was put, I remember I said "snugly" in place under the ramada to hold fresh drinking water.

When all these things were finished, a family came to our home in search of a place to live. My parents agreed to give them the room at the west end of the house for as long as they had any use for it, for my parents had built the house of two rooms for this purpose. The Sánchez family took the room, happy and thankful, and my parents smiled to see them happy. We children were happy too, because we had three new children to play with. They were friendly children. One of the boys, Juan, was the nephew of the head of the family, Loreto Sánchez. From this time on we also played with our girl cousins. Our pastime in the evenings was to go out and play "London Bridge is Falling Down," singing it in our own way, "*Florindichi, Florinda, Florinda canastita de algodón*" [Dear Florinda, Florinda, Florinda, little basket of cotton].

Loreto Sánchez and my father were both devout Catholics, and going to church every Sunday was a pleasant affair for both families.

Our *tevat kus* [household cross] was in front on the north side yard. Very close to the well, the two fathers would stand facing the ramada and the cross. They would say in Yaqui,

[13]

"Our heavenly Father, we are going to church to hear Thy word and to amend our souls in prayers. *Dios achai em vale' epo.*" [God the Father, be it Thy will.] When this short ceremony was ended, the fathers would say, "*Hantebu!*" [Let's go!] It was nice to see the two men heading the little procession starting off for church. First we had to cross many vacant lots and then walk six blocks and around the school yard until we came to the Cathedral San Agustín downtown. It was somewhat old-fashioned, for it had not yet been remodeled to its later beautiful structure.

Every time when we came from home to the church, the preparations for the service to start would be going on. The candles would be lighted, then the bells rung. The priest officiating would come out with the paten held on both hands. From this point I behaved as taught in doctrine.

After three consecrations of the Mass, the service was over and it was time for all to go. Out in the street, our group would come together, all talking our language, starting back home. Our procession in the street took the same order and kept the same itinerary back to the tevat kus at home, where my mother would deliver the Holy Mass to the Virgin Mother Mary: "*Im te santo misa teopo vetana em mampo yecha.*" [Here we place in your hand the Holy Mass from church.] Then all the children would say, "*Diosta te vaisae Deo gratia.*" [To God we give thanks.]

One time on the way home, I asked my mother why the priest was angry and scolding the people. At home, when we were in the ramada, she told me of the priest and said, "*Hinabaka,*" meaning sermon preached.

A baby was born into the family of my uncle. She had to be baptized, and my uncle, living among the Yoris, talked with my parents about coming to our place to have them hold the baptismal ceremony for his child. This affair is called the *bola* in Yaqui.

The next Sunday, having arranged with the child's godparents, my uncle brought them. The child was already dressed in baptismal attire—a silk cap which went on her hairless head making it look like a silk ball, a silk dress, and white shoes. The godparents took the child in their arms and took the same route that we followed to go to church.

The parents remained in the ramada to wait until the return of the godparents with the child. While waiting, they were preparing the ramada for the dance. The musicians, being on hand, started. My uncle had to dance, so he dressed for it. At the bola only one Pascola* dances, attired in his hat, work clothes, and leg rattles. On this occasion all the relatives took part in performing for the dance: my uncle danced Pascola, being the child's father; my father was harpist; my oldest brother Encarnación† was violinist. The music and dance were on when we saw the baptismal party coming. They said they were a little confused, and going by the tevat kus, they lighted a bunch of *trikis*, firecrackers, standing in front of the cross. When the parents came out, the godparents delivered the child saying, "We are very happy to have fulfilled your request placed in our hands not long ago."

After the baptismal party came from church, the dance and music continued. Then at three o'clock, food was served to all present, and after the meal, soda pop for the children and wine for the men. When all had had their meal, the godparents of the child and the parents went to the tevat kus with the child in her baptismal attire held in the godmother's arms. At the tevat kus, the godmother placed the child in her parents' hands and then gave them the certificate from the church saying, *"Inimetopohtim tepohtim"* [a bronc impressed with a branding iron]. The name of the child was Lupita.

Finally, the parents stood facing the cross, and the godparents walked toward them, stood with them, and all walked around the cross three times to seal the compadre relationship formally. In a brief talk, the godparents

---

*Pascola Dancers function as ceremonial hosts of Yaqui household fiestas. Besides dancing, they often entertain with jokes, stories, and pantomimes. Traditional Pascola garb includes a carved oval face mask, waist jinglers, and cocoon leg rattles. Yaqui refugees began rebuilding their unique church organization and ceremonial structure soon after they settled in Arizona.

†Encarnación was an older son of Martín Savala, a half-brother to Refugio. He could have either accompanied his father to Arizona on his initial trip or come later on the train with the rest of the family.

urged the parents to see that the child should be trained in Christian doctrine as commanded by the Catholic church. By this time the *canario* was playing to end the fiesta. After thanks were given by the parents, the fiesta was ended, the dance and music stopped.

Still living in the same house, we heard that there was a natural fountain called El Ojito de Agua [The Little Eye of Water] nearby in the Silver Lake region. We went to see it springing naturally out of the ground. All the people who saw it were convinced that it was a natural spring until it was discovered that it was a leak from the city water main which came from the city water service that was located near the Santa Cruz River. When this pump was moved, there was no more Ojito de Agua for us at Barrio Libre.

To the west of us was a little Yaqui village called Mesquitalito, being in a mesquite forest. The bigger village, Mesquital, was directly across the river from the city water pump. That place was known for Yaqui fiestas by all the people of Tucson. Mesquitalito was a block from the Ojito de Agua and was also known for Pascola fiestas.

Tucson was very pretty on my side of town. We had the Santa Cruz River, Silver Lake, and El Callejón in the Silver Lake region. There was a beautiful grove of ancient cottonwood trees on both sides of the Callejón, an *alameda* [shaded street]. The Santa Cruz River flowed abundantly, and a dam was built right where the Callejón came into the river. This provided a swimming pool for boys and men. To make this dam, first a ditch was dug across the river to get down to soil, not sand. The irrigation canal was built to water the Tierras Flojas region—the University of Arizona experimental farms.

We Yaquis called Tucson, Too sone. Main Street we called *Muina Kaya* [Molina Street] because the Eagle Milling Company was on it. Their wheat field was between the El Paso and Southwestern railroad yard. In my boyhood appreciation, everything was interesting. All was fun; it was fun to ride the streetcar through downtown and north to the University of Arizona campus. It was fun in school in the baby class with the sisters of the convent and fun on Sunday church trips.

"...My mother, being so active, soon found ways to put us two younger boys to work...."

But at this time my father took to drinking and caused a separation. He told my mother that he would wander off and leave town, going to Yuma. She replied, "I will stay home *inusimake* [with my children], depending on Divine help. Divine help go with you, and when you come again, you will find me here waiting for you." My father said he was going to the mining camps in Ogilby, California.

My mother, being so active, soon found a way to put us two younger boys to work to bring in food. She made tortillas and tamales and we sold them among the people in the neighborhood. With the money, she bought the material to keep her laundry business going. Because the laundry that she did had to be delivered by us, she often had to send us into "enemy territory," where we were prey for the little bullies. My brother Fernando has always been my guardian, so in town he had to do the fighting. It was the Yaqui in us when we got into a fight. Often he fought with two of the bullies and beat them. We made them run—after us, but they ran anyhow, ran out of breath because we were too fast for them. We beat them and thought ourselves go-getters.

When we had the time, we went to Silver Lake Dam. Here I had to learn to go in deep water. The first time my brother and another boy had to hold me by the arms to take me into neck-deep water. Before this I had been only in knee-deep water in a stream. I learned to swim by starting in shallow water until I could float in the deep where I had walked the first time.

It was July, and now the time came when we had to move. A tall Mexican told the news to every family living along the arroyo going down to the ancient willow tree on South 11th Avenue. We had the help of a neighbor, Ambrosio, and his son Miguel, who had a wagon to move the whole building which my father had put up before he left us.

We built the house from the material that was in our first house, the walls and the tin for roofing. The place we chose was on the north side of the arroyo near a well-known Mexican dancing place, El Puente. Nearby lived Martín Coronado, the Yaqui butcher for the Durazo Slaughterhouse, whose daughter Josefina was the wife of my oldest brother Encarnación and mother of my niece Yzabel. My brother Fernando and I were the builders under the supervision of my mother. My older brother was already married, so the house was shelter just for us four. It was a huge square box of lumber with doors on both the north and south sides. We had the box put up with the rafters and were working on the roof when my mother came with all our belongings in Ambrosio and Miguel's wagon.

One of those summer cloudbursts broke on us suddenly and, of course, got us all wet. Only my mother's and sister's clothes were found dry in the trunk, so I was dressed in their things for the night, since it was already after sundown. After the storm, I had fun watching the flood in the arroyo nearby. Nothing serious happened to us, thanks to Divine help, so we passed the night in our new home.

At this time my mother started making menudo for us to sell. My brother and I took it out every morning for our customers to have for breakfast. We also continued our schooling at the convent, though it was a long distance from our new home. We went after delivering menudo very early and came from school with time enough to help our friend Martín, the butcher in the slaughterhouse, where we got all the meat for our use and for our Aunt Eulalia's too.

One day while crossing a fence on the way home, I had an accident that crippled my right leg. I stepped on a mesquite thorn which went into the flesh about one inch. My brother pulled it out with great effort. Afterwards, he lighted a candle and with the drippings covered the bleeding and stopped it.

As I said before, my brother Fernando was always my guardian, so when we had to go to our aunt's home, he carried me on his back leapfrog fashion because I was crippled from the thorn. This was done often since my mother was working in a Mexican restaurant. Fortunately, before I was crippled, my brother did not have to carry me to school.

My mother was informed about the wheat harvest on the San Xavier Papago Indian reservation. The idea was to glean after the reapers, picking up all that was left. Julián Apaleo

[Harpist], was living at San Xavier with his wife Jesusa, relations of the Coronados with whom we lived at "El Puente." He had a wagon and a two-burro team, and he took my mother and us three children to his own dwelling at San Xavier. From there we went to the field of the wheat harvest. I was water boy for our family. The field was on the road west of the Santa Cruz River, and from there I walked to the river to get the water in the *tahoe* [a dish-shaped hole dug until water flows into it naturally]. When I was coming, my singing was heard by the reapers and gleaners. My sister-in-law told me I was the singingest soul there was. My favorite song was *"La Valentina,"* also some school songs and, of course, *"Florindichi, Florinda."* In Yaqui, my favorites were *"Kone"* [The Crow], Pascola music, and "The Yellow Bird." Of lullabies, "Little Grey Wren" and "Little Saint Horny Toad" were best.

After working all day, we would go home to Julianita, the daughter of Julián Apaleo, and she would have supper with some nice wheat tortillas ready. Julián Apaleo was a hunchback known for his trade as an *abatellero,* or *batealeo* in Yaqui. He made kneading troughs of wood in two shapes—round and long—with four legs. These he dug out of solid wood, a block of cottonwood, so the trough was of one piece. For spoons of wood, the size of frying spoons, one piece of mesquite was used. His business was to sell them to make a living. Also there was Emilia whose husband was Yori mix. She was the sister of our friend Martín Coronado, Yaqui butcher for Alfredo Durazo. Emilia and her husband Emilio had their home right at the east foot of "A" Mountain, where the spring was then. This spring was one of Tucson's landmarks and the source of the acequia. Tucson was pretty then, and it remains pretty for one who grew here to see and appreciate. All my cherished memories are here.

When the harvest was finished, the next thing for us was to go home, and we had our house already put up—no job of building this time. Emilio had a big wagon drawn by two horses, and my mother arranged with him to bring us children home with our picking, which was only a half a bushel of wheat. He made the way by the east side of the Santa Cruz

River. Crossing the river and turning due north, we came to a little Mexican settlement called Los Reales across the river from the Yaqui settlement El Mesquital, precisely the location of the city water service pump which had given us El Ojito de Agua near Mesquitalito. We came to Ajo Road where the two buildings of the Papago School were and later the St. Joseph Orphanage. After passing this, we came to the arroyo where our home was, the home we built during the storm. Already at home, my mother made a deal with the Mexican merchant who had a grocery store. This man's name was Leyva, a well-known old-timer of Tucson. He paid her four dollars for the wheat.

When we came back from San Xavier, my brother and I continued working in the slaughterhouse which was across the road from our home. We picked dried mesquite beans to feed the pigs for the slaughter. At a nickel for a sack, we made good boy-wages on this job, and we had all the meat we could use—free.

Our house was on the same lot as Juan Coronado's, a cousin of Martín. His mother was an aged woman, a *limosnera* who went by asking alms among the people. She walked into town as far as she could and came back with her bag to feed her great-grandchildren. Her son, being an old man, worked as a farmhand for a Mexican named Chulo where the Callejón went into the river and Silver Lake Dam. With him, we could get watermelons, cantaloupes, *calabasitas tiernas* [tender pumpkins], green corn, tender green beans, green chilis, and tomatoes to go with a soup bone, so we had an olla of *wakabaki* with all the trimmings. Wakabaki is the food made of soup bones served at Pascola fiestas. The Pascolas say it is "*Waka,*" —Yaqui in Pascola talk.

Juan Coronado was getting four dollars and fifty cents a week, six bits a day, with all the provisions to help his mother and her grand and great grandchildren. We, on our part, were making that besides what we did peddling food for mother. We were content depending on Divine help. Food was available in many ways for us. During the time of saguaro cactus apples, we went up the hills across the river to bring the red fruit down. We made a long pole which the

Yaquis call *hiabuia,* but Mexicans call *wichuta.* This pole has a sharp point at the end and cross arms in the shape of the lance carried by Pilate in the Yaqui Easter Ceremony only minus the tiny tunic. It is used to push up the apple and bring it down on the little cross.

There was a large Chinese garden field between the orphans' home and the river. There, by asking permission, we could get sweet potatoes, carrots, green chilis, and onions, a complete *salsa de chile verde* to eat with *frijolitos de la olla* and *casuela;* beans and steak. Also, my mother made some popcorn just like that we buy now; in those days there was no store popcorn to buy. Then the Yoris got the idea to sell it back to us. My mother, grinding the popcorn on a *metate* [stone grinder] made corn *pinole,* which is just as good as any cereal for breakfast or any mealtime. We ate it with *panocha* [brown sugar] and water instead of milk. The same process is used with wheat, which is roasted and ground to pinole for a stout meal—invigorating.

My mother somehow visualized my father coming home. From that, I perceived how she loved him; that is, she had faith in him. The only thing that she would say was that she told him she would be waiting at the place where he left her. She asked an odd question—would we be pleased if he came. We chorused in one voice, *"Hewi, hewi, hewi!"* [Yes, yes, yes!] three times for emphasis.

We had come back home from San Xavier in summer, and now it was winter. One cold Saturday night we heard a knock at the door, and there was my father. We could see he had been told where we were by a man who lived across the road at our other place. My mother was prepared for him as if she knew the day and time of my father's coming. She had some fresh tamales ready for him, so he had supper right away, praising greatly the reception. However humble the reunion was, it was as joyful as in a king's palace.

A mental faculty like my mother's is called *seataka.* A person gifted with the virtue of seataka is very intelligent, always on the Divine side in dealings and performance, with a lovely personality. My mother and father were both of the same nature. My mother said that telepathy was accomplished by

Divine help, for God moves hearts and minds in mankind. Therefore, seataka is a Divine gift, having the capacity to desire nothing more than Divine nature, whereas *yoaniya* is devil nature.

My father was a harpist of outstanding merit by gift. There came a man who was learning to be a violinist and seeing my father back at home, he came to learn the three frequencies of Yaqui music. They are *campanilla* [evening], *partillo* or *una vahti* [midnight], and *vakothia weye* [dawn]. These two men *malehto* and *novisio* [Maestro and beginner], started discussing yoaniya—the magic world. My father strictly advised his student to refrain from applying to yoaniya to be a good violinist. He told him, "With true desire and depending on Divine help, you don't need anything else. Apparently you are a person of seataka, which is on the good side. Yoaniya is evil. It is true you acquire ability from yoaniya to be a gambler, a good horse rider, a thief, but it is useless for the art of music, which is acquired by Divine help."

Yoaniya can be taken by magicians and tricksters. I have been tempted so many times, being susceptible to it, but I go for what is natural, not supernatural, being satisfied with God-given nature. Yoaniya was essential in ancient times because the people lived by it, but there came *o'owim susuakame* [wise men], who classified yoaniya as infernal. However, it is still being practiced by people who see it to be popular among their associates.

One flute and drum player told me that he acquired his ability to perform in dreaming. He saw a male king snake on top of the water, and when he picked it up, it turned into a flute, which is the instrument that he plays along with a slender drum. One Pascola Dancer told me that he first fought a wild male goat and overcame it. Then he stood up and saw two rattlesnakes that came and wound themselves on both his legs, turning into the leg rattles dancers wear.

The true yoaniya was described by one man who, having the desire to see the mysterious places, was taken in by the supernatural spirits in the forest. He said he was sitting at the edge of a lake when an old man came to him saying, "I know your desire to see our home. Come now and I will show you

[23]

"...so we had to move again. This time it was to the north part of town..."

the place, but be sure you don't get frightened with whatever you see." He took him close to a cliff, where a monster of a snake held its mouth wide open. The old man told him that the mouth was the gate to enter the city, so he had to walk into the mouth of the snake. When he came out on the other side, he found that he was in a beautiful place where he saw all kinds of amusement. The old man said, "Take any art you want." There was gambling, cowboy roping, horse training, music of all instruments. This man took the art of marksmanship with bow and arrow. He was still living when Porfirio Díaz was invading the Yaqui country to annihilate the tribe. He was known by the name Kukut, and with firearms he was a sniper. He was required by the spirit to bring in more believers to yoaniya. The spirit of yoaniya wants souls to forsake Divinity and serve the devil. For this reason the person of seataka does not need to ask the yoaniya for anything, because his inborn capacities are God-given.

The man who came to study with my father learned to be an accomplished violinist by Divine help.

After my father was with us six months, the railroad coming from El Paso claimed the land where our home was, and also the Coronados', so we had to move again. This time it was to the north part of town, across the tracks from Barrio Anita, because my parents preferred the Yaqui side. The cemetery was just across the street from us. This third house we were in was borrowed from another woman who had lived with us in the SP section living quarters.

But my father soon decided to bring our homestead from the south side of town since all the wood was in good condition. The site for rebuilding was just a short distance from our third house, a little farther north. The lumber was hauled by our friend Ambrosio on his wagon. My father paid for this with money that he brought from Yuma. When the house was set up with the ramada and patio and a new olla for water and the tevat kus, my father went on another trip to work in the yard at Yuma for the SP section.

[25]

2. GROWTH

Merging of Labor and Love

How things are natural in the wild
When the flowers, streams and the light
And the trees offer the shade so mild,
And protect the feeble bird aflight
Like the mother's tender love for a child,
Add to pleasure the most sensual delight.
                                    –Refugio Savala

Again, Tucson was pretty on my side of town. The irrigation canal from Silver Lake Dam went through, so the *seya aniya* [flower world] was lively and lovely, and there was a willow tree grove across from our house.

My married brother Encarnación was living on the south side of town in Barrio Libre. I continued my schooling nearby where I began with the sisters, and I moved from the baby class to first B class, finishing in the A class when I stopped because of the distance.

After my father had been away six months, there was a stepfather for us three children. With our new father we got a new sister named Eloisa, and she claimed she got a mother, a sister, and us two brothers. Our new father was not a railroad man. Best of all, he was not a drinking man. He was a big man, a heavy-set six-footer who worked adobes by contract. In this work, he made men of us two boys. He ran the molder for four bricks of prepared mud, while my brother Fernando

[27]

ran the wheelbarrow. I would prepare the mud with straw and dung. We got thirty dollars for a thousand bricks. In a week's work we also put time into laying out the adobes for the sun to dry them and into stacking them for delivery.

Then the time came for our father to work out of town up on Cañada del Oro, which is on the west end of the Catalina mountain range. He was given a big green wagon with a horse team to take the whole family, and we loaded all our possessions and headed up north toward the Catalinas. We came to a park, the last grocery store, then crossed Rillito River. No bridge was put up in those days, so we went across the river, but there was no water, so the crossing was on the sandy riverbed. Then we came up to the top of the hill. Then we reached Oracle Junction, and taking the road to the right, we started into Llano Toro [Bull's Plain], a cholla forest with cattle roaming. They were decorated with cactus spines all over, even their faces. Our father knew the desert, and when we came to a ranch at Toro Cañada creek, he told us that it was the old post where the stagecoach took relief coming into town. In those days ore from the mining camps was hauled by mule train, and these we saw in town. They stopped for the mules to drink at the city water trough.

Our destination was reached when we came to Rancho Samaniego. The Cañada del Oro was flowing with a torrent of clear water, very beautiful. Our father was not working Sundays, so he told us about the way he came to Arizona. He crossed from Mexico at Douglas, going through Cochise County to Willcox on to Bowie and on to Safford, San Carlos, and Globe.

In our camp, we had a large tent to live in. The foreman had a Mexican wife, so he could talk Spanish. They lived in a building made of lumber. Our father told us we did not have to work, so we became again two playmates, but the ranch foreman's wife soon put us to work with her own boys as *gok bakeom* [walking cowboys], herding the cows to the corral early in the morning for milking. We drank much milk every morning as gok bakeom, and we had dinner with the foreman's family at noon. What we liked very much was the *kuahada* [cottage cheese]. This is the cheese which has not been put in the molder. This woman made the molders so big that when the cheese came out, it was about the size of a *tampaleo kubahi* [Pascola drum].

Every day after being gok bakeom, we had all day to go places. Going upstream, we found a good swimming hole. This was one pastime for us, and so was walking into the canyon to see the spring water flowing into the main stream. This canyon was deep, the walls on both sides solid rock. In the solid rock bottom, we found little bowls made by hand by the Indians of this river, for the purpose of catching rain water to drink when water was scarce. My father called them *tesa akim* in Yaqui.

Truly, we were enjoying ourselves here more than in town.

The study of Cañada del Oro was of much profit to me. I learned all about ranch life since both my parents had great experience. I learned the Yaqui names of plants and fowls and about taking bees for wild honey. The *siba wikit,* cliff bird, is a day bird and sings at dawn. *Kauruaktea,* a night bird, sings all night.

The perfume flower plant is the Spanish *vinodama* [*kuka* in Yaqui]. You can sense the perfume from a long distance. My father told me how the Indians knew God by this perfume.

Before the white man, the Yaquis saw God in this creation. They saw him in the firmament's heavenly bodies, his spirit in the perfume of the *sewam* [flowers]. They would say, *"Wame'e buero chokim ieffering* [Go the planets when our earth is suspended], 'For there is nothing covered, that shall not be revealed'" (Matthew 10:26). The Yaquis, not having any Bible study, many times tell whole chapters of the Gospel, as my own father gave me the definition of the fifth commandment: "Thou shalt not kill; do not be unjust, unkind. Do not take little animals to be a nuisance. They are made to be with us. Rather be a life saver. If you see a fly in a bucket of water trying to save itself, stick your finger in the water, let it crowd up, and snap it into the air. Here you save one life as precious to God as yours."

My father also told me of an aged Pascola Dancer who gave, in a fiesta closing sermon, a verse from the seventh

[29]

chapter of Matthew, "Enter ye in at the strait gate" (Matt. 7:13). In telling the deceitfulness of the broad road he said, "But the road to heaven is a narrow footpath in the ground, narrow for not being much in use, for there be few that find it." The name of this Pascola Dancer was *Wahu Chahi* [Falcon], and the sermon was given at Mesquitalito in Tucson.

Another story he told was of Peo, which means Pedro. Peo was a big liar and deceiver all over the eight villages of the Río Yaqui. One day a priest came riding a mule. He met Peo and asked him to fool him as he had heard. Peo said, "Father, I have to get my book with which I do my tricks to deceive people, but wait here and I'll go get it." The priest said, "Take my mule and go get the book." So Peo took the mule but did not return to the priest again. This man told his lies so realistically, he even fooled himself. He told one person in Guaymas that a whale was lying on the sand at the seashore. The word was passed all over town. He saw the people running to see the whale, and when he was told about it, he started running also to see it. When he arrived where the people were, there was no whale. There was confusion, and people asked who had said there was one. Peo himself was asking the same question.

All these stories were told in Yaqui by my father in Cañada del Oro. Then the time came for us to go back to town. We had to go home because my mother was pregnant and also because the work was finished. When my father was dismissed, he was given the same green wagon and horses. I was exceedingly sorry to leave, but we said goodbye to our ranch friends: *"Adios, hasta la otra visita con el favor de Dios."*

When we pulled out of the canyon, we were again on the Llano Toro. Up here we saw the canal which brought water by force of gravity from up the river so that Llano Toro was made a farmland. They raised wheat and barley. It was wonderful, for the river water was turned up on the hills without a dam. We were on the same route as we came on, passing the *cuesta* [hill] and the old post. Then we started going around the west end of the Catalina Mountains. The huge mountains seemed to be standing at the same distance, but Tucson became visible. There was no hurry, and my father never used the whip on the horses because they went fast enough at ease until we arrived home. We caused a sensation with the neighbor kids. They asked me if we saw genuine Indians, and we told them that we were the genuine Indians up there.

Before I went away, I had been attending school at the convent, but now my father decided that I should go up to public school. I was placed in first grade, A class.

My father had a big house of his own and moved us all from the house which my true father built of the original material acquired from the SP yard. The move was made because of the coming baby.

Since winter was upon us, we were glad the house was a solid enclosure. The house also had a fireplace in one of the rooms, where we could burn big logs of mesquite wood.

No plans were made for the baby, but my parents were very joyful and said that whether the child were a boy or girl, as heaven willed, *o'ou o hamut teweka bale' epo* [it would be a blessing].

My father started the new ramada for the bola two weeks before time. The green willow branches were just across the track from our place, and it only took one whole day to build it, including the tevat kus and *tinaja* [red olla]. One week later the baby arrived, a boy. Sunday of the next weekend was the bola with a violinist, a harpist, and one Pascola Dancer. Everything went as at my cousin Lupita's bola, except that the musicians were not our relations. The violinist was a blind man who lived right at our backyard with his nephew. The harpist later lived in Pascua.

After the bola I had a little baby of my own to play with, which greatly delighted me. When I saw the *tepohtim* (baptismal certificate from the church), it said February 15, 1913.

I continued at public school after my baby brother's baptism. When we had been at the San Xavier wheat harvest, I had been the singingest soul, but at school I was silent. For this I was left in the room after school with another silent boy. The teacher asked us to sing anything we could for her, and I sang "Rockabye Baby on the Treetop." The other boy sang it with me. The teacher, somewhat amused, told us to sing in

[31]

class or else stay after school. From that day on we were good singers. The teacher was very pleased and told others in school. I was slow in arithmetic, fast in reading and writing, also making good marks in art with Crayola drawings. The principal at that time was good with the paddle, being a big lady. This I know because one time when I came in too late, she crossed me over her lap and gave me a good paddling so that I cried like a baby, which I was not anymore.

Out in the schoolyard playing was allowed until lunch time. When a whistle blew, we ran to the front door on the south side, and each teacher placed her children in military formation. The piano started the march tune, and the children, first class first, went into the lower and second floors of the building. Then we all went home for lunch. We also performed this after lunch and in the morning at nine o'clock.

My brother had an accident, spraining his ankle. He was in bed for a long time, so I was forced to discontinue school. In the city work was started to pave all the streets. My father started to work, and I was taking lunch to him at the job each noon.

The house we had left vacant was borrowed by a person from the University experimental farm. It became the rendezvous for drunks, and one Saturday night, it was burned to the ground. It was a great loss of effort, time, and labor.

By this time my brother was well again, so we started going to pick cotton in Flowing Wells for two dollars a hundred pounds. We both always worked to pick fifty pounds to make one dollar. We got paid on Saturday, with all the men working for daily wages. My mother was no longer working as she had the previous year because she was nursing the baby, Chémali, for José María.

After cotton picking my brother and I started work in grown-up men's jobs on a farm, baling and irrigating. At this time we moved across the arroyo, which crossed the railroad and a canal. At this point in the canal there was a flume of galvanized tin sheeting. This was called Caro Vita, having a swimming hole at the far end. It was truly a pastime place for all. Here we lived in front of the blacksmith shop.

At this time Father bought a big wagon to haul wood;

then, having the need, we bought two good burros. With these we packed up again to go south to chop wood for a Tucson fuel and feed company, getting twenty dollars a cord. I went with my parents to camp. We took a big tent, the same one we had in Cañada del Oro. My father was a good chopper; he was cutting and I was carrying and stacking. I had a light ax to help, and my father had an over-sized ax. By evening we had put up two full cords and called it a day.

It was winter, but the mesquite forest was very thick. We had a commissary at camp for food, and we got water from a windmill. It was raining much, so my mother stayed in the tent with Chémali, burning wood to keep warm. My brother stayed at home until two weeks later, when he came just to see the fun. We worked together to cut one cord a day. In another week we started back home—sweet home it was. At home we had an adobe house. It was not up-to-date, but a home. Being back together with my two sisters, we worked where work was until war started to put us to work for the railroad.

When the war started, a work train was assembled to take laborers northwest on the Southern Pacific track to Jaynes, Rillito, Redrock, Picacho, Casa Grande, and Maricopa. It was a commuter train, going out in the morning and coming back to Tucson in the evening with extra gang number ten, campo diez. I was only fourteen years old, but because of the shortage of men, I was hired. I was as green and tender as a pumpkin. When it came to learning track language, I was back in the baby class again, but I never fell asleep. A foreman told me in Spanish to get the "Yaqui." They called the track jack "Yaqui." The clawbar was called "chiva," goat. I had many teachers, and they made fun of me, but, in turn, it was also fun for me. Though young, I was a man in stature, so heavy lifting was play to me, and the pick and shovel, toys. I had to learn the names of all the pieces to make a "steel stew": bolts, pikes, rail anchors, tie plates, and angle bars.

While the campo Yaqui was in operation, a regular fruit express train wrecked in Marana. The men working in Tucson yard section gang were sent to inform the number ten extra gang men to gather where the work train picked them up every morning. It was night when the men came, shouting, "*campo diez, campo diez!*"

When we arrived at the wreck, we found four cars lying on their sides. Work went on until daylight. At eight o'clock, a work crew came with a derrick. The side track was not damaged, so the crane worked from there, picking up the four fallen boxcars. An oil tanker was just derailed, and this was pulled up by means of frogs, and its wheels placed on the rails again. Two rails were twisted, so the last car was lifted and held up on end by the crane, while good rails were put under it to fix the track. The men spiking the rails worked under the lifted car. All were highly experienced.

The eastbound passenger train 110 was sent to open the line at nine o'clock. That day the roadmaster and the division engineer were present to supervise the job, and our foreman was praised for the way he had conducted all the manual work. Our work train was made up of one chair car and a flat car, so we climbed in the chair car and arrived back in Tucson asleep.

After the wreck, gang number ten continued as before. We were working at Wymola between Redrock and Picacho when the work train was recalled to the Tucson depot for the men to register for the draft. I was rejected and told to go to school. My brother Fernando registered but was not called for induction.

When we were laid off from the work train, my father was hired again by the same contractor who paved the streets going out of town. He was hired to work at a rock quarry west of Tucson, so we loaded again to go camping. We pitched our tents again. I had my two burritos and a light wagon, so the first week I was sent to town for provisions. I hitched my two pets to my little wagon, and at sunset, I was off with my bedroll, water, food, and clothes. Night took me just as I passed the Robles Ranch. The road was under construction, but they had not started work where I was, so I pulled to one side of the road for the night. I rolled out my bed in the wagon after I turned loose the burritos. While the burritos were grazing, I was in the wagon asleep. Then cattle started coming and passing by me, cowboys following them, shouting. For all this, I had a sweet sleep all night. At sunrise, my burritos came to the wagon. I knew they had drunk *yuku ba'ampo* [in a rainwater pool] because of their muddy feet. I warmed my food and ate and hitched up for the remainder of the trip. The burritos just waited for me to climb up on the wagon. They started and took the road turning toward the sunrise. By and by we came to where the cowboys were in siesta. They took a drink of my water and bade me and burritos good wishes, caressing the burritos.

I proceeded and arrived at Calera Hill. Here I came upon a man and his family eating. He asked me to eat, and I had rabbit which was roasted on open, live coals. These people were from Altez, a Papago village. I joined them because we were neighbors at the camp. I was sent ahead of them, having a lighter wagon. My burritos were anxious to go, making quick steps. They knew that on arriving, I would feed them baled alfalfa hay. The last night they had eaten *kopaim*, milk weed, which they also liked very much.

I arrived in the afternoon and had time to go to the farm for a load of watermelons, cantaloupes, chiles verdes, tomatoes, calabazitas [little pumpkins], and tiernas [tender] green corn, all summer delights. With all these things, I was ready to go the next day. After midnight, I started back to camp. I was informed that I would see a *fantasmo Tejano* [Texas phantom] rider in the pass at Gato Mountain, which I made at dawn. My burritos would react if there was any such spirit. For myself, I had no fear at all. So I came again to Calera Hill by daylight. There was a natural water pot in the west side of the hill, and from this I got water for the burritos and went on, not urging them because we were only halfway.

I met an old Papago who desired a watermelon, which I gave for no money because we could not understand each other. He knew no English or Spanish. This is where my three tongues failed, for I tried Yaqui also. So by gesture, I made him know that I gave it to him at no charge.

After I arrived in camp, what I bought in town for a nickel, I sold for ten cents; all prices were doubled. The farmer had instructed me to do this, so I made good money, but spent it all and was poor. I agreed with my mother's idea that the money I made was to keep my business going. The commissary at camp was not adequate for all needs, so my parents also had need of provisions. I only made two other weekly trips when the quarry stopped. The concrete bridges for which the quarry provided rock and gravel were made. My father and Fernando worked three weeks while I was loafing and making trips to town. These trips provided money for myself and my two big sisters, who were not spendthrifts. What I provided was enough for circus days and even an occasional movie.

While we were at the quarry, my father told me this story: King Lion and King Cricket were nature's most powerful. King Lion went out to review his domain. Walking, he stepped on something and heard an angry voice saying, "Who is disturbing my palace?" It was King Cricket whose palace was a round cake of dung. Lion said, "You cannot talk to me like that. I am king of this whole forest. If another kingdom exists in this forest, I will destroy it." Cricket replied, "I am king of all the insects." Again Lion said, "I'm king of all the beasts. My beasts respect me, and if one does not, I kill it." Cricket said, "I do not kill my insects for doing so. I would be destroying my own kingdom, thereby losing God's kingdom." When King Lion said that he was going to destroy King Cricket, Cricket would not see that without putting up a fight. As Lion challenged him, he accepted it and war was declared. A suitable place was chosen for the hosts to meet in battle. King Lion, being powerful in ground forces, assembled his army of wild animals. King Cricket, being powerful in air forces, assembled his mighty Black Squadron composed of *biko* bees. The biko bees, having a poisonous sting, had power to destroy hair. Using a remarkable strategy, King Cricket sent the black bees first. They attacked and peeled the hair of the beasts, leaving every beast hairless for the second squadron, which was made up of stinging bees and yellow jackets. Those honey bees were not sweet to the enemy, and the fierce beasts were powerless and had to retreat. King Cricket came out victorious.

This was one war without killing, just as King Cricket desired. My father used this story to instruct me not to fear wild beasts because the king of beasts who caused trouble was vanquished.

When work ended in the quarry, we went back home. When we arrived there, to our surprise, Juan Pistola was the subject of much discussion. The newspaper said that a Yaqui chief had been found—General Juan Pistola, commander-in-chief of the Yaqui Indian tribe. He had become the designated chief when a group of Yaquis attempting to enter Sonora were taken by officers as they were crossing the border. Because they had no one to represent them in Tucson, Juan Pistola offered to help. His true name, as we knew him, was Rafael Muñoz. The name Juan Pistola had been assigned to him at Durazo's slaughterhouse because his broken thumb was bent at the joint, making it look like he was holding a pistol.

The border incident and designation of Pistola as chief caused a controversy among Yaquis north and south. I was on his side, but I was a little too young to be concerned. One point in his favor was that he caught employment for us during this period of depression after the war.

This was the time when my brother Fernando got married to his first wife, and the wedding took place at our home. A Yaqui marriage is much like a child's bola. Two Pascolas dance, one for the bride, one for the groom, with the Pascola and musicians on the bride's side wearing ribbons. The bride's Pascola also wears an ornamented comb in "her" hair, an imitation pearl necklace, and a red ribbon in "her" hat. Both wear just leg rattles and waist jinglers rather than complete Pascola regalia. The Pascola on the groom's side starts dancing first, alone. Then the Pascola on the bride's side comes in when the bride comes from the church to the tevat kus. The Pascola impersonating the groom receives the Pascola impersonating the bride saying, "My wife." This begins a comic imitation of the real marriage. Both Pascolas perform an affectionate love act. In the ramada at my brother's wedding, both Pascola newlyweds planned for home and family in the future. He told "her" how he would persevere in love and "she" made him promise not to look at other women. He said, "Emphiba" [only you].

[37]

What was done at this wedding was nothing compared to what used to be done in the past, when the Pascolas would give a comic imitation of going to bed together the first night and an enactment of a charge of jealousy against the husband, where the "wife" was chased around the house with her water pot and told that "she" had gone to the river with another man. These acts, though, are not performed anymore. Now the real newlyweds are made to eat together from one plate so their love will endure.

By this time my true father was back from Yuma, living with my brother Encarnación on the south side.

After Fernando's marriage, the SP required all those who worked on the extra gang number ten to go up to Mohawk Summit in the Yuma district. Fernando was sent first, by the L. H. Manning commissary company, which was then cooperating with the SP railroad. My brother went, taking his wife, and was accompanied by his father-in-law, who was also called. The camp was the same type as that of Palmer Gauch on the Benson-Nogales branch, and the foreman was the same man who had run the work train in Tucson.

When my brother was established, he came home and took me back. When we arrived at camp, the outfit was at Kim, three miles east of Mohawk. The foreman had all the same men who had worked for him on the train in Tucson — extra gang number ten. The camp was mobile and moved as jobs required. From the Kim siding, we moved to Wellton at the present Phoenix branch junction.

At the time I came, a group of Río Yaqui Yaquis arrived, and here I saw for the first time a genuine *chukui teta* [black stone]. It was an exceedingly beautiful *piedra imán* [stone magnet]. When the owner lifted it from the case, it picked up the steel, gold, and silver, so its appearance was like a jewel. The owner told me that at sharp noon he had seen a black bull standing right on the place where the black stone was. He had to attract the bull away to get the stone. To do this, he had to do some bullfighting, which though he seemed likely to lose, he won. After a good fight, he got the piedra imán, which was actually concealed deep in the bull's horn. The stone had many strange powers. It protected the owner from being hit by lightning, and, since he was a gambler, the magnetic stone drew the money to him. It also made him strong enough to lift pieces of rail without injuring his body.

This same man also revealed to us the *choni*, which he said was the scalp of an Apache Indian. It was a round piece of skin with braided hair. There was a little red bow at the end which made it look like a woman's headbraid and ribbon.

A choni's power belongs to the arts of yoaniya, and it is used by those who forsake God. The choni can be used to strangle sleeping people, as it does its owner's bidding. It is very jealous, and if the owner goes with a woman, the choni kills him. On the other hand, it is very useful for herding cattle, especially for rustling. When a single cattle rustler was met by lawmen, he passed by them, the choni driving the best head of cattle on ahead so that he drove half of what he was taking by the lawmen.

Those who use the power of the choni embrace yoaniya. They say, "We have made a covenant with death. With hell we are in agreement" (Isaiah 28:15). This evil in the following of yoaniya had been confirmed by one *moreakame* [bad witch]. When she was cursing God as she was about to be burned alive, she was told to say, "God help me," but she refused, so she was tossed onto a pyre of burning green wood.

These stories prove the statement of the *o'owimsusuakame* [men of wisdom] who follow seya aniya and godliness and reject yoaniya, the infernal. It is true that yoaniya was all the Indians could live by until Seahamoot, the prophetess, predicted the coming of baptism and the cultivation of plants from seeds. The story of Seahamoot makes clear the benefits of divine power over infernal power:

THE SINGING TREE*

A big dry tree with all its limbs almost crumbling to the ground appeared in the wilderness every day from sunrise to sunset. This tree was vibrating like the chords of a harp, the sound of which was audible a great distance around. Every day people gathered to hear it.

---

*Reprinted courtesy of the *Arizona Quarterly*, vol. 1, no. 1, Spring, 1945.

Wise men from all parts of the country came but no one knew the significance of the sound of this tree. When everyone in the country failed to find an answer about this living tree, an old man stepped out of the crowd and stood before the wise men and spoke: "There is only a slight hope for us to reveal this great mystery which has bound us in confusion for a long time. When I was young, traveling with my father, we found an old woman in the forest. This old woman will interpret the meaning of the sound of this tree, for she is very intelligent, and wisdom crowns her with unmeasured understanding. This woman, if living, is our only hope." Thus he spoke and the wise men after conferring gave the old man an answer. "To lead us out of the obscurity of doubt, it is our will to unmask this mystery, so if you think this woman is wise enough, go forth and bring her. We will make arrangements so that you may depart by sunrise." The next morning the old man and a score of young men moved toward sunrise into the wilderness.

After many days of hardship in the forest they observed from a distance the abiding place of the old woman. It was late in the afternoon when they arrived at her hermitage. The old woman did not show surprise. It was as if she had been expecting these visitors. The messenger upon his arrival saluted, standing far away, fearful that she might turn loose her pet tiger to devour them. She offered them welcome under the shady ramada to rest. This woman had dwelt in the wilderness since the death of her husband, with her only daughter, a young maiden whom she called Sehamoot.

When the messenger had settled down, he told the object of his mission. Having explained about the tree, he said: "All the inhabitants of the country are in a profound confusion over this tree. You are the only one not questioned. We ask you to come and interpret the tree yourself, for you are in the grace of cultured wisdom." Though the woman knew these things very well, she pretended ignorance and declared solemnly: "I am advanced in days and the journey through the forest is perilous." This she was saying when at the rear of the hut footsteps sounded. Her daughter arrived with a young stag she had slain. Her mother called her tenderly, and a sturdy young woman appeared before the men. She sat down timidly beside her mother as if she sought her protection.

Raised in this remote wilderness the girl could get along better with the beasts than she could with a human being. She had loved and respected her mother who had brought her up in all good things. The mother explained how she had prepared Sehamoot in all manners intellectually, and how many years ago she had been told that these things would come to pass. Then she spoke to her daughter: "For this occasion I have prepared you. These are the men you knew were coming since their departure from the living tree." Then the mother told the messenger: "As I must fail to comply myself with your request, I will send forth my daughter. She will interpret the meaning of this message the Almighty sends to the people of the earth." And the old man rejoiced upon hearing this answer for the star of hope shone vividly in his mind.

He mentioned that this would be pleasant news to the people waiting anxiously for an answer, and he asked the girl if she would consent to go. To this she replied timidly: "My mother desires it. In obedience to her I shall go." After she had accepted the petition she prepared the game brought from the forest.By sunset they were eating and Sehamoot became more familiar with the men with whom she was to travel. Evening occupied her mother in instructing her, and the next day at dusk the girl was ready to go. Her mother placed a pretty white tunic in her bag which she would wear upon being presented to the people.

The old messenger told the young men of their great responsibility in taking the girl away from her home. Farewell was said and they departed into the wilderness. They had not gone far when the tame tiger roared a very sad grunt. Sehamoot almost turned sharply back, but she realized that her mother was safe with the tiger to guard her. She herself knew every art of self-defense in the forest even better than the men who were traveling with her. During the long weary journey she defended herself and the men in a very skillful manner no man would risk to do. She led them windaway from the beasts so they did not scent them even at a near distance. She knew when a beast was near and how to avoid it.

The girl was enjoying the journey. She was not even tired when the men began to light up their countenances, seeing their destination at hand. Presently two men were sent on to announce their approach. When the message was received in the village everyone went to the place where they expected to meet an old woman, tired after the long journey. Instead, they were surprised to find a rough, sturdy, wild-looking young

[41]

woman who did not show the slightest sign of weariness. She was dressed in the neat white tunic her mother had made for her. The most enthusiastic people from the crowd came close to her with the object of kissing her. But this she thought was a challenge and recoiled back in position to charge upon them.

The old messenger had a hard time correcting the enraged girl. When she was again quiet in her mood, the people were afraid to come near her. In presenting her to the wise men the messenger said: "The old woman failed to come herself, but her daughter she has sent to take her place. In presenting Sehamoot to you, I do not fail to fulfill what I promised in taking up the journey into the wilderness, for she will interpret the sound of the strange old tree." The wise men were happy, for this would unmask a great secret and their wisdom would improve. So they received Sehamoot with honor and did not delay in asking the great question about the living tree.

When the girl prepared to speak, silence reigned all through the multitude of people. Everyone was staring at her.

She listened to the sound of the tree. Then her voice rang clearly in full tone. "This message the Creator of all things sends to the people, a testament that he will establish with the earth: that it must produce all sorts of subsistence for every creature upon it; trees in the forest shall bear edible fruit in abundance; the vegetation of the earth will sustain the beast and the fowl and even the tiniest insect that has life in itself; another thing called seed will also come upon the earth; every bush, shrub or tree which does not bear fruit shall be cut down and the ground cleared for the good seed, then tilled with an instrument called the plow. Thus the ground will be prepared.

"After the ground is prepared and seed is placed beneath the soil it shall come to pass that, from the seas, water will be lifted in clouds and carried by the winds to the plains in the form of rain. The seed under the soil will burst forth into life and if cultivated properly it shall bear fruit in such quantity doubled, that one seed will produce one hundred, and this shall be for the maintenance of the people.

"But there is another thing to come in exchange for the benefit the earth will provide. It is called death. Together with the sustenance, all creatures upon the earth will receive also death, for death will not spare even the tiniest insect that has life in itself. And it shall come to pass after death that all substance will be swallowed by the earth in payment for the nourishment given during life."

[42]

These things did Sehamoot tell the people, while the strange old tree vibrated like the chords of a harp when touched by a passing wind. Then it came to silence and remained so forever. The wise men tried to conceal this wisdom from the people, but there was a great change among them. All those who accepted the word remained in their homes and those who did not receive it gathered and danced the farewell dance and disappeared into the morning air, going underground to establish their own kingdom.

The coming of baptism and the planting and cultivating of seeds described in the story of Seahamoot required work. That is why it was straight-away rejected, and many refused to receive baptism. Those who would not accept became *Surem* and went underground and formed their own kingdom. The place where the farewell dance took place is *yo yis wakasapo* [witch dance place], and nothing grows there. It is bare of any weeds.

The ants of all species are supposed to be the Surem. Having refused the seed, now they are the most seed-packing insects of all. They live on humans' food, the seeds. *Kichul* [Cricket] is their king, also called *Tukarilhat*, which means night.

After learning that the yoaniya was infernal, I also learned that it was pre-Spanish, for it was from the Spanish that baptism was received and the *si'ime wa'a* [saints' names] were derived. The God of the white man was revealed by the missionary priests, who translated prayers into Yaqui. I am happy that many Yaquis follow the Christian faith, so there is no return to the practices of the yoaniya, because we are no longer as susceptible to it.

Being with these Río Yaqui Yaquis, seeing their amulets and hearing their stories almost made me accept the yoaniya, but the influence of *seataka* was stronger. *Taka* means body and *sewa*, flower, but *seataka* has nothing to do with the body; it has the most influence mentally, bestowing self-awareness and assuring memory, keen judgment, and intelligence against evil power.

When I was with my brother Fernando at camp up in the Gila district, my father built a small adobe house on the south

[43]

side of Pascua Village, later called Adelanto. They had previously informed us of the move, so we paid our fare from Mohawk and came to our parents' new home. This place was not suitable for my sister-in-law, who wanted to be with her parents after being absent a year, so we moved back to the adobe house near the canal, the one we had left to go to camp. My brother's wife was well pleased, and Fernando and I both went to work at the rock quarry that was on the side of "A" Mountain just west of the city. My brother's father-in-law was the powder man, and we were feeding the crusher using mining handtrucks. My other brother, Encarnación, and my true father were still working at the EP and SW railroad.

Juan Pistola was living with my parents at the time we came back from camp; he had moved in with us when my brother took his wife. I had known Juan Pistola since the time of the house at the Arroyo "Puente" near Durazo's slaughterhouse. Now he was an aged man with a young wife named Lola, the older sister of Julio who years ago had been with us admiring the Ojito de Agua and who had been a baby Pascola. He had danced in a baby Pascola outfit with men Pascolas.

Though Julio was taken to be half-witted by those who didn't know him as I did, he was, in all respects, a normal person but without schooling. His sister, Pistola's young wife, had gone to first grade. She was the older, but Julio was the breadwinner, carrying wood to support the family and their aged grandfather, who was a *tampaleo* [drummer-flutist]. When she was older and married to Juan Pistola, she bore him a daughter who was eventually married to a gambler who was shot by a Negro at Jaynes.

Like Julio, Juan Pistola was illiterate; however, he was conscious of the need for education, so he sent us big boys to public school.

Shortly before this, I had applied for a job with my father's foreman and was hired, so I went to the section house. While working here, I went to night school to study English. When I returned from the section house, Juan Pistola again sent us to school, where I was put in fourth grade and learned grammar. I started writing and became a word hunter in English and Spanish. The dictionary was my hunting ground. It was after the depression, so we could attend classes, but I had my job, so at sixteen, I was allowed to leave school.

In those days, after working south of town, I came back to the north side to be with my brother and my parents. The Garcías were living at Pascua plaza, and fiestas were held at their place. For this reason the site was selected, and Pascua Village was planned to bring all Yaquis together in one place suitable for ceremonies. My mother chose a lot next to Ignacio Maestro, and my brother and I built her a typical Yaqui homestead. The lot is still there, even the *te'owe* tree which my mother planted just to see a desert bloom. Te'owe is called *vagote* by Mexicans and palo verde by Americans.

When I was settled, I took to writing and made it a hobby, a mania.* Miss Thamar Richey frequently came, encouraging me and contacting Professor John Provinse at the University of Arizona. As much as I dislike publicity, my hobby put me in the news as much as Juan Pistola, only with less apparent personal merit. "Yaqui Poet Produces Belles Lettres Here," the headline of the *Arizona Daily Star* said. Much better would have been "Yaqui Is Going To Talk." With this, I went on the air for the University of Arizona radio station. By the time these things were accomplished, I was popular, pounded with questions all the time. My response to this was a desire to learn the guitar. I took it up, depending on Divine help. My prayers were not uttered, but just meditation, and I sought not money or popularity but fun. I desired to compose my songs to my own music, which I was able to do by Divine

---

*At this point in the narrative, Savala severely telescopes time, leaping ahead of the 1912–24 period to document the development of his writing. Although he did begin writing in the early 1920s, it was not until 1927 and the forced unemployment of the Depression that he produced the greater portion of his work with Miss Thamar Richey's encouragement. In the mid-1930s, while working with John Provinse at the University of Arizona Department of Anthropology, Savala made his contribution to Ripley's "Believe It or Not." The headline he mentions is from the June 20, 1941, *Arizona Daily Star*. The university radio broadcast took place shortly thereafter on October 26, 1941. In Chapter 4 of this book Savala again describes these events, this time adhering more closely to their actual chronological context.

help through meditation. This method is unorthodox but effective. Any person can accomplish greater things by Divine help. I advise anyone to do things in the same manner; it is good. Do all your work in terms of the fun you get out of it and you'll enjoy it.

At this time I had a desire to see my writing in print. With the help of the university faculty, who trained me to use the international alphabet, so I might give information in Yaqui, this happened. Yaqui culture was the subject studied in the Anthropology Department.

The only time I got money for writing was when I was offered and accepted $100 for a "Believe It or Not" story. The check I received was a drop in the bucket in Depression times, but my desire to see my writing in print was fulfilled.

My great uncle had come up, walking with a group of young men, from the Río Yaqui in Sonora and had been living with us one year, when a memorable event came to us Yaquis. A notice was sent out that all Yaquis could return to the Río Yaqui with all belongings, cattle, wagons, and farm implements. Transportation was to be provided.

My uncle went with the first group. Next to leave was my brother-in-law, the husband of my older sister Agustina, who was the little girl who had given me a little rag doll to suck when I was an infant, the little heroine of the first eventful moment of my life. My brother-in-law and his family made all the arrangements to go. My mother also went to join my uncle and my sister; my little brother Chémali, ten years old, went too. En route, at Guaymas, Chémali was lost and left behind. My brother-in-law walked back and found him and put him on the train.

My mother's destination was Potam, her home pueblo. When she arrived at the home of my uncle, who was expecting her, he gave her a reception, killing a ram for *wakibaki* [soup].

While my mother was in Old Mexico, my brother and I went to New Mexico with the SP extra gang number seven at Deming in the Río Grande Division. Robert Bosworth was foreman; Tomás Mazo, assistant boss. It was good for me to see a Yaqui in this position. My uncle, Félix Esperanza, was also an assistant under the same foreman, but in the Tucson division.

In 1923, after we had worked in the Deming camp one year, we heard that the Río Yaqui Yaquis were being given transportation to the fiesta in Magdalena, so having the money, my brother went to the fiesta in October and brought the whole family back home. At that time, our home was on the west side across the river from the deaf and blind school. The house was between the canal and the river in front of a small jungle of mesquite and catclaw trees, which provided just the little play yard for Chémali when he came in his little Rio Yaqui attire—rawhide sandals and a straw hat with a chin strap. He had learned to make his own sandals, and, to my surprise, he spoke good Yaqui, like a grown-up, so he could relate to me his experience at Guaymas. He had stalled, watching departing soldiers at the same time the train left, so he followed it, walking on the track. My brother-in-law told me the kid was not a bit scared or crying when he found him, and he ran with him to the train. Chémali told me that they rode in empty cattle cars, swept clean and that the women had used their *hipetam* [mats] and pillows to lie down on. Chémali had ridden in boxcars before, so he was traveling in class this time. All these things he told me in Yaqui and described in detail.

Once he said the kids called him a sissy because he was not in school. He replied that he was not a sissy if school was all that was needed. He said he would go to school to be normal and not a sissy. *Nawia* means sissy, and he disliked that very much.

During this time my mother and sister were with us at home, and my brother Chémali was playing at "shooting Yoris" in the backyard jungle. His gunfire was not "bang! bang!" or "pow! pow!" it was "poom! poom!" or "pum! pum!" repeated rapidly.

It was September of 1923 when I had to go to the Salt River Valley with two of my friends. One of them was Anselmo, the son of Guadalupe Báltazar. Anselmo was white for

[47]

a Yaqui, but he spoke Yaqui fluently. We landed at campo diez, camp 10, on the west canal, one canal north of Chandler. It was the Salt River Valley Water Users' camp. Being a section gandy dancer, I was not used to sloppy ditch clearing work. To be out of the ditch, I took to working with the scythe, cutting brush on the borders of the ditches. My feet were dry, but I was soaking wet from the waist up. During one of these sweating periods, I became the prey of a *moreakame* [bad witch], and he got me. (This *Yoeme* [Yaqui Indian] had a pretty wife and was jealous because she served dinner for me and was with me while I ate.) I fell too deeply asleep. I was conscious that I was stricken by envy and hatred, and I planned to fight this evil with Divine help. My plan was not to hurt the moreakame but by Divine help to relieve myself. The next day, away from camp, I was lying by the canal on the ground. I was helpless, slowly sliding down to the water. If I had rolled into the deep water, I would have drowned. I was lying in this desperate position when the workers came, and my two buddies dragged me out of danger.

The next day I was given all my papers to collect my pay at the office in Mesa. I went in a wagon with a camp boy and lodged at the home of Dolores Gómez, the father of Miguel Gómez, the blind accordionist who played on a corner in downtown Tucson. This man knew all the selections in Mexican music. He didn't speak Yaqui but understood every word of it. When I came to his parents' home in Mesa, I had dinner with them.

Having already collected my pay in the afternoon, I went to the packing shed to lie down in the cool shade under the platform. A man passing by saw me and went to camp and told my friends I was dying under the shed. My buddies came again to see if I was all right. I told them I was ready to leave for home on the evening train, so when they went to camp I stayed and caught the train to Tempe. At Tempe I transferred to a gas-motored doodlebug to Maricopa, where I caught a train to Tucson. I told the conductor to let me off at the end of the double track to walk home. When I arrived at my home, my mother was alone. I refrained from telling her that I was sick, but she had already visualized it in her even-

[48]

ing dream, so she was not very much surprised. She said she saw me in discomfort, not in need, so I got in bed, not in continuous pain but unable to move my left hand, wrist, and arm.

The following morning my knuckle was not swollen, but when I touched it, I felt an acute pain on the side, so that I could not do anything with it. I gave my mother the money that I had brought from camp, and she went and got a *yuemhitebia,* a curing expert—expert because he cured by experience, spiritual or natural. This case was spiritual, evil being involved. The yuemhitebia performed the cure in the pattern of Christian Science. He asked me if I believed that Jesus Christ is a *hitebi* [curer]. I said He was and is forever; faith has much to do with the cure. He then applied some Yaqui tobacco leaves saying, *"Senyor emvale'epo"* [Lord, Thy will be done]. My trust in Divine help and his simple performance cured me. My hand was as good as ever the next day. He who believes does well.

One week after I was cured of the palsy, I was called back to the railroad job with the same foreman. The camp was between Lordsburg and Deming, New Mexico. Tomás Mazo had been transferred to another camp, and the new assistant foreman was a white man from Texas.

3. EXTENSION

Protecting and Providing

The burrow crane, it lifted rails,
The adzing machine, it planed the ties,
The screw machine, it tightened bolts,
But still the sweat ran down our eyes.
                    —Refugio Savala

In September 1924, extra gang number seven was moved from Deming, New Mexico, to Yuma, Arizona. One chair car was placed on the camp cars for women and children. We had no kitchen or dining car, although it was a family camp. The September 16 Mexican fiesta was forgotten on the trip, but it was fun to ride 300 miles on top of camp cars, making rest stops in Bowie, Benson, Tucson, Gila Bend, and finally arriving at Yuma. The camp was at Ivalon, three miles east of Yuma which later became the Yuma east yard.

We had all our equipment unloaded—tools, hand cars, push cars, and one motor car and trailer. The new material for construction was still on a flatcar—ties, 110-pound rails, spikes, plates, angle bars, and compromise joints. All the material was brand new out of the foundry. Extra gang number seven was called on the job for skilled labor. It was composed of Yaquis, about 125 men, all expert steel construction workers.

The job was to construct a new yard in Yuma. A little steam engine was hauling gravel to fill in where the new yard was planned. The men said that it looked like a pack mule carrying a canvas water bag, because the water container was built on top of the engine between the smokestack and cab. When orders were given, the men started tearing up the old yard all of the way down to Prison Hill. We had no track machinery then, so all the work was done by hand. We were pulling and lifting rails, new and old, with hand tongs. One tong takes two men, one on each handle.

The camp was moved to the "Y" on the mesa between the cemetery and orange orchards, where we passed the winter. We were at this location when *Waehma* [Lenten season] came.

The few Yaquis of Yuma made *junta* to talk of Waehma, the Yaqui Easter ceremony. The camp Yaquis were bidden by *uhbuani tua Vahiliostempo* [obligation to God]. We had Ochoa Maestro in camp, a Head Maestro. The Yuma group sent Señor [Christ figure carried by ceremonial participants] to us for *limohna* [contributions]. The *uhbuani* [request] was joyfully accepted in camp. A man named Juan Lucero conducted six weeks of Friday processions, Palm Sunday, and Holy Week. The spirit of Lent was the atmosphere in this small group, this small congregation of the Lord's people. Ochoa Maestro made arrangements to be second to Lucero. Our foreman understood all this Yaqui movement so well that he was happy about it.

The temporary chapel was made at the home of Félix Esperanza.* His house was under the hill on which the city water tank stood. The available space was occupied by the fourteen stations of the cross. I did not get to see all the performance, only part. The three Pascolas were from Yuma. There were seven masked Fariseo soldiers, the officials all as usual. The Matachinis got together twelve men with the camp musicians. Only those who took part went [into the chapel] at the time of the chant of the Gloria. The place we

---

*This may have been Refugio's Uncle Félix Esperanza, with whom the Savala family stayed upon their first arrival in Tucson.

were was in plain view for watching as they assembled, so we walked up the hill to witness the Gloria, that is, to see the Yuma *Gloria Pahko* [Holy Saturday fiesta]. It was altogether wonderful that so few Yaquis could present the whole Easter ceremony. On Easter Sunday, I went for the farewell sermon delivered by Lucero. He based his text on the gospel of Matthew. The Maestro delivered the opening similar to all sermons. He also described the transformation of Fariseo soldiers. He quoted the words of Jesus saying, "In the last you will come again to me. I will then make you pretty and new people again. You will come to my church. I will teach you. You will be my disciples thereafter." He also explained about the performance, how the Fariseo soldiers shed the masks and ran into the church. They surrendered under the feet of the crucifix on the altar. As the Lord told them, they surrendered and were again human beings. The Maestro then said the Apostles' Creed: "He descended into hell. By the creative power of His Father, the third day He rose from the dead. He went up to heaven to sit on the right hand of God the Father Almighty and will come again at the end of the world to reward the good with eternal happiness and the wicked with everlasting pains of hell. Knowing this, we must prepare ourselves today for salvation. Now is the day of salvation." Telling that Christ died for our sins, Lucero quoted Isaiah 53:4–5, "'Surely he hath borne our griefs, and carried our sorrows.... But he was wounded for our transgressions, he was bruised for our iniquities....' Jesus had power to destroy his enemies. 'The Son of man goeth as it is written of him...'" (Matt. 26:24).

The Easter ceremony in Yuma was successful. After the fiesta, building the new yard continued. The main line from the south made a U-turn and went out facing south. Out on the main line a turn like that would require a "Y". The engine would go into the "Y," coming out backwards and going into the main line facing the opposite way from its original course. This U-turn was a wonderful engineering accomplishment.

It was sharp noon when the first train came into town on the new main line which was then reported finished. After granite gravel had been dumped on all tracks, we raised the track to standard level. I had been working with a small crew, and every morning we took water to the job. We loaded five fifty-gallon wooden barrels on a push car. Here I made a grievous mistake. When the push car started coasting with five water barrels, I tried to jump on the car, and my right foot slipped. I fell with my left foot stuck under the push car, and one wheel ran completely over my leg below the knee. It was a miracle that my leg was not broken. I was sent to camp; but no doctor was needed. This accident happened right under the east end platform of the Pacific Fruit Express ice plant. It was a tremendous weight to run over my leg. The flange of the wheel remained impressed on my pants, and the skin was marked with the same flange but was not bleeding, so I walked to my sister Eloisa's, the daughter of my stepfather in Tucson. Her husband was the nephew of Loreto Sánchez, who had lived with us when we first came to Tucson. I told her about the accident, and then she put me in bed right away. I stayed until I was healed and then headed home. My brother Fernando arranged for passes for both of us, so he came with me.

Our home was at the same place, next to Ignacio Maestro in Pascua. My brother told my mother about the accident, and she brought a man, a sprain setter. This man placed the nerve cords and stretched the leg so the nerves got back in place, and I started walking without difficulty. My sister Eloisa had made a *manda* [vow] for me to San Francisco Xavier, so I walked from my house to the San Xavier Mission with four silken wax candles. *Sea cantelam* are long yellow wax candles adorned with *vara de San José* [St. Joseph's staff] which cost only $1.50 a box. So I took four of them and was freed from the vow.

Coming back from San Xavier, I dropped in to see Eloisa, who was back from Yuma. When my sister saw me, she said joyfully, "I am glad to see you not on crutches." From then on I started being well enough to play baseball.

After the accident I went to work in the yard section of the EP and SW railroad. The foreman was in need of workers to construct what was called the Polvo branch, connecting the two main lines from El Paso with Davis-Monthan Airfield in

[54]

Tucson. The branch-off was between Aldona and Cruz on the EP and SW line from El Paso. Juan Martínez was with us and Juan Sánchez, my brother-in-law. In our gang were ten men. The project was to lay new ninety-pound rails for a one mile stretch by hand, using tongs to lift. We loaded the frog on a push car first and slid it down in place. The frog has to be placed with all precision in relation to the stakes. The job was out of the yard limits, and the switch engine crew was sore about having to bring the frog to us, so we unloaded it, and they went right back. We were only glad that once having the frog, there was no stopping until we would meet to connect. After laying only about fifty rails, we ran into a deep arroyo. To cross this we built a trestle with old ties. Then the bridge gang built a bridge on it, so the job proceeded. The next obstacle was a crossing for the Benson Highway.

The gang to meet us from Polvo was the Wilmot section. When we connected about midway, we started dumping slag gravel. The ties were newly creosoted. When the gravel was put in the track, it was raised to the stakes according to the plans, and after the track was given the standard elevation, we started dressing. The black slag was made to look like it was made in cement forms instead of cement trawls. It was tamped with square-pointed shovels. The subgrade, being of dirt, was kept clean of weeds.

In those days the railroad was still of importance, but look at those tracks now [in the 1960s], all bushy. . . . We left, that's why. When we gandy dancers get together, we talk of how fussy we were, fussy about weeds and low spots.

The project of the Polvo branch was finished. It took four months to complete the whole job. After this, I continued working in the same section. We went to the job in the morning and came back at five o'clock. This kept on until after New Year's of 1926.

My brother Encarnación did not work with us at Polvo because he had been sick and was gradually getting worse. He was in bed at home, and his wife was taking care of him to the best of her ability. My brother was Caballero capitán in the fiestas of the South Tucson group of Yaquis. He continued sick in bed until Palm Sunday. On Holy Thursday, he

"...The Matachinis got together twelve men with the camp musicians...."

sent for me. He had made a last request to the *Kohtumbre Ya'ura* [heads of the Easter ceremony] to have the whole assembly in his sickroom. But this was not the reason he sent for me. Rather, he had a presentiment that I would be writing about ceremonies. My brother told me, "If you write about Yaqui ceremonies, put in all the performance exactly as it is done. All about the liturgy can be taken from the book of the Gospel. *Evangeliom si'ime ayuk bueituk Jesús ta pasion* [in the Gospel is all contained because it is Jesus' passion]. You can describe the prayers and *alabanzas* [praises] as events too." He had finished all that he desired to tell me when we heard the flute and drum sound in the background. The Kohtumbre came in and did what is done in the church after processions.

On Thursday of Holy Week, I stayed with my sick brother. At eleven o'clock I went home, still in Pascua. I told my mother about conditions concerning Encarnación. There was not much to discuss, but we waited for the best. On the Saturday of the Gloria Fiesta, one of my buddies needed to make a trip to bring his sister from the northeast part of town. She had to present two *angelesim* — "little angels" — for confirmation in the Easter farewell circle. I went with my buddy on his request, since his sister's need was urgent. We returned, bringing his sister to the fiesta.

At midnight I was standing with the crowd watching Pascola and Deer Dances when a man tapped me on the back. He told me abruptly that my brother had passed away and that he had been sent to take me to the home of the deceased. He said, "Come. I have a car ready to take you." We arrived at three in the morning. Such is the fate of mortals. He died on the fiesta of his devotion. My elders forgave me for being absent in that time of distress when I told them the circumstance that caused my delay.

The *velación* [funeral service] was made Easter Sunday evening. The burial was made Monday at ten o'clock in Holy Hope Cemetery.

My brother had life insurance, and my sister-in-law was the beneficiary. One week after the funeral, the certificate came, but it was placed in the hands of a person who intended foul play. This man told my sister-in-law that he could collect the money for her. She sent for me to see about the matter. This man had taken the insurance certificate to the office of a lawyer. It happened that I knew the lawyer's office, so I went and told our foreman. He went with me to the office, and when we entered, the certificate was on top of the desk. The foreman took it saying, "This is the paper that I came for." The lawyer only said that he was glad the foreman could handle it. The foreman took the certificate to the depot for final processing, and he instructed me to tell my sister-in-law to tell the manager of the funeral home when the check came. The check came after another week, so we went to the mortuary, and the manager helped us to cash the check and pay the funeral bill. He took us to the bank. The check was for $1,500. My sister-in-law put $1,000 in deposit and took $500 cash. She paid $300 for the funeral, including the tombstone. She kept $200 for *lutupahko* [death anniversary], and she also paid the priest of Santa Cruz $7.50.

My brother had a daughter named Yzabel by his first maiden wife, and after her father's death, the girl stayed with her step-mother, calling her mother. My sister-in-law placed her in a Catholic school.

When everything was well settled, the same man who had tried to cheat us about the insurance came with another proposition. He said that the girl's grandmother wanted her. Moreover, he said that the insurance money was to be divided; that is, $750 for the girl and $750 for my sister-in-law. In this case, he could not proceed because it was not lawful, but this man's intentions were too conspicuous, as anyone could see. When I interfered in his fraudulent schemes, he called me his political enemy. Even when he saw that his work was all exposed, he still wanted fifteen dollars for service done in collecting the insurance money. I told him we knew that the lawyer had not sent anyone to get the insurance money. But finally he was glad to put the matter off when we saw him, because he admitted that he had not given any service in the matter.

When all things were put well under control, my brother's death anniversary ceremony was still many months away. Seeing that I had ample time, I went to Tempe to work in a camp on the Phoenix branch, extra gang number twelve. We were in Sacaton in September. One evening as I was getting in bed, my friend Juan Martínez came to me, telling me Fernando had been murdered. I asked my buddy to take me to Tucson right away; we left that evening to arrive at my home at three o'clock dawn. My mother told me everything. The event happened at the home of my brother where he was living next to my Aunt Josefina Escalante. He had been drinking with another fellow, and in a fight, my brother took an ax and tossed it after the man. When the ax fell under his feet, the man took it and swung it backwards, thus hitting my brother on top of the head, making a gash which took ten stitches to get put together. Fernando was at St. Mary's Hospital. The same buddy who had brought me home took my mother and me to the hospital to see him. Martínez had told me that Fernando was unquestionably dead when he saw him. Actually, he had been unconscious, and he recovered.

In this case, the man who kept trying to cheat us again took over, but we rejected him. I only paid thirty dollars for Fernando's treatment at St. Mary's.

After this I started working for Mountain States Telephone Company. I was getting fifteen dollars a week, and seeing this, the cheat came to my mother to collect forty dollars, saying he was working on the prosecution of the man who had hurt my brother. My mother believed him because he came with a detective from the sheriff's office. This man told my mother to pay in terms of five dollars a week. He was a drinking man, and he did this to satisfy his vice. I bought him some corn moonshine. He played it smart; I played it thrifty. I only paid three dollars for one gallon of the stuff and thus settled the debt. Forty dollars would have taken more than two weeks of my earnings. It was all too silly, but I got rid of this unlawful person for good. He got his own medicine and quit going on like this.

In March 1927, one week before Palm Sunday, our lutupahko was made at my sister-in-law's home. It was made one week before the anniversary because the Kohtumbre Ya'ura were busy at the Lenten fiesta. After the lutupahko I went to the employment office of the SP and found that three

[59]

of us workers of extra gang number seven were on the list to be shipped to the Shasta division. We were all relatives, and at that time living together. We were used to these shipping-outs in Arizona, but going to northern California was new to us. We made our bedrolls and came to the office. I had collected seventeen dollars before leaving and took seven dollars to my mother to say goodbye. I told her about the trip being distant. The experience, she thought good. I went to California and was absent for two whole years. When I came back it was 1929, three years after my brother Encarnación's death in the 1926 Lenten season.

The train to take us was to leave at four in the evening. We checked our hand baggage to Los Angeles and boarded a chair car, three men together. By sundown we were passing by Pascua Village. Going out of the yard limit, we were thoughtful, but California was a charming illusion after all. We were on passenger train number forty-three, westbound. Traveling all night, we arrived in Los Angeles the next day, having passed Yuma at midnight through the yard we built. When we arrived at Los Angeles, a man came into our car. He took us in a pickup truck to the commissary to eat and to get food for the rest of the way. We were each given a roll of bologna and a loaf of French bread. We were told to be at the depot to proceed on the evening train. At sundown in the waiting room I could see the sun going down right behind the city hall building.

Our coach was hooked to the train going out at eight o'clock in the evening. More men were put in our coach. In addition there were three more coaches. Of my two companions and myself, only I had left home with ten dollars, so I bought a little food for us. All the other men had been shipped from El Paso. On the way, the Texans ate canned sardines and soda crackers.

This was still in steam engine times, and we were crossing the Mohave summit. The train man told us every time we crossed a tunnel. Going down the Tehachapi Mountains, the track ran above a tunnel which we had already passed through. Then we came to a valley. Caliente was the first section at the foot of the mountains, and in another hour we

[60]

came to the Bakersfield oil fields, then to Fresno at noontime. We ate our lunch, and the other men ate their sardines with crackers and water.

It was eleven o'clock when the train pulled into the station at Sacramento. The man in charge of the shipment of SP workers gave us meal tickets to a restaurant where we ate and had coffee. We filled up the restaurant where we filled our bellies. It was a Mexican restaurant near the depot. This was a midnight supper. After eating we walked to our car at the depot, where we were told to get some sleep and be ready for breakfast. Having lost some sleep the previous nights, we slept well and went to eat breakfast at eight o'clock. Our train was to leave at ten. We were on the Cascade and Shasta division, the branch-off being at Suisun where the Sacramento River comes into the bay. The next town as we went due north was Marysville.

From there we kept on going alongside the Sacramento River. We came to Cottonwood, then to Castle Crag, named for a rock formation. The next place was Dunsmuir, the office of the superintendent of the Shasta division. We got off and drank water from a fountain labeled 100% pure. Three more miles and we were at Shasta Springs. I said, "This is not Ojito de Agua but Ojo Grande de Agua!" Seeing the water cascading down the rock cliffs, blessed were our eyes, for we saw what others had desired to see. Rich people spend huge amounts of money to see all the magnificence that we *kia polove* [poor people] saw, which was *uhyoli* [beautiful]. One mile above Shasta Springs, we came to a horseshoe turn called Cantara. This was the curve to go up out of the canyon. Then we reached our destination, a lonely railroad section named Mott. It was in August when we arrived in late afternoon. Here we saw snow-covered Mount Shasta.

It was the August after my twenty-third birthday. The camp was on a side track. We saw a young lady of our acquaintance, and she recognized us. When we came to her she introduced us to her mother, who made us come into their car. When they had been well informed of all things in Tucson, they told us of a vacant camp car, which we took to bunk in. Doña Lencha was the mother, who took us for boarders,

[61]

so the next morning we had breakfast in her car and went to work. It all went nicely, and we slept well in a warmly heated car.

On the job, we were again with the same gang as at Yuma, and it only took a short time for us Gila monsters to climatize. Being August, the cold was not yet severe. We had been working steadily for one week when a report came to the foreman from the Forest Service unit that we should go to fight a forest fire at the foot of Mount Shasta. We made all preparations to wait for a truck to come for us. We made a big campfire on the driveway from the main road as a signal for the driver. Then we saw a truck going on the highway. It stopped but did not turn on the driveway to come to us. Seeing this, a boy said, "*Se vino! Se vino!*" [It's come!] as the truck passed on. The foreman said, "*Yo pienso no es*" [I guess it's not it]. Then we remained silent. Only the foreman was talking in a low voice with the timekeeper. I could hear the gurgle of the water in the river and the crickets chirping. I was pondering this forest fire job, it being my first time on one. I had been told of all the hazards—that the fire would travel on the top of the trees scattering the fire below. On these things I was pondering when the truck came. It was an open army convoy truck. We climbed on and soon were en route to the smoky region of the fire, our truck in charge of a man from Mount Shasta City. He drove east from there on to the fire camp. The camp was very much like a circus ground, with a truck loaded with provisions and a big water tank car.

The fire was not in a pine forest but in the thick shoulder-high manzanita brush. The line was started from open ground. We made a gap that was like a deep ditch dug in the ground, hard to climb out of. The fire, fanned by strong wind, burned like oiled fragments. Some smart leader asked me, "You wan'na smoke?" I said, "I smoke my brand, but your brand is too stout for me." We were going up the ditch, that is, the line, when some carriers came with bags of lunch—bread and wieners. After the vittles came the water to wet our smoky throats.

The fire jumped across the line and chased us out. Walking as we could, by sunrise we landed up on a rocky hill away from the raging fire. I looked on the dead tall white pine trees burning on the top. With the white ashes at the bottom, they looked like candles on a birthday cake (santo taewa kekim bena).

The truck to take us to camp was parked below our hill. To get down to where it was, we had to walk across the hot ashes. Those who had thin shoe soles surely got the hot foot!

The Forest Service did right to let nature take her course, the wind driving the fire away to the lava rock piles at Black Buttes. There was no brush to burn there, so the golden bearded monster was driven away by the wind.

There were two SP gangs, seven and five, fighting the fire. Gang five, all Texas Mexicans, called themselves Texicans, and gang seven, all Yaqui, called ourselves the New York Yaquis, for New York Yankees. We spoke many languages and couldn't understand each other, but we all understood dinner call. After dinner the railroad workers were dismissed, so we came back to our camp by evening. The following day the foreman, using the motor car and trailers, took our gang to Black Buttes to see how things were. Not a thing combustible was left where the wind had driven the fire. It was interesting to see the lava stones piled as if they were placed by hand. Manzanita brush, like Arizona greasewood [creosote] brush, goes up with fire like oil. Manzanita is the Mexican pinisika and bears an edible berry. The tiny berry is like that of the cumaro, an Arizona tree found in abundance on the east side of the Santa Cruz River. Between Sahuarita and San Xavier, south of Tucson, this tree grows up as tall as telephone posts.

After the forest fire, the camp was called to a railroad emergency job—a landslide of a high cliff which fell on top of the main line at Siskiyou, Oregon. We left Weed in the late afternoon and made Siskiyou at sundown. The next day we went to work below the Siskiyou tunnel with the regular camp. Parked on a side track, the steam shovel on a flatcar had tractor wheels. Working that day, we opened the line for service again. Then the camp was dropped back to Mott section to raise track.

The work at Mott was below the "Y" where the booster brought up every freight train out of the canyon and turned after pushing. One of these boosters returning from the "Y" overrode the flagman placed above the job. We were in a point with a high cliff on the right and a steep cliff down on our left. If the engine had derailed, we wouldn't have escaped. The roadmaster was with us, and he told the engineer in a kindly way not ever to repeat this error. As nothing serious happened, the roadmaster was considerate and reasonable.

There was a short tunnel near this place below Mott section. A little way down was the horseshoe curve, Cantara Loop, where the track crossed the river to go downstream.

After the track-raising job, we remained in Mott doing night work. The September rain was causing landslides, so there was need to watch night and day. This also provided overtime pay: fifty-six cents an hour was seventy-five cents an hour for night work. One good thing in this cold country was that whiskey was available. Yaquis don't drink much and pass out quickly. One Saturday night the section men were drinking, and they desired us to join them and sing Yaqui songs like *"Sawari ba'ata"* [yellow water] with guitar. Soon two of these men got into a brawl, and one began beating a little short fellow, using a brakeman's club on his head. We Yaquis went in to stop the fight. The bleeding was terrible, so one Yaqui brewed some bitter herbs and bathed the short man's head with them and stopped the bleeding. The man who had beaten him thought we had turned against him, so he went to his room and came out with a gun, a forty-five automatic. My friend, Juan Alvarez, who saw where this man had dropped the club, took it and struck the man with the gun on the left cheek to prevent him from killing one or more men. The stricken man, falling, tossed the gun close to the foreman's porch.

The next day was Sunday. Because of this incident, the section foreman put the law on us. Alvarez, the man who had struck the gunman, was in his camp car alone and sent for me to be with him. He told me he had intended to take away the gun to avoid the killing of one or more men. Soon the law came, two homely-looking men. Of the two officers, the younger was in charge. He was considering the condition

[64]

and situation. Juan, the man who was sought, walked out of his car to see what was to be done. I went with him. Then the section foreman accused us both together. He testified to having seen us both when the man was struck.

The officer in charge arrested us and took notes on the case. He told our foreman that it was a charge of drunkenness at Dunsmuir. The timekeeper wrote our time checks payable at the depot, and at noon sharp we were behind bars, like the real thing, enjoying every bit of the experience. Such fools we mortals are.

The officer came and told us that we were to be bailed out. He took us to the depot to get our time check money. From there he took us to the judge who fined us ten dollars apiece for being drunk. We had enough money to pay and even to have a couple of beers. Then the officer himself took us back to camp. Company regulations required that our names be changed so we could start working as new hired men, losing seniority. Mine became Tomás Flores; Alvarez became Juan Gualberto.

The matter was settled, and after the work in the Mott section was finished, the camp was moved to the town of Weed below Black Buttes. There the camp was assigned to a big job up at Grass Lake, a railroad station with a population of ten persons—four section laborers and their wives, and two telegraph operators. Grass Lake, being fully packed with tule grass, had a wooden runway built to the middle of the lake for visitors to walk on and enjoy the mosquitoes the size of houseflies.

Our project was to destroy and pick up the old branch connecting Weed to the main line of Klamath Falls. Temporarily our camp was on part of the branch. We pulled out of Weed at three o'clock dawn, so we had no meal until noon when the women brought our lunch. Work was impractical with the camp on the track to be torn up, so the camp had to be moved to the next switch ahead, Morrison. From there we could see the main line, but we were in utter wilderness. The switch ahead of us was Cougar, but no one lived there. With the camp on the side track, the work train would come to the job and pick up the old material. There was no crane to pick up the rails, but the roadmaster was a veteran railroader, and he made the Dunsmuir wrecking crew put a steam shovel with tractor wheels on a flatcar. The old track was cut off fifty rails away from the turnoff.

When the work train arrived, orders were to break and leave ten rails, so ten rails were left connected and shoved to the center of the track. One empty flatcar was coupled in front of the steam shovel. The ten connected rails were hooked with a giant heavy chain and cables to the coupler of the empty flatcar, and the engine started pulling backward, dragging the rails one car-length on the ground. Then pushing forward, it placed the shovel in front of the rails, and a rail tong hook was chained to the shovel. The joint bolts were broken with chisel and sledgehammer, so the rails were lying loose on the ground. The shovel then picked them up and loaded them on the flatcar. This operation was repeated until the load was finished. Then the car was staked and placed on a side track, and an empty one brought.

When the job came to the highway crossing, the camp was moved to Morrison. In the same way the work carried to Morrison, where the camp was, the work train coming every day with the steam shovel and empty flatcar. All the old steel was salvaged for junk, and the rails for secondhand grade. In all we made up four carloads of ninety pound secondhand rails, figuring forty rails on each flatcar. In the afternoon we went to pick up the old ties. The track bed was left bare, the old ties piled up and burned. The foreman said, "Anytime we finish this work, we quit," meaning we would have the rest of the day off if we finished early. That evening we received a big batch of Tucson Yaquis. In picking up the ties, Canuto, the oldest man in the gang, kept encouraging the boys just like in a battlefield, *"Kate'em am mahawe kialim velawim"* [Do not be afraid; they are like tender grass]. The newcomers made the gang much larger, and by evening the curve was like a circle of *luminarias* in the dark, every pile of ties burning like a lantern. This finished the job far enough to move the camp to Gale, three miles from Weed. Here we received our paychecks. Mine came in the name of Tomás Flores, the name I got for being in jail at Dunsmuir.

After being two months in the wilderness, we were in need of clothing. We invaded the stores in town, and my friend Juan came back with a pair of over-sized shoes which were too big for him. He said, "Being so long without seeing a new pair of shoes, when I put them on, I took them as they came."

One day we went one mile away from camp. There my nephew Pedro, one of the three of us from Tucson of the same family, was dismissed. He went back to camp. Sánchez and Escalante, my other relatives, got passes for the three of them to Tucson, so they went home. Then camp was moved to Black Buttes above Weed Town. Here I arranged for my name to be put back on the payroll accurately. This place the Rio Yaqui Yoemes called *hiak batueta benasi hiapsa* [like living on the Yaqui River], for the abundance of wildflowers and water, including *maza'asia gotoboli* [wild roses] and *San Miguelito vara prieta* [St. Michael's black staff].

I went to Weed one Sunday. I had a woman friend in town and stayed with her three nights, laying off the railroad for three days. When I returned, I was charged reasonably. The regulation was that no man could stay away from work three days, and the foreman said I had violated this rule because I was not sick. That same afternoon I left camp for the highway to take the stage [bus], my clothing rolled in my bedroll. At Dunsmuir, I collected my time check, twenty-five dollars. At the Manning store, I was sent to a section at Mistletoe, Oregon, a lonely section on the northern slope of Siskiyou Mountain. When I got on the train, the roadmaster was in the same car, and he remembered seeing me on the old branch job. I rode with him until I got off at Mistletoe. He was going down to Ashland where he had his office.

It was in June when I arrived, about four o'clock. Mistletoe was very pretty, with beautiful scenery down below and up above. There were five Mexican nationals in the section. I walked a mile, through a swamp to an apple orchard, to the highway to get some food to get started with. Then night came. The houses were old boxcars with windows and doors, and mine was full of trash and mice. I swept it clean of trash, but the mice were in their own home, not to be chased out. Mice are made to be with us, so are we made to be with mice. Bedtime was anytime in Mistletoe after I said my prayers: *"A mina omnium pidelium per misericordiam Deus requiem cantim pace, amen"* [May the souls of the faithful departed, by mercy of God, rest in peace].

I was doing my own cooking on a small stove, burning tie wood. I was alone in my house when two men who were placed to live with me came. We three got along nicely. One of these two men was a very small fellow. The other was of medium size, whose name was Calixto. The little fellow was called Cortito, or Shorty. There was another, a big man who was a bully. He was always teasing the little fellow, making his life miserable. I was told he had beaten another fellow previously. I was always talking in favor of the other fellows, seeing the big man abusing and cursing them. I did not get in a scrap with him, because I would have had to use a pick handle. The big man knew it and started behaving more like us. This man was alone in his bunkhouse. Then the little man was put with him. They were always in heated argument. Late one Sunday afternoon, when the foreman had gone to town, Calixto came running into my room, because they were fighting. I ran to their house and found the little man had the big man cornered, wielding a mean knife at the big man's belly. The big man ran out of the house desperately frightened, the little one after him. Running, the tall fellow grabbed a pole which held up the clothesline, but when he tried to turn to face Shorty, he fell on his back. The little man climbed on him, still with the knife in his hand, but the big man caught the hand with the knife. I came and dragged Shorty away, and he went with us to our house, so nothing serious happened. The little man's real name was Pablo. The big man was Santos, and from then on, Santos was a saint.

We were a five-man section gang. I was making good money doing overtime, so I could send fifty dollars home to my mother and Fernando monthly. Every evening I went to clear the way for passenger train number seventeen. This was because of the landslides constantly rolling down on the track.

In order to get overtime, I walked up to the Siskiyou tunnel, which is a mile long on the summit. Coming back home,

I rode the engine booster down. The booster pushed the freight trains up from Ashland to the top. To make the grade, the train had to zigzag. All these trips down were joy rides because of the magnificent scenery. Looking down the valley, I felt like I was on an airplane ride. This perspective I had also enjoyed in the Sacramento River canyon the year before when I arrived in the Mott section from Tucson. My memories of Tucson, while I was in Mistletoe, were of the toasted evening horizon, the pink rose color dabbed on the Catalina cliffs.

All this went on until winter came, then Christmas season. Not looking for a white Christmas, I saw it. We had whole forests of Christmas trees decorated with snow. At the foreman's home, his wife read St. Luke. I told the Yaqui story of the Immaculate Conception: Mary rose one morning feeling very happy. Her heart was overflowing with happiness. She took her red clay *cantara* (pronounced kantra, like Barbra for Barbara). Everything was very beautiful. The spirit of God was in the sewam [flowers] this springtime morning. Mary arrived at the river singing a pretty shepherd song her mother had taught her. In a whirlpool, she found a rose floating round, round, and around. She desired to have it. She waded into the river, and as she dipped her cantara, the rose floated into the cantara. She took the rose out and dropped it down her loose robe. She inhaled its perfume to her heart's desire.

Mary wished Joseph to see the rose, and when she came to him, he was also happy, whistling merrily upon his labor. Mary said, "Joseph, I brought a most beautiful rose for you to see." But when she searched her breast, she did not find the rose. She was grieving, saying she had lost the rose, but Joseph knew the rose was there, for the place was filled with its perfume. Joseph said, "Why do you grieve so for the rose? In this life pretty things come and remain for a brief time with us. If the flower is lost, all we can do is forget it." But the rose was not lost; it was within her. The Yaqui "Hail Mary" says, *"Tua et katek em tompo yoremta Jesús"* [Truly within thee in thy womb forming, Jesus].

Time passed until Mary started showing her inevitable condition. Consequently, Joseph, being a just man, was of a mind to leave her (Matt. 1:19). This he decided to do the next morning. He told Mary that he was going to the country to get wood for his work. As much as she loved the country, Mary was to stay home. She was sad, being still a tender young soul. She took it as she could.

Joseph, in the country, left the mule to wander and graze. Soon he was overcome by thirst and heat, and he went under the shade of a big tree and became unconscious.

At home, Mary was mindful of him delaying so long, and she decided to go and find him. Joseph, lying unconscious, heard the mule bray as though seeing one she knew. Presently, he heard Mary's voice. This inspired him to sit up. Mary shouted in her familiar way, "Joseph, you are thirsty. I have brought you some water." She had a red bowl in her hands, and Joseph drank and regained consciousness. Mary said, "Come in the house," and he found himself in the patio of his home, beside his loving wife whom he had left. Mary was talking by the spirit: "Joseph, we have a glorious gift, a gift from our heavenly Father. It is the joy of us both, his parents. This child will be the joy of all our people too. The rose cannot be forgotten, Joseph. We shall keep it forever in reality."

I told the story this far in Mistletoe on Christmas evening. After all, Mistletoe is the symbol of Christmas. I had the pleasure of being in the foreman's home, I know, because the other men could not talk the English language. I meditated, "My heavenly Father, my country is truly beautiful *(tua uhyoli)*, being Thy gift. Thou hast given it to me by means of consequences, amen. I love my country as I love Thee, amen."

My friend Calixto was a poet, writing in Spanish. He had published his compositions in the *Los Angeles Herald*. I was also writing verses in Spanish to set to music. We had a guitar, and I rehearsed them among us just for a pastime. I wrote a short song in English about hobo girl Lou:

[70]

Well, I don't know where I'm going.
I am riding away once again,
And I don't care where I will go.
I am riding away on a train.
I only know, as all lovers do,
That on the road I am happy with Lou.
She will be smiling always with me.
Listen, the engine whistle ahead.
That's the other town where we'll get us some bread,
And if we get caught, we will tell the truth,
That we are bound for the valley for fruit.
Let times be hard, as hard as can be,
If we are together, the happier we'll be,
And when we pass the next town below,
We'll be in our home, down in Mistletoe.
After this trip, what will you do?
I will be loving my hobo girl Lou.

Thus the Yaqui and Yori poetry mingled in Siskiyou. We were off six days from Christmas to New Year's Day, so I took a trip to Salem with Lou.

4. RETURN

Mining, Writing, Gandy Dancing

When all the rails are measured right,
And the switch point down on the headblock tight,
And the stock rail bolted right in line,
And the frog in position nice and fine,
The foreman then begins to name
All the aces of number one.
It takes good maulers to run a gauge,
And over a mile is a long, long run.
— Refugio Savala

Now it was January 1929, and the spirit began to urge me to go home to Pascua. Having completed the six months necessary to get my pass, I had already informed my brother of my coming in Lent. It was in February when the arrangements were finished.

The train going east was due at Mistletoe at ten o'clock. On February 15, I walked three miles to Ashland to get my pass and came back in time to pack my possessions. A one-room waiting shed was the train stop. It was as it had been with my father waving his handkerchief in Sahuarita long ago; I swung my hat below my waist. The engineer answered, stopping where I was, and I boarded a chair car and met a Mexican. I believe all are friendly. This man gave me good advice not to go astray by taking to drink. He said, "You have triumphed. Your happiness depends on your behavior."

By this time we were on top of the mountain. I took a last look at the scenery below, going like a whirlpool. We entered the mile-long tunnel and went through it. We came to Holbrook, and beyond this was a river of clear water. Going over the bridge, I saw salmon in the transparent water. This river goes to Yreka, a mining camp on the south slope of the Siskiyous. Then we were zigzagging down the grade, and I looked out toward Weed Town and the ninety-mile stretch of open country. Nearing Weed, I saw the cottonwood grove below town. At Weed I did not get off to see my woman friend of the past. Going out of Weed, I saw the Black Buttes yard, which I had left to go to Mistletoe, then Mount Shasta where I had gone to the forest fire. How well I remembered the birthday cake candles.

Three miles below was the Mott section, where I first came. Then we traveled on down the horseshoe curve, Cantara Loop, on to the beautiful Shasta Springs (*Chata Rin* in Yaqui) and Mount Shasta (*Munchahta*). Then we passed Dunsmuir where I had spent one hour behind bars with my friend Juan. Another landmark was Castle Crag, then Cottonwood, and next, Marysville, and the Suisun turnoff.

In Benicia, the train went onto a large boat to cross the bay. Here I was feeling our car moving but heard no sound of wheels. Then the train pulled off the boat at Martínez. I had a stopover in Oakland, and from there I took a ferry to San Francisco. In San Francisco, I stayed two nights at a hotel. Here I went slow, with my money talking. Seeing that I did not prevail over the question of money, I checked out, went to the Oakland piers, and checked my baggage to Tucson.

I enjoyed the trip from Oakland to Los Angeles, going by the coast. My pass allowed a stopover in Los Angeles, but my money was going fast, so after one night in Los Angeles, I went straight home to Pascua, arriving for *Tako Pahko* [Palm Fiesta]. I arrived in the daytime to greet my mother and sister Agustina. I was dressed in a black leather jacket and a Tejano Stetson hat called *mo'obe'i* in Yaqui. The taxi driver thought I was one of those Indians off the reservation. He said, "How come you talk so good English?" I replied, "Because I try and I am tried."

I felt grown up at the age of twenty-five years, but my mother treated me like a baby. To our mothers we are all babies.

Now my mother had tamales on the table and led me to them. She gave me the same reception she had given my father years ago.

I was glad to be talking in Yaqui without difficulty. The Yaqui language is omnipresent in my mind, whatever the discourse. I'm glad my language has never been robbed of its beauty. It still keeps extending to all the margins of any language. The legends have been translated from good old primitive Yaqui. It also adapts to English grammar.

When I returned from my long absence, all my gang, seven buddies were back in Tucson, but my brother-in-law was away in Hayden. After a week he came to get his family, my sister and the children. Gabriel Robles was the husband of Humo's wife's elder sister, and it was he who took my sister to Hayden for my brother-in-law. She told him to bring me too, if I wanted to go, so Humo told me. My friend Manuel Suárez was to go with us.

It was morning when we left in Humo's 1925 Chevrolet touring car. I left my mother well provided with food and money. We took the Oracle road, the route going the Cañada del Oro way, only we turned at Oracle Junction and came to Oracle Station. From there I saw the mountain range beyond Hayden. Turning north, we went down the grade to Magma, there across the Gila River through Winkleman and on to Hayden. The road into town was in a canyon, the town nestled in the canyon too. Here we turned off toward a hill on San Miguel Street. At the north end, the street crossed the track to the smelter. My sister lived at this end, above the railroad track.

Manuel Suárez lodged at Humo's home on the south end of Miguel Street with our boyhood acquaintance—Celedonio from the Sasco smelter. This man was a Yaqui-minded person. His closest friends were all Yaquis, and I had been one of them since boyhood.

When I came to Hayden I was not prepared to work, but Celedonio took me to the foreman in the concentration plant. The foreman in charge of the laborers was a Sonora man who talked enough Yaqui to say, "*Vivata ne mika, Pascola.*" [Give me a cigarette, Pascola.]

Our gang was to do manual labor. I got the job doing everything, even to dish-washing after parties. I worked the job for a dollar an hour, getting paid every fifteen days.

My brother-in-law was working in the smelter and placed Manuel Suárez there too. Celedonio was in the mill. My brother-in-law was dumped out through a chute into a gondola, but he landed upright and did not get hurt. My friend Humo was doing contract work with four other men, unloading concentrate out of gondola cars. They were getting paid eight hours' wages for unloading one car, a job which could be done by noontime to make a day.

I made one trip to see my mother and came back again to work. While I was home, my mother told me Fernando was in the Rillito section, working with his family, but home on weekends. I left some money, telling her that I would go back to Hayden to work. It was August when I made the trip, riding the stage. When I returned to my sister's, she was happy to know about our mother being well. I told my sister I would work the rest of the year in Hayden. My plan was to go home to stay after Christmas. When Christmas came, I spent it at Celedonio's home. We were drinking moonshine liquor. I even went to the bootleg woman's home. At midnight I went to my sister's, and she had some tamales. We ate all together, and I was telling how I had Christmas in Mistletoe the year before. Christmas without tamales is like Christmas without a tree.

The same man who brought us to Hayden was visiting the Humos, and when he left, I hitched a ride with him and came home. Seeing me gone, my sister followed after me with the family. They came home with a plan to go picking cotton. This was already the beginning of the Depression time, so my brother-in-law desperately sought work at the Hall Ranch in Coolidge. My mother and I asked my sister to leave the children with us. The Welfare Department was offering a charity work project, so I enrolled the four children as my dependents and was given three days' work for the food necessary.

My mother had another lot in Pascua about three lots

away from our house, and she wanted to move over there, so I tore down the old house and started carrying it to the other place. I had a two-wheeled hand truck and carried tin from the city dump. I got big sheets from old car bodies. I had to cut them all in pieces, so I could load them on my hand truck and haul them. When I had enough roofing sheets, I started putting up the building according to my plans to make it double the width in length. I had posts to make it twelve feet high for roofing. It was February of 1930 when I moved my mother in on the east end which I built like a porch with a roof. This part of the building served for a kitchen. The building was so big, it had a kitchen, dining room, and bed chamber. But it was far away from the well where we were getting water, so I made a four-disk, rubber-wheeled, hand-drawn wagon. On this I placed two tall, empty carbide cans to haul water in. So I had water for laundry, kitchen, and a few plants. I also placed a square-yard wooden box on the wagon and hauled food from charity. Working three days, I got two sacks of flour, oatmeal, and plenty of rice. But there were no potatoes, no lard, no frijoles, no coffee or sugar. The load was heavy.

I was living alone with my mother when my brother Fernando came to town to the place where he had been chopped on the head with an ax. The place where I lived with my mother was where Dr. John Provinse came, guided by Miss Thamar Richey. I offered him a stool to sit on, but he sat in a squatting position. I was surprised, not knowing him to be an anthropologist. I had my writings all packed in large envelopes to give him.* Reporter Bernice Cosulich of the *Arizona Daily Star* took the writings and put me in the news. She quoted from the story about the forest fire in Shasta and the

---

*This modest but varied body of work included poems, tales, character sketches, and brief narratives. These writings had been produced by Refugio during the Depression years, with the encouragement of his Pascua teacher, Miss Thamar Richey.   After describing his meeting with Dr. John Provinse, Refugio proceeds to somewhat compress the course of his writing career. The personal events described in this chapter occurred from 1929–1934, but the work with Dr. Provinse, Dr. Spicer, and Mrs. Painter took place from 1935–1955. It should be noted, however, that the essential chronology of Refugio's account is accurate, and that he was in fact producing the major portion of his creative work during the years spanned by this chapter.

[77]

"birthday candles." About ten years later, when I was teaching Dr. Spicer the Yaqui language, I wrote about the fire in Yaqui. I chose two passages for language illustration—*"Vempo hiba nau molmolti noka"* [They only together in low voices spoke], and *"santo taewa keki cantelam venasi vete"* [burning like birthday cake candles]. A few years after this language study, Dr. Spicer recommended me to Mrs. Painter. She had previously asked for a description of the Deer Dance, so I brought it to this first interview with her in 1948. What caught her first glance was my handwriting, all in print. Upon reading the material, she noted the poetic accent in the clauses. Then she noted the description of the dancer's regalia, the gourd rattle in each hand. Here is the Deer Dance description I gave to Mrs. Painter:

THE DEER

The deer hunter's song[s] are very beautiful in composition. The poetry is characteristic of the life in the wilderness: the human, the beast, the fowl, the bees, the amphibious animals, to the tiniest insect, the mountains, the streams, the rivers, the valleys, the meadows, prairies, the forests, the flowers, of all seasons—Spring, Summer, and Winter —the wind, the rain, the clouds, the celestial body stars, moon, and sun.

Three men are seated on the ground with faces toward the sunrise, with the hats lowered upon the forehead. One of them (with a pan full of water), beats a gourd bowl floating bottom up in the water, with a short stick bound with corn ear barks to produce a muffled noise. The other two singers each have a thin rod made of red hard wood exquisitely carved into many teeth laid on top of another small gourd cup on the ground. With the right hand the singer holds another wooden wand, which he wags on top of the toothed rod; the sound it makes is something like filing iron. With all this noise, the songs are almost inaudible.

Out of these hunting songs, the "Deer Dance" was originated. The dancer's bonnet is made of a white rag; above it the deer head is securely mounted. With it on his head, the dancer imitates the deer going down to a stream of water. He is half naked with a skirt made from a *rebozo*, a Mexican shawl, and a

[78]

wide leather belt around the waist decorated with innumerable shells of deer hoofs hanging loosely on chamois strings. He has in his hands a pair of gourd rattles which he wields harmoniously with the songs. His movements are quick and blitheful. Bound to his legs are the curious rattles made from the worm cocoons. This kind of rattles we call "tenoibim."

Later, we had a brief talk with Dr. Spicer. For some reason Mrs. Painter said, "I will be killing two birds with one stone." I had the same alternative, because from that day on, I, being *polove* — poor fellow — was with the high class people. We had our interviews on the University of Arizona campus in the museum building, upstairs, until we had to translate a sermon from Yaqui. This had to be done at the residence of Mrs. Painter. She had a recording of the sermon at her home. The sermon was recorded from the actual Easter farewell sermon, the author being the Pascua Head Maestro, Ignacio Alvarez. I would listen and write it, first in Yaqui, then English. We would divide every page in sections for reference. In this manner, we translated as many pages as were required. When we had it all translated, it was published for the purpose of study.* I saw the printed copy and Ignacio approved it. Here are some of the lines:

In the seven weeks, embracing his holy book, the Maestro prayed for it, looking toward heaven; he begged for that flower (grace)† like this.

Until during these many days, that holy fulfillment was made, right there where your holy temple stands.

In the presence of Our Leader God Jesus Christ, in His house, where the heavenly light comes down, truly came down on the maestro, he asked for the holy flower in the prayers said toward heaven.

---

*A Yaqui Easter Sermon was published in 1955 as University of Arizona Social Science Bulletin No. 26. Refugio's name appears on the title page along with that of Muriel Thayer Painter and Ignacio Alvarez. The volume contains a literal interlinear translation of the sermon as well as the free translation which Refugio quotes from here.

†Flowers and grace from heaven are synonymous in Yaqui ritual thought.

Now then, it was shown to you like that, that Our Father's flower, that Our Father's blood.

He, Our Father, hung on the cross with open arms; the blood, touching the earth and splashing down, spread all over the world.

Up yonder, where sits the Lord, the Most Holy Trinity, on the holy throne, up yonder, were truly made the pretty flowers which have been created down upon you.

The good holy heavenly light came down to each of you, to every baptized person.

But with that holy prayer that the maestro prayed toward heaven, right there while he was praying, the holy light was sent down to him.

The following Eastertime, the Maestro took his place to preach, but he told us that he was not in condition to deliver a sermon. He then pulled out the little book, and going by it, he delivered a sermon. He also mentioned the usefulness of the book of the sermon in print. Obviously he valued it as his cherished possession.

I was able to record and translate the sermon because I always learned recorded songs. Learning songs from phonograph records, I sang them as a pastime, so my ears were well broken in for this occasion.

As the Depression struck Pima County, I composed a song in Spanish, a narrative story about charity workers, such as I was. The *corrido* was fully packed with humor, telling how things were going in charity work. The verses in the corrido told again how sad it is to see people work just for food. Men greatly intelligent were seen with us in line. Also women were shouting to those of Pima County, "Be of good cheer, sister! We shall go today and work for our flour!" I had the corrido printed by the Mexican paper *El Tucsonense*. I was charged seven dollars for the printing of 100 copies. Selling it for five cents a copy, I made fourteen dollars. In Depression times, as poor as I was, I was content with fourteen dollars. I would have been content just to have gotten my seven dollars out of it. I paid for the printing by making chairs of willow tree branches which sold for seventy-five cents apiece.

When we went to work for money we were very fussy, not wanting to work too fast. But though it was the Depres-

"...I left home town one day on train...."

sion, I never got in too tight a spot. I even made Pascola masks of soft cottonwood roots, and I made the resonator we call a *sonasum,* with brass disks encased in a wood frame. These two pieces sold for $1.50 a set in curio stores. So we always had frijolitos de la olla and fried potatoes. We concluded all this to be Divine help, as in our prayers we praised the Lord in songs in Latin, the Miserere, Psalm fifty. This could be done, my mother being a Cantora, and I had the book. This was not done for people to hear, but for the Lord, who hears in secret. We kept doing this, for mother needed the practice.

In 1931, my brother-in-law Dolores got sick at the ranch near Tempe during Lent and died the same year during Holy Week. He was brought to Pascua on Good Friday. The Kotumbre Ya'ura took charge because he was a *cabo,* corporal. After his burial, Frank Acuña, field boss for Hall Ranch, brought my sister to us. Juan Se'elai, when my sister became widowed, proposed to marry her and to come to Tucson for her later. He didn't come in the same year, so my sister stayed with my mother.

The SP was in need of men, so I went, my brother with me, to camp at the Dragoon section. When we arrived in camp, Lauro Martínez of Pascua was with us, as were Lauro Suárez and Tomás Suárez, but most of the men were of Barrio Libre in South Tucson. The two Suárez men were the sons of Lino Pascola of Pascua.

We went with the job down to Benson, laying new steel. It was all done with track machinery. By the time we came to Benson, I had a song composed, "The Steel Stew." This was first in Spanish, but after a short time, I translated it into English. This is "The Steel Stew" in English:*

> *I left home town one day on train.*
> *It was in search of work in hard times.*
> *I was so very lucky again,*
> *And I go to work for the SP lines.*
> *Are you boys ready to go to work?*
> *Asked the foreman Joe Cataleno.*
> *Yes, sir, we have been ready*
> *Since we left the cottonfields, you know.*
> *Early next morning, the work train was out*
> *With material for track:*
> *Boxes of bolts, spikes, and plugs,*
> *Rail anchors, tie plates, and angle bars.*
> *The falling rails,*
> *Oh, they rang like bells.*
> *It was for us only fun and play,*
> *While the other fellow, who don't know the steel*
> *Was scared through the day.*

I always had to be a witness in cases of grievous incidents. We were coming from Benson, going up the steep grade to Sibyl when the friction wheel came up, slipping to the top. The foreman parked on level track and took a handful of dirt and started rubbing it on the running disk to which the fric-

---

*The corrido is a Mexican narrative folk ballad characterized by great fluidity and spontaneity. Refugio composed several variants of "The Steel Stew," one of which appears in the Interpretations section of this book.

tion wheel was slightly pressed. The running disk dragged his hand into the wheel to cut off the thumb and two forefingers. The white boys took him to Benson and had him treated. After emergency treatment, he was brought back to camp. His wife was pregnant, so we did not tell her right away. Then he was taken to the Tucson SP hosital for final treatment. After this, an investigation was made, each witness telling in a statement how the accident could have been avoided. I had been sitting over the running disk and saw how it had happened, so my statement was this: "It could have been avoided if we had first stopped the motor, then wiped off the grease on the disk that caused the slipping friction wheel."

After this severe blow, Joe continued on the job, directing work and always cheerful as before. He only kept his arm in a sling for a short time. To lay a new switch, he depended on his expert workers to assemble it.

From Dragoon, the camp moved to Bowie, from there laying steel up to Stein's Pass, New Mexico. We finished that job; then the camp was put on the road to come down to Mesa in the Salt River Valley. When we came to Willcox, a Chinese cook was off the train when it pulled out. Desperately, he ran after the caboose and caught it as he could, dangling like a rag, holding to the side bar. One big man on a flatcar where all the camp equipment was loaded, managed to catch him and pull him up again to save him.

My brother had been laid off with a group of other workers. He was in Tucson, living with his family. My mother was at the same place with my sister and children. In September 1933, a group of men was brought to our camp at Mesa. In the new group—which arrived on Mexican Independence Day, September 16—came my brother. That evening, the camp was pulled out, this time en route to Yuma. We did not go to downtown Yuma, but the camp was placed on a siding, Fortuna, eleven miles east of Yuma. Next morning we were unloading camp equipment when the motor car was rolled down on two heavy poles. One of the poles jerked and whipped a man on the ankle, putting it out of joint. This man was laid to bed in camp after his foot was put in a cast.

The camp then moved back to Blaisdell. From there we worked on curves up to Dome, transposing rails until we came to Granite Spur, the SP rock quarry where granite gravel was taken. From this quarry had come all the gravel to fill the Yuma yard. We continued on, all the way from Yuma to Wellton, transposing rails on the Dome curves. A work train came from Yuma to pick up a load of old rails. An air compressor was used, the steel cable slipping off the pulley. One man kept it in place with a lining bar. One day a new man was put on to do the work. Because of lack of knowledge, he was not doing it right. Joe Cataleno climbed up to show the new man how to keep the cable in place. While he held it in place, the cable whipped, and the bar hit Joe in the head, knocking him off the flatcar to the ground. This was not so severe as the hand accident, but the rule was changed so the air crane was not used anymore. From that time on, we loaded the ninety-pound rails by hand. This was in three-time, yelling, "Up! High yo! Heave o!" In Mexican this yelling sounds, *"Apa! Hai! Yo hiva!"* On "apa" the rail goes to the waist; on "hai," over the head, held in the hands; on "yo hiva," it is tossed onto the flatcar. These old rails were curved, but still of use. When they are put in straight lines, they straighten up if the track is lined with lining bars.

When we cleared this job of all scrap material, we started drifting in toward the east from Wellton through Mohawk, Stoval, Stanwick, Aztec, and Sentinel, on down to Gila Bend until we entered the Tucson district. From Gila we went to Maricopa, Casa Grande, Red Rock, Rillito, and into the Tucson yard limit. In Tucson we worked raising track.

When the work in Tucson was finished, the camp moved to Pantano, a pretty place. From there sprung the water that flowed in the Rillito River, enough water to make a good sized dam for irrigation. The fruit orchards below Vail were irrigated from the canal from the dam. The Colossal Cave mouth was in view from our camp at night. The work was on the well-known horseshoe curve of Pantano.

Hiram Gailey came here to join camp number one. He was a resident in Mesa where we had been before going to Yuma. Gailey was a student in railroading. He came to us in this steel construction camp, and he got a broad knowledge. He did wonderfully being assistant foreman to Joe Cataleno. Later he became foreman of the extra gang number one. Still much later, he became general foreman of all the maintenance-of-way camps. In 1933 I was sent from Yuma to extra gang number one at Mohawk where Gailey was now foreman of the camp. We came, not doing construction work, just raising track, putting new gravel and new ties, and tamping with air tie-tampers. This required motor air compressors. I had been a flagman on the west side since the time of the Cataleno gang. We came doing this work from Mohawk to Maricopa. When Gailey was made general foreman, he had to be in the Tucson office, being of the Tucson division. All the Phoenix and Yuma men were laid off.

At this time Catáleno took over extra gang number one again, which again became a steel construction gang. We started one section west of Maricopa at Heaton. A work train came every morning with a giant compressor for the air spike hammer. The spike maul was used by those driving the gage. The rail was put to standard gages, spiking its quarters, centers, and joints. There were four men to point every spike for the air hammers. The hammer was put on the spike and pressed down until it was driven in.

On the train crew there were five men—four brakemen and one engineer. Flagging for this job, I had the responsibility of a train man. I was protecting the job and the work train. The big air compressor could not be set off the track, so the work train had to take the side track to clear for a passing train. The engineer of the passing train would blow three long whistles as the call for the train flagman.

When the Tempe branch-off was renewed, the camp kept moving as the job advanced south toward Tucson. As the job moved on, I kept moving with them. I made a watch case to carry in my pocket. This I fashioned of the blind plate of the engine number on the headlights. I rubbed off the black paint until it was sparkling bright. I was very fussy about my job and had a regulation railroad watch and a trainman's timetable. The timetable contained train schedules: regulars were eastbound, extras were westbound; locals went by engine

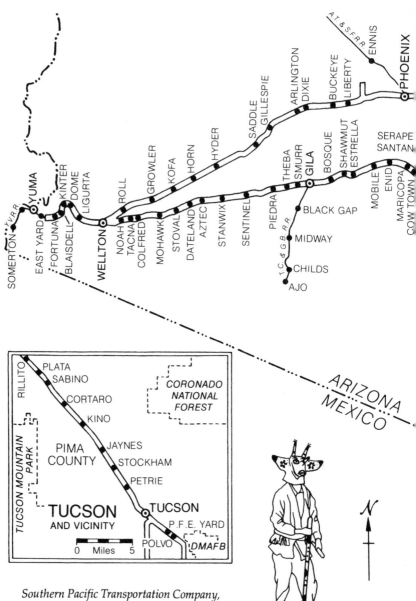

Southern Pacific Transportation Company,
Tucson Division.
Adapted by Nora Voutas.

Arizona Section Points on the Southern Pacific Line

number. This was in Arizona; in northern divisions, trains were numbered according to southbound and northbound directions.

After we finished with the air compressor, work went on with the burro cranes on the track. We came to Picacho, Queen Creek branch-off. When we came to Red Rock, the Silverbell branch was put in condition for big engines to work on. Then camp moved to Rillito.

The heat was affecting the steel that was laid, pressing the rails tight. When six inches were cut off, it just drew close together. The same thing was happening in Benson district. Ties, dragged by the rail anchors, could not hold the run. This was due to the downhill run of the steel. This steel run had us on the run too. The camp was rushed to the Benson district.

We passed through Tucson the evening before July 4. I rode in my bunk car. The camp was placed at Tully, a horseshoe curve, the morning of my saint's day. We were only three persons in camp: the cook, a flunky, and me. All the men who spent the night in Tucson came in the afternoon. There were coyote howls, fox yelps, rattlesnake hisses, every sound to celebrate July 4. The fun is what counts.

The next day, we went to round up the steel running wild. We had to transpose the track on all the curves to control it. This continued until September, after summer. The same trick was applied west of Benson to Mescal.

All this time we made weekend trips to Tucson by freight train, coming and going, so I learned that my mother was sick from a foot disease. This I cannot describe adequately, but it was an ugly lump of the sole skin. My sister and the children were still with her.

When I was absent again, Miss Richey placed my mother in the Southern Methodist Hospital. They operated on her, and she was sent home. Every trip I made, I came to see her, and my sister took care of her until she was able to walk again.

On another trip, I was told of my father being sick. Fernando and I both came home to stay. He went to his family, and I went to mother and sister. My brother and I were both given a chance at WPA work on a control road up on Mount Lemmon. We were getting food and clothing for one week of work. My food order was as when I worked three days a week in 1931. The clothing order was eight dollars in any store downtown. I was able to provide well for mother and my sister's kids. It was 1934, and we did not attempt to move in search of work, for the Depression was still licking its tail. My mother was doing wonderfully, but my father was failing fast. At this time I stayed at my brother Fernando's home to help him with my father. This was the time when I wrote most of a long poem, "Jesus, Mary and Joseph," written in three parts.

Two legends, "Otomcowee" and "Seahamoot," were published.* I have already told the story of "Seahamoot," the prophetess who predicted the coming of baptism, the white priests, and seeds to be planted and cultivated. "Otomcowee" tells of a prehistoric bird which made its abode in Otomcowee, Skeleton Mountain:

THE LEGEND OF SKELETON MOUNTAIN

In the pleasant shade of a ramada, a boy who was almost a man reflected his face in the water in the olla as he dipped the gourd cup to drink.

It was in summer. A drowsy old man sat on a buckskin stool with his back resting against the wall of the carrizo that formed the jacal of his abode. The old man had just risen from the noon siesta. The adventurous boy asked his grandfather: "That mountain yonder is so beautiful and high—why is it called *otomcowee*, Skeleton Mountain?"

The old man sighed and replied: "In olden days a monstrous bird was invading our eight villages and a person was lost every evening. The victim was followed and always was found on top of that mountain. Piles of bones were found there and skulls of victims who were carried away by the great fowl.

"Now there was a young woman who was greatly loved by her parents. She was about to be a mother. As it was summer

---

*These legends appeared in the *Arizona Quarterly*, vol. 1, no. 1, Spring 1945.

[89]

the young woman was sleeping outside the house, outside the jacals and the shelters. At midnight the bird swept low along the river course to where the young woman lay asleep. She was already in the bird's claws when she screamed. But it was too late to save her.

"The young woman's father followed the bird which had taken part of his soul. Other good men went with him also, taking weapons. It was far and high to the mountain top, but they reached it by morning. As usual, a new skeleton was found, and among the bones, a child. He was alive. The child was taken into the village and was greatly loved by his grandparents.

"Years passed and the boy was old enough to know that he was an orphan. He studied with great interest the art of archery, which he soon brought to command. There was no other Yaqui to bow and arch so sure as this boy. When he had prepared his weapons, he called all the people in the village together. 'I ask permission to go into *otomcowee* and slay the giant fowl.' But the council answered: 'Many are the good men who have tried to kill the bird. Always they have failed because it is a farsighted animal and vanishes into space when men seek its abiding place. But if you think to go, go. If you require help, it shall be given.' And the boy again spoke, 'I shall go.' Then the young man chose an arch of great power and three arrows of the most exquisite art, and everyone knew his skill as an archer. And so, many offered to accompany him. But he did not consent, saying, 'In three days you may follow me. Whether I fail or prevail will then be known.'

"Early the next morning the boy was ready to go. Thus he instructed his people: 'If I fail, you will see that beautiful carrizo grass in the patio of my house become deathly pale. If I die, so will the grass die. If I am sad, so it will become dry and withered.' Then he said farewell and the drum announced his departure.

"The abiding place of the winged monster was high in *otomcowee*. Before midnight the boy stood just below, within an arrow's flight of the top of the mountain. On the west side of the mountain all night he remained wakeful and unsteady. When the first rays of morning showed in the east he was greatly surprised to see the enormous bird swinging round and round the top of *otomcowee* making a noise like a huge wind, until it settled down to its nest on the mountain top. The boy cast one arrow into his bow and moved closer, making his first attempt, which missed. Never before in his life had an arrow of his gone wild. The creature did not even notice it. Another arrow was placed on the bowstring and sprung with force at the bird. This one also failed, though the bird made a movement as if preparing to fly. The boy was disappointed when his aim again failed, and he recalled the warning voices of the older people. He had only one arrow left. If this failed, the bird would escape.

"In the village the carrizo grass began to wither. Quickly the people sent out a score of men to climb the mountain. The grass had only become dry, it had not withered away, and the men went forth against the boy's will. Travelling fast, they made themselves ready for any disaster that might come their way.

"With his last arrow the boy aimed at the bird with care. This time he did not miss. The arrow struck the great bird through its neck. With hoarse cries it tried to fly away. It rose into the air but could not sustain its flight. Down it dropped, striking the cliff, rolling over the slope of the mountain, scattering the trees of the forest, rolling down and down, the boy running wildly after it, a club in his hand. When the bird caught at last in a stump of a tree, the boy came upon it and killed it with the club. When he had done this he shouted and jumped about and sang. At this moment the men arrived. They were afraid to come near the vast animal until the boy assured them that it was dead.

"Meanwhile, in the village there was great rejoicing, for they had seen the carrizo grass become green and bright with life again. Everyone ran all the way up to the slopes of *otomcowee* to see the bird which had taken so many innocent lives from the villages. Now they were no longer afraid. The boy was taken back into his village and was considered thereafter a great hero."

In this manner did the grandfather tell the story of that mountain which is called *otomcowee*, Skeleton Mountain. The sun was low and the heat was not overwhelming. The boy who had listened intently went out into the field with a sharp hoe to work in the young corn.

My father had perfect mental ability in his sickness. He said, "I don't want to be in a hospital. I will not find rest on earth. The Lord will give me a true rest when I depart from earth."How well I perceived these words as those of a dying man seeing the end.

My father endured the sickness all October and November, while my brother kept the room warm, carrying in live coals from the outside fire. In mid-November I remained by the bedside to do what had to be done. It was one week before the end of the month, and I placed my small cot by my father's bedside to make him as comfortable as I could. We Yaquis have in common taking things as they come.

On the evening of Christmas 1934, I came home to my mother. She was a devout Christmas celebrant with her songs and prayers. I sang "Gloria in Excelsis" in Latin, and returned to my father. After a week, during the night before he was to die, my father was talking. He imagined he was traveling in a camp outfit from Stein's Pass, New Mexico, on the stretch down to Bowie. He was saying that I was dying by his bedside. Then he said I was dead and asked to tell the fireman to stop the train. "We shall place him in a grave safely and go." When he awoke, he was conscious but did not tell any more. He knew me and told me to bring in Fernando. When Fernando came in, my father made a request in the name of the Trinity to have the Maestro come to his bedside. When the two Maestros, Tomás Maso and Chico Pajarito, came, he told them the reason for his request. He prayed in a loud voice "The Lord's Prayer," "Hail Mary," "The Apostles' Creed," and "The Act of Contrition," all in Yaqui. After the prayers, he gave the Maestros leave and thanks. Then one of the Maestros read the Extreme Unction from the book. While the reading was going on, my father asked for water, and my sister Agustina gave him a bowl of water. After he drank, he saw the spirit depart. He extended his hands, saying, "It's gone. Now we shall never find it." Those were his last words, and he expired. We placed him in front of the tevat kus for the night ceremony.

It was the last of December 1934. We could not afford a coffin, so we made one of twelve planks, a casket covered with gray cloth. When we had placed my father in the box, I went home to get my mother and sister. They had come for the night but had taken a ride back to Pascua with Juan Martínez at dawn. In the morning, we thought the homemade casket might be unlawful, but it passed requirements and the undertaker took my father. Only members of the family made the procession in a Model-T Ford. The burial was New Year's Day 1935. We came back home in the afternoon, and at five o'clock, Lencho, a friend who lived across the street from us, came with a list of names that the foreman Cataleno was asking back to camp. Straightaway my brother consented to my going. Lencho said, "Be ready for the eastbound passenger number forty-four."

5. ACCEPTANCE

Cycles of Grief and Joy

Let time be as useless as can be.
Far away I go at evening
Where the beauty I love, I see,
Where happiness abides enlivening,
Describing this loveliness to me;
There sorrow changes its meaning.
                              —Refugio Savala

This time we shipped to Mescal west of Benson. We worked this district January through February, then moved to Red Rock, where we had worked on the Silverbell branch. The boss had the same old crews together again. A shipment of new steel came, to fill up a mile-long strip left from previous work from Wymola to connect at the west end at Red Rock. The big compressor was put off the track and the burro crane put on. I was in my old position, flagging. The weather was mild. By the end of March, we were going to town often to enter fiestas.

In April my mother started getting sick. She had had a chronic blood disease from long before, and this caused skin eruptions all over her body. At the time, Fernando was in the hospital, so I took her to various doctors in town, but they could not help her. The last one I took her to see gave her a white lotion which cured the sores. It was applied superficially on the eruptions and eased the pain. The skin cleared up, so she was not complaining and was, in all appearances, in good health.

When I got my April check at Red Rock and came home, my mother was sick in bed. I was one week at home when one morning I found her spitting blood. Fernando was with me, and I arranged with him to take her to the hospital. It was late afternoon when the ambulance came and took her to Southern Methodist, where Miss Richey had made arrangements. The next morning I went to see my mother. She had spattered the wall with blood. I took my sister to her, and she recognized her just vaguely.

The last of April, when I went to the hospital in the afternoon, I was informed that I would have to put a special nurse on, because my mother had need of one. I told them to put one on, and they told me it would cost seven dollars a night. Having arranged this, I went home.

The second day, I called the hospital at seven in the morning, and they told me that my mother had departed after midnight. The priest had been with her. She was to be brought home at ten o'clock that morning. I ran home and told my sister and Fernando, then ran arround the village to get my mother's godparents. They arranged everything for the night *vigilia* for departed souls. Moreover, the Pascua Kohtumbre Ya'ura took charge of work needed, because she had been a member of ceremonies in the church.

I informed all my relatives across town. A cousin of ours—Lucía Savala—and her husband, my stepfather and his second wife, and the Maestros came. The ramada was set up by our Kohtumbre men, and firewood was brought. It was the day of Santa Cruz. In the evening the pueblo wanted to take my mother's body to the fiesta, but my Aunt Josefina objected because we were in mourning. When the Matachinis came, they would not play the *scape*, the Escape dance. The *Yo'o monaha*, oldest dance leader, who was from the Río Yaqui, pointed to the three Marys which were brought from the church to the distant cruz table, the altar set up beyond the patio cross for my mother. All these little things had to be observed, so procession music was played to escort my mother to the portal of the dead, the funeral ceremony altar.

She was brought in a coffin from the mortuary, but for the burial, a hearse was not provided. One of her godparents had a platform truck with sideguard racks and benches added. It was a cotton-picking truck with a stepladder on the back. The women and children climbed on the truck and all Pascua went to the burial. This was after the night of the ceremony of the Finding of the Holy Cross on May 3, 1935.

Just after the burial, Juan Gonzáles came. This was Juan Se'elai, who had been married to my sister on the ranch near Tempe after the death of my brother-in-law Dolores. He came to take her back to the ranch because he had promised for her kids' sake. He had his own pickup truck, so my sister agreed right then.

My sister's three-year-old child was left with me and a boy of school age. The first evening, I made ready the bed for the little girl, but she refused to get in, saying that she had to say her prayers. She rose, walked to the little altar, lighted the candle, and knelt down. Her opening prayer was Spanish: "Los ángeles Tu alaban, Padre eterno" (The angels praise Thee, Father eternal). She asked me to join her, and when I knelt down beside her, she made the sign of the cross. She said the "Lord's Prayer," "Hail Mary," and "Glory Be" with me. After her prayers, she walked to her bed. Lying down, she was muttering. She said aloud, "Now I'm ready to go to sleep." With this little performance, grief for my mother turned to joy. I was providing for the child, and she had learned to say her bedtime prayers.

My nephew went with Frank Acuña to his mother at Hall ranch, but the following weekend he returned to me again. The next Monday, the boy was going back on a freight train, and I just had to go with him. To do this, I left the little girl with my brother Fernando. The Phoenix local, Number 903, left Monday evening, so we went to the SP east yard and took an empty boxcar. We arrived in Coolidge at midnight and saw flashes of light flaring. I thought they were the train men. The boy knew the way, and we walked to camp to my sister. When we got into bed to sleep, I heard the barking of many dogs. Presently one came where I was, growling meanly. It was from a posse from Florence which was on our trail. The officers came and checked and found it was their mistake. The next day people in the camp investigated to see who was taken. This was similar to incidents in Dunsmuir jail and Mistletoe. I was glad to see the three came out to be insignificant.

I persuaded my sister to come and take the little girl, so her husband took half a day off and took her. Now I was on my own at home, since my nephew went with them.

Catalina García was alone, too. Her husband had left her to go to another woman in 1926. Since then she had remained at home with her two children. She and I were long-time acquaintances, since she had been my mother's intimate friend. Catalina and I started getting together to talk about our being alone, and she said that we could make a living together. She had a broad knowledge of family maintenance. From this point of view, I went as she suggested until we were mates. Being alone was not loneliness, but fate predestined us together.

In these days, the owner of a gasoline station came looking for a handyman. I was at home, and he asked if I would do some work for him. I agreed, at two bits an hour, starting at eight o'clock. I chopped all the weeds, raked, and swept the yard, and mixed some cement to make a base for posts. When I finished at five o'clock, I had four dollars. This man was just starting then. Later he built a restaurant on that spot.

That same day Catalina had arranged to go cotton-picking. The Reed ranch truck came, and she took a bed spring and mattress. I took blankets and a quilt for covering and a box of groceries I bought with the four dollars which I made that day. We went to the ranch that evening. I left my house to Fernando.

When we came to the ranch, I had to rent a house to live in. Our friends the Vásquezes were already well established at the ranch.

Nicolasa, Catalina's sister-in-law, called Catalina *ako* (older sister). I often called her "Lina" for short.

The next day was opening day for cotton-picking at the ranch. This was not new to me, but I had always been a slow picker. But the fun and experience from it pays well. The fun I had was in figuring out the wage at seventy-five cents per hundred pounds. Later I learned to figure it by decimals, not fractions. Our evening amusement was a phonograph with popular Mexican songs. I would sing some selections the men would ask for.

I picked cotton one week and then went to work on the ditch gang. This work was clearing ditches, clearing them of all brush. We were getting fifteen dollars a week, good enough for a slowpoke picker like me.

In November we came to town for Anima, All Souls' Day, when we have a table serving for the spirits of the dead. This second day of November is a memorial day for both Yaquis and Yoris.

On the return to the ranch, I was left, because the car in which Aunt Josefina came was overloaded. On November 3, I returned with Ignacio Maestro. We almost had a disaster turning into the Reed Ranch alley. A speeding car met us right on and rubbed the fender of our car. What damage the other car took, I don't know. Ours got a scratch to show how close it came. I got scared like when "the falling rails rang like hell" in "The Steel Stew," but we came home safely, not departed souls. On Memorial Day all the workers had gone to town, taking a day off with leave in Marana.

By this time Lina was in need of clothing, so we made a mail order from the Chicago Sears catalogue. It was a small order, so we got it soon, COD, at Pima Mercantile in Marana. She only got one dress and some under things to amount to fifteen dollars.

Now the San Xavier fiesta was nearing after November, and I planned to work until then and go, depending on Divine help. Then in December, I took my heavy coat and as I walked toward Rillito a man with a load of wood gave me a ride. At Pascua, he invited me to join him in going to the fiesta, so I went. When I left the ranch Lina said she would stay and wait for me. I had nothing in mind but to go and come back.

At the San Xavier fiesta I was walking from the road to the dance when I heard one word shouted—"Compadre!" This was my sister Agustina, sent here to bring me to her by any means, because one of her daughters, the youngest, was to be married. She told me insistently, "So I am taking you on my trip back." By this time she and her family were at a ranch near Chandler. My sister Eloisa, who lived with them, had an expensive dress at my home that she had left when she went to the Salt River Valley in 1931. On the way, we stopped at my home to take it along with my clothing. I had my clothes in a small trunk, so both things went in the car. Fernando was not home because he was living in Eloy at the Milligan Ranch. I had sixty dollars entrusted to my sister-in-law Eulalia, Fernando's wife, so on the way I came to her to get five dollars and proceeded on to Hill's ranch near Chandler. Agustina lived in a big ranch house with the family, and she made room for me in the big house. I picked cotton with my two nephews, Cuco and Epifanio. We weighed our pick together. The cotton was Pima long staple.

Then all was prepared for the wedding of my niece Angelita. We all went to Guadalupe on the weekend, and the wedding was performed at Guadalupe church. There were two Pascolas to represent bride and groom. Their performance was like that at Fernando's wedding in Tucson. Eloisa was Angelita's sponsor.

On Sunday evening, after the ceremonies, we went back to the ranch and my sister prepared for *lutupahko* for my mother. This was to take place in Higley, another Yaqui settlement in the valley. We joined another party who also had to do a ceremony for their dead.

We were in need of money, so with my brother-in-law, I went to Eloy. My sister-in-law who had my money gave me twenty dollars. With that, we returned to Higley, and the ceremony was done. After this, I had to return home. My brother-in-law Juan took me to the depot with my things, and I took the bus, arriving in Tucson at night. Then I took a taxi and came home.

The next day, I went to my brother's to see him and his family. They were just ready to leave for Coolidge, and they suggested that, being without a job, I should go with them. It stood to reason, and I went with them to the ranch. My niece,

Lola, Agustina's oldest daughter, was there also. I picked with them for three days, weighing my pick alone. The cotton was also Pima long staple.

I was sleeping in the tent which my brother had put up. It was a heavy canvas tent to resist any weather. I dug a hole at one corner to put live coals into to heat all the room. During the week I was restlessly conscience-striken about Catalina, seeing that I had left her alone at the ranch with her words, "I will wait." These same words were my mother's to my father long ago.

On Sunday evening I went to my niece's tent while her husband was having supper and told them about what was done in Guadalupe and Higley and all about how I went to be with Agustina and her family. Making my talk brief, I went in to get in bed.

When I got in bed, I could not sleep. I still had my railroad watch, and I knew the time of the Phoenix local train by the timetable. At midnight, I walked to Coolidge station and took the train at two o'clock. I rode to Picacho and got off at three o'clock. On the walk to Red Rock, I found a lone man warming by a fire. I talked with him until daylight, then I walked to Red Rock, where I met one of my section buddies and deliberately spent the morning with him. When I was going, a Yoeme from Rillito picked me up. He dropped me on the road to the Reed Ranch.

The first thing I did was go to my Aunt Josefina. She asked me if I came to Catalina and added, "Come, I will take you." As she walked with me she said, "She was waiting."

Catalina and I came together again after the short separation, both happy. And now my job was also waiting, which meant so much to both. I continued working on the Marana field job.

There were two other SP gang workers in Marana picking cotton; one was Manuel García, second Monaha of Barrio Libre. The other, Ramón of Río Yaqui. We had to wait until New Year's for SP work.

Cataleno's camp number one was taken over by Jim Becket. This foreman was from Texas, speaking good Spanish fluently. He was instructed to take all extra gang number one men. Juan Gonzáles, the assistant foreman, and Lencho got us together. We Marana men were informed to move into camp at Red Rock. I talked to Juan Vásquez, and he was allowed to use the ranch truck to move. It was the last day of January 1937 when we started work.

Becket told González to get an experienced flagman. González said, "I have just the man to take the west part." So I was a flagman again. The shipment of steel arrived, and we distributed it from Wymola. Here "falling rails rang like hell" again, but ears used to it took it as fun.

This was the time when Social Security first came into force. We filled the blanks for them to get the cards with the account number. When the cards came, most of them were lost. I did right to put mine upstairs in my good furniture where I still have it for reference.* My bookkeeper is also upstairs, and she keeps track of everything for me: addresses, all dates, especially dinner dates. Her name is Señorita Memoria. Everybody knows her around here. Her advice is, "Always remember not to forget," or "Don't forget to remember."

The work started at Red Rock and was to go west. We did not get our checks in February. The camp kept moving west—Casa Grande, Maricopa, Estrella, Gila Bend, Sentinel—laying steel all the way. It was March 6 when we got two checks. We went as far as Mohawk, and it was Holy Week. Many of the workers, being Yaquis, went to Tucson to the fiesta, but Manuel and I took a round trip pass and went to Marana. I came to Catalina to see if I could move her to Tucson. When I told her that I was going back, she said the ranch truck was available, so she prepared to take everything back home in the truck. I talked of this to the ranch owner, and he said, "Juan will take her as he brought her." Catalina took fifteen dollars, which I gave her, to start with. Catalina was not going that day, Sunday, but my pass was for that day, so I had to leave. Manuel and I waited for passenger train H3 at Marana and boarded at six-thirty by my watch. We rode part of the night and arrived in Mohawk in time to

---

*Savala is humorously referring to his own memory.

work Monday. Everything went as straight as a mainline for us cotton pickers, whereas the others who went to the fiesta spent their double checks.

At that time I was waiting to come near Tucson to go home. The steel being laid to Mohawk required the camp to retrace our route to surface the track—raising track, changing gravel, tamping with air gun tie-tampers. So we came close to Rillito, and in July 1937 I went home.

When I arrived home, Fernando would not let me stay alone where mother had died, so he gave me a small hut in the middle of the lot at his place. When I moved in, I fixed the hut as I do section houses. There I lived alone doing my own everything because I was used to it.*

At this time, the Pacific Fruit Express yard was being constructed, and I went there to work. Robert Bosworth was the foreman. Bob had extra gang number seven foreman in the Shasta division, and all the men who were with him there were here with him. Bob was called to this job because Cataleno was section foreman in Jaynes. Juan Alvarez was not there, but the two Pascolas were, Cruz and Romero. This big job was finished in a short time, July and August of 1937.

After the PFE work was finished, I was idle, but things had to be done for money. During this idle doodle time, I went to the commisary which shipped SP workers. They sent me to the Globe yard section to an Italian foreman, Geraldo Iloa, whom we called Jerry.

I came to Bowie and took the doodlebug on the Globe branch, 125 miles from Bowie to Globe. I arrived at quitting time. The foreman had my belongings loaded on a motor car and took me to a section house. I had all the food I had need of to start. The foreman gave me a SP meal ticket good in a Chinese restaurant. By this time, I was already a heavy winebibber, but only beer was served with food on the meal ticket. That was not what I would prefer to drink in such a time and place.

---

*While Savala does not explicitly discuss an end to his relationship with Catalina, this obviously occurred sometime during this period. She did not join him at any time during the months he worked in Tucson, even though she was also living in town.

[103]

I was alone in my room the first night and went to work the next day. Then a man came to share a room with me, a young man, Benito, whose father was a section man in Cochise. There were five colored men in our gang. These Benito disliked. He was always talking of going home to his parents in Cochise, but he was never ready to quit his job for that.

Nelson, a white man who was in the gang, was also rooming with us. The section house was of two rooms—kitchen and bedroom. The three of us cooked on one stove. When I made wide round tortillas, Nelson called them tarpaulins.

When Nelson went home, Benito decided to go home also, but he desired to take me to his parents in Cochise. I knew the roadmaster, so he arranged for us to transfer to Cochise section number four. I had filled out the form for alien registration at Globe and carried a copy with me. It was September of 1939 when we came to Cochise to Benito's parents. The foreman was Jimmie who spoke Spanish very well. The job we came to was to grease every joint, taking off the angle bars and putting them back on bolted. Then came an outfit of two camp cars—the bolt machine operator and assistant. I had worked with these two men in the steel gang previously. They would tighten the bolts that we were greasing and put them together when we finished greasing our section. We took to a regular daily routine: putting new ties, raising low spots, tamping with a pick tamper.

I was living with these good people as if of their own family and was with them Christmas 1939 and New Year's Day 1940. Then I was moved to Dragoon where I stayed in one room alone, doing my own cooking.

From this time on, the roadmaster moved me around like a checker on a board, filling vacancies where they were, from Dragoon to Stein's Pass, New Mexico, to San Simon, Arizona, to Gary, New Mexico. Gary is an hour's Sunday stroll from Lordsburg. I told the roadmaster that my next move would have to be Yuma. It happened that on March 6, payday, I was in Lordsburg, walking back to the station when I met the foreman, and he gave me a pass to Yuma and my check. The next day I boarded the passenger train to Yuma. I was with my Aunt Eulalia and family in Yuma by April 1940, when Selective Service registration came, so my Selective Service office had to be in Yuma. I remained there, working in the yard with Kelso the foreman. When my work ended, I came to Tucson to Fernando and the house where I had lived before going to checkerboard moving. Then I joined a floating gang in Gila Bend, which is a camp that moves from section to section, the section foreman being the foreman of the gang when it moves into his section. In this camp I went to Spur, Theba, and Sentinel west of Gila Bend.

So I passed 1941, a little here, a little there, at home with Fernando. One floating gang came to Jaynes, six miles west of town. I worked in this camp to the yard limit and walked to work.

On September 1, 1942, I received notice to report to the Selective Service office. Seeing this, the foreman gave me a pass to Yuma and I went. My name was on a list of selected draftees ready to go to Phoenix for final examinations. On the evening of the fifteenth, we had supper at a cafe in Yuma, boarded the bus to Phoenix, and passed the night in a hotel. The next morning, examinations started early. When we were at lunch on an upper floor of the hotel, September 16, a Mexican fiesta parade was on the street. In the afternoon, those who passed the examinations were made to swear an oath. How proud we all were, with broad smiles impressing the officers. In my roster there were two young Mexicans and one colored man. The others were all white and over thirty. I was thirty-seven years—too old—but passing the test made me in the army. That evening we boarded a Santa Fe Pullman train. We traveled all night to get to Los Angeles, where we transferred to the San Pedro train. The first train left me, but the station lady arranged for me to take another. The group I came with knew this and was looking for me when I got off. I climbed on the truck with them and came to the reception center.

Next morning, when we fell out for calisthenics, it was still dark. After chow they shouted, "Get in line for haircut and clothing!" Haircuts cost thirty-four cents. Clothing sizes varied. Shoes and socks were to be of ample size; mine were thirteen B and provided good foot comfort.

[105]

The first day we were dressed in fatigues and had aptitude tests. After dinner we played softball. The rest of the afternoon until suppertime, we policed the yard. Night came and we went to bed—no pajamas—just shoes, hat, and top clothes off. Talking was heard by the sergeant. It was to be silent at all times.

Next morning, when we rose we had to learn to do our beds. This was our second day at the reception center, and the same day we were given OD uniforms to wear in the evening for shipping out the next day. That afternoon we were all together for the roll call for each branch of the service. I was called to the air force unit.

The coach cars to take us were parked on a spur in front of the camp, and as we boarded we were directed to our cars. Ten cars were filled, all going to different camps and fields.

We would not know where we were going until we reached our destination, but I knew when we left Los Angeles that we were on the Santa Fe Railroad which goes straight through the state. After San Bernardino, we crossed the Sierra Nevada. Having traveled all night, we were in mid-state. At Needles, we crossed the Arizona state line, and in the afternoon we came to Kingman and Flagstaff. Reaching Winslow, we crossed to Gallup, New Mexico, and went on to Belen at the Río Grande. When we reached Amarillo, Texas, the troop coaches were hooked onto the Burlington Railroad.

Before reaching Wichita Falls, Texas, our train took a side track. A troop train we met was full of trainees who shouted, "You'll be sorry!" When we arrived in Wichita Falls, several buses were waiting to take us to Shepherd Field, three miles north of the city. It was about sundown when we were shown our barracks.

Getting up in the morning, we made our beds army style, and whoever did not make it right was put on extra duty. Dressed in fatigues and leggings, we marched to the mess hall. All was brand new to me, a gandy dancer. I liked breakfast very much, as did the others.

Back at the barracks, a sergeant gave the necessary instructions. We learned the general and special rules, and the orders were given. We were of the sixth squadron, and we were informed about the squadron commander, the base commander, and the location of our orderly room. This much we learned the second day.

The third day at six came the holler—"Fall out for roll call!" We marched to the mess hall first and then to the training field for calisthenics. Next the sergeants took charge of their trainees and made platoon formations to teach them steps. Standing in formation, we were taught to right face, left face, and about face. These were performed by the sergeant for us to see.

Oh, the sergeants! Some were tough, some considerate. But anyway, the training was done with good results. I liked them tough because I wanted results for myself. I desired to learn to gain advanced rating, but it was as fussy as flagging trains. Here I had no responsibility but was the same as a hired man, subject to orders and getting them, plenty.

After we learned the footwork formation, we were given guns and began to learn to handle them without killing each other. We learned to shoulder arms, right and left, to present arms, and to trail arms. After learning these, we learned sighting. Then we were taken to the range to learn firing. On the rifle range I did not aim well, and my shooting report was average in standing, sitting, and prone positions. Lunch was brought to us on the range. Service club girls were there selling cokes, candy, and cigarettes. We spent the afternoon cleaning up the field and went back to camp in time for retreat.

The next day we were given a test for classification, and I qualified for guard squadron. For this reason I was moved to the guard squadron barracks. The base guard house was the stockade, which was the military police school. Every evening we went to the city on MP duty. A group of us on this duty graduated in November of 1942 and were ready to ship out.

Of those who were ready to ship out, four of us MPs were to go together all the way—one German, one Russian, one Italian, and one Yaqui, me. Before the names were called, we were asked if any of us wanted to stay on for permanent duty. The answer was "No!" Then our four names were called, and we went in a recon truck to our barracks to get our bags for travel. It was near sundown when we came to the depot. Of the four, the Italian was my close buddy. Neither of us knew where we were being sent. The Burlington pulled into the station, and MPs directed us. Only other MPs saw us new MPs leave Wichita Falls.

The first city we arrived at was Amarillo. There was a curfew in this city for soldiers, but the MPs seeking out late-stayers did not bother us when we told them we were from the train. The station master placed us on a Santa Fe train, and we continued the trip riding in a Pullman car.

Our leader told us we were going somewhere in California. I knew the way. Leaving Texas and traveling across New Mexico, we crossed the Rio Grande at Belen. Then we came to Gallup and crossed into Arizona, passing through Winslow, Flagstaff, and Kingman. Needles signaled the California border, and before crossing the Sierra Nevada, we came to Barstow. We were eating our meals in the Pullman diner, soldiers first. Civilians had to stand in line for chow instead of us rookies. We had dinner in Barstow and were in San Bernardino late in the afternoon. We arrived in Los Angeles in the evening, after eating supper on the diner.

In the morning we had breakfast before our train departed at eight A.M. Leaving Los Angeles we started going north. Going up the Mohave Mountains, I was in familiar territory. I was telling my companions about the tunnels and curves all the way. As we passed the Caroco tunnel, we went under the track we had just passed over. At this time we were having dinner. When we came down to Caliente, I told the boys about Bakersfield, and when we passed through there, they said it was good to be with one who knew the way. There was no stop until we came to Fresno at night. We got off the train and went into the waiting room, still not knowing our destination. There was an officer there, and an army chauffeur came in, gave a salute with all precision, and took him to a car. Later a soldier in fatigues came and told us that he had orders to take four non-coms to camp. When he mentioned Shepherd Field, we knew he meant us. He led us to a convoy truck with a tarpaulin cover. The fog was low; the night was dark. We had come to Hammer Field. I took my overcoat from my barrack bag and put it on, for the fog was getting us wet. It was eleven o'clock when we reached our barrack, and it took one hour to get us booked in. We were no longer called non-coms.

We passed our first night at Hammer Field. We had to take our mess gear to eat breakfast from, and after eating we had to wash it clean to pass inspection. There was a swimming pool to look at, it being winter, and a beer joint not to look at, me being broke. The beer joint was so close to the pool that beer was served out on tables there. This was our first day knowing our destination.

The second day at the field we had physical training—calisthenics, football, baseball, and foot races. Mass formation drill took up the afternoon until retreat. That evening I took a pass and went to town. Dressed in full OD uniform, service cap, and belt, I went to a photographer and allowed him to take my picture. One I sent to my Aunt Eulalia in Yuma, one to Fernando. In the picture I am holding a pair of dress gloves which I bought.

I drank beer in a Mexican joint and ate a Yori supper. We were not to get our November pay until the end of the month, but my Shepherd Field pay was holding out. In the army loan sharks can make you poor fast, so I hoped to evade them, maybe.

Hammer Field was a replacement center, so shipping out was frequent. The four of us were reserved for a purpose, though—KP. Also, we were to keep together permanently. We did guard duty regularly and motor patrol. We got our pay on November 30, 1942, and in December continued on duty as before.

Having my alien registration, I had it checked at Shepherd Field. I was often called from the training field for interviews about application for citizenship. Although the application was to be completed later, interviews kept me busy until the Christmas season.

I went to town Christmas evening, and when I came back, I was on the list for KP Christmas Day. So I had a holy day as an MP on kitchen police duty. After mopping the floor and carrying out dishwater, I was put to filling up Christmas bags for everyone in camp. There were three of us, and we started opening neatly wrapped bundles. Soon we were almost buried under paper and box trash. At dinner time, food was so abundant that we could not eat it all. When we came back to the barracks, our Christmas bags, as we made them, were on our beds.

After Christmas fun, we went to the Skull Valley rifle range. We took bedding and pup tents, leaving the field at four o'clock, in time to set up tents for the night. We crawled into our one-man tents, and in the morning rose up to wait for chow. Breakfast was brought from the field by truck, and we used our mess gear. There were only fifteen men to stay all day on the rifle range, so the first practice started after breakfast. I was mindful of my failure at Shepherd Field. Targets were 200 yards away. Positions were: first, standing, gun slung; second, sitting down; third, prone. Orders were called: "Prepare!" (meaning to place the clip in the chamber), "Ready on the right! Ready on the left! Fire!" Five rounds were fired in each position. I was not disappointed, especially with my standing position mark. After the first practice, lunch was brought on a truck again. In the afternoon the practice was repeated. It was a profitable day. We all had fun in Skull Valley.

You start to like where you are, and you have to move. The army is like that. When we returned from the rifle range, we four were on the list to move, not knowing where, only that the move was sure.

The evening of December 27, we boarded a train at Fresno, going north to the Tracy line. We came to the Oakland piers at night and from there went on to Martinez and across the bay to Benicia. From Suisun turnoff, I was on familiar territory. We took the Sacramento River route through Cottonwood to Castle Crag. Dunsmuir, my town, we passed at dawn. By daylight we passed by Shasta Springs, then went on to Cantara Curve, out of the canyon up to Mott, place of my memories, then to Shasta City below snow-covered Mount Shasta.

We were in the dining car eating breakfast at this place,

having traveled the night asleep in our Pullman berths. The army provided all these facilities, shipping us in and out. Going farther, we came to Grass Lake, an old branch reminder. Here we were over twenty miles from Shasta, and it was late afternoon. I knew where we would be by night—Klamath Falls, Oregon—because of the route we were on. We had supper at about eight P.M. There were two signal corps men in the car with us four, and we traveled all night, still confused about our destination. One porter said we would be in Portland by morning, and it happened that we arrived there and went into the waiting room.

We had traveled the Cascade route, thereby missing the Siskiyou route. The divide started at Black Buttes below Shasta City.

Now we were in the SP depot on northeast Morrison Street, a street which became a bridge crossing the Willamette River, which divided the east and west sides of the city. We had breakfast, still on army account. I had enjoyed the trip exceedingly because I knew all the way, and also because I had traveled in class as monied people do, eating and sleeping while going. Only the air force personnel moved by Pullman accommodations. Others moved in troop trains, doing KP in fatigues.

We waited only another hour until rescue came. A soldier came with orders to take six men from Hammer Field. Unanimously we were from that field, so we climbed on an open convoy truck, going across the bridge and out of the city to the gate of the Portland Air Base.

We came to a supply room with a sergeant in charge. This man was so big he made a sarge-and-a-half in one. We were dressed in full ODs, service caps, and leather belts. The supply sergeant made us strip these things off and put on fatigues. He gave us each cartridge belts to wear from then on. We were put in the barrack next to the orderly room, and a corporal taught us the base rules.

Being booked in, we were put in guard squadron 864. As a rule, guards do not stand in line for chow but go one by one to eat. Every week we had Saturday inspection of barracks. Beds were made hospital style, with white collars. Failure to pass meant being put on extra duty one week. To be a good soldier meant passing all inspection days right. A good soldier is hard to find, they say, but I say that we were all good soldiers.

We also got inspected every day at noon at guard mount. Uniform for the day was prescribed: fatigues, field jacket, leggings, cartidge belt, helmet. All guards stood in formation as the officer of the day inspected each gun. He took it from your hand, inspected it, and tossed it back playfully. He reminded us about haircuts. We stood facing the guardhouse, and at the call of our names, we made a snappy about-face turn, standing at attention in saluting the guards. We went on duty at noon, each taking his post. We were given a password and said "Halt!" to anyone who came near. If in three "halts," he did not obey, we were to load the gun ready to shoot. The officer of the day was there to see that we discharged our duties properly. We were to be sure he was the officer of the day we had seen in the guard mount, then salute him, present arms, and report that we recognized him.

When my relief would come at midnight, I would give him instructions I had received when taking the post. The corporal would be driving the truck, and I would stop him with three "halts." When he stopped, I would be sure to stand in the dark according to the rule. I'd be taken to the guardhouse to sleep, eat, and sleep. Sleep was precious in that line of duty in order to be alert the next day. Walking the post was done as general order commanded it, in military manner, alert to everything within sight and hearing, using the field telephone to report every hour. At the base I was given many posts to guard.

It was in March that I was put at the bomb dump. It was camouflaged to appear like a city park from the air, with a small natural lake in the middle. We used shotguns to guard here, for safety with the explosives. The place was beautiful, or it is my weakness to worship nature. I saw the cottontail conies come timidly down to the water, the tiny snails climbing up tall pine trees. The pheasants were of as many colors as the flowers. "Heavenly Father our country is beautiful. We love it as we love Thee. We will fight to keep it. We desire to win depending on Divine help." This meditation in the bomb dump was like that in Siskiyou. Love for country is love for God, the fulfillment of the law.

My relief would come at noon, and we would go to the base for the rest of the day. The guard squadron had permanent KP duty, day and night. Off duty, we could get a pass and go to town evenings. Man shortage was severe in Portland, and girls brought their own cars to take GIs to town. I was not one to go with a girl but took the bus. The bus to town came at five o'clock at the base gate. There were cars parked at the gate like quitting time in war plants. All these cars came to take GIs for a ride to the city.

I took a room in a hotel where I met a Mexican. He had no whiskey ration card, but I had mine. Ration was two pints a week, so I bought one and we drank it. Then we went down to a joint that we both knew at the end of the bridge. I took one snort too many and ended up in jail. I was in the city jail among civilian drunks. At court time for civilians, MPs took me to the provost marshal. My trial was not for being drunk but for being out past pass time, which ended at seven o'clock. I was taken back to the base, where I was put on extra duty one week.

The yard outside our orderly room was in need of a new lawn. I knew I could lay the lawn alone with tools, so I told the detail sergeant to get a truck to get a load of soil. We got the truck and went to load the dirt. The other boys needed gloves, but I did without. A shovel is my wing gear. Five yards were enough for a small job. After I had laid the Bermuda grass, the men made fun of me, seeing the orderly room yard. I was always "yard bird" now—"yard bird" first class.

The two signal corpsmen who came with us from Hammer Field were with us in the same barrack. One was old enough to get a discharge, and he applied for it, got it, and went home. My discharge was also due—thirty-eight was the age limit. I was asked if I had a job to go back to. They told me to write a letter to my employer, so I wrote to the superintendent of the SP Tucson division, and in fifteen days the answer came. It was a letter with the SP sunset emblem, with the sun setting and track going into it. There was a job waiting.

I made all this known to the squadron commander. The

last interview I had was with an attorney in the office, who checked on my being an alien in the army. Then I was sent to my final physical examination and found to be all in one piece to leave. May 3, 1943, at five o'clock, I was at the finance office. An officer gave me my discharge, my pay, and a war bond certificate in deposit. With all my papers in a big envelope, I prepared to take the evening train. I was given my reservation at the ticket office. It was for a chair coach to San Francisco. The fare was twenty-five dollars. I was entirely on my own on the trip but in familiar territory from the start. We rode all that night and the next day until we reached Klamath Falls at ten o'clock. From here I knew which would be the next town. Grass Lake is not a town, but after that we came to Shasta City and went on to Mott section down into the Sacramento River horseshoe curve. I was enjoying all the beauty of Shasta Springs anew. The train was going on the west side of the river, and we came to Dunsmuir, as when I had come from Siskiyou, Oregon. It was evening, and we came to Marysville and the Suisun turnoff. Traveling all night, it was day when we crossed from Benicia to Martínez on a bridge. The conductor saw my ticket to San Francisco and said I had to get off at the Oakland piers; I got off the SP train and waited for the ferry boat. I arrived at the San Francisco SP depot at night. I was in OD uniform, service cap, and belt. Inquiring, I found a kindly person who took me to a hotel. It was good, as I had known it before, and I slept that night in a two-dollar rate room.

Pondering in bed at the hotel, I remembered the separation of our "big four." PFC is private first class, and I had been a PFC then. Now I was a poor four-F civilian. My last fifty dollars of army pay had to do the money talk in this poor period I was in. The one hundred and twenty-five dollars mustering out pay I was given was going.

San Francisco was too wet for a Gila monster like me—water, water everywhere and not a drink. I went to Chinatown and got too wet and ended up in the hoosegow. I spent the night in uniform with civilian drunks. At nine o'clock, MPs took me to the provost marshal. He said, "If you are on pass, why didn't you go back to camp?" I told him that

I had been discharged, and I was taken to my hotel to get my papers. Then I was brought back to the office and given my billfold with seventy dollars. A new full pint of whiskey was not given back to me, but I was released. The MPs took me to the hotel to get my suitcase; then I was taken to the SP depot to prepare to go. The agent gave me a reservation to buy a ticket the next morning, and I went back to the hotel. I told the MPs I would keep to my room until morning when the Daylight would leave at seven. When I arrived at the depot, the train was parked to leave, and I went in the coach. A lady had her reservation in the chair beside me. Leaving Frisco, we crossed the Golden Gate Bridge, taking the Tracy Line through San José.

On the main line we came to the Fresno turnoff, going south past Salinas. Coming to San Luís Obispo, we were on high hills. At La Maron we were again at the seashore, seeing the Pacific Ocean.

The lady sharing the reservation with me didn't have much to say all the way. Once she walked to the end of the car and bought a doughnut, which she gave to me. I took it and ate it, having only eaten lightly. Coming to Santa Barbara, the lady said she was home. She said, "I'll see you." I said, "Yes, mum."

When I came to Glendale, I saw the camouflaged war plants. Then I came to Los Angeles and walked to a barroom, where I met one of my section buddies. I spoke to him by name, but he didn't know me. Then I went to the depot to fix up reservations for the rest of my trip.

I sent a telegram to my uncle in Yuma, telling of my coming the next day, then took a room for the night. I caught the train in the morning, arriving in Yuma at nine o'clock. I took a taxi and came home, where I changed into civilian clothes sent from the reception center but kept the GI shoes.

The reception was food and Yaqui music, my uncle playing violin with a Mayo harpist. My cousin took me around to see our friends in his car. There were so many questions, but I had all the Yaqui answers.

Now I was in dry Arizona and not to get myself wet again. I was ready to come to Pascua, to call it a day. I remained in

Yuma one week with my uncle's family, during which I helped my cousin to wire the outside wall of his house. We plastered the outside and laid a concrete floor inside.

While still in Yuma I went to the office of the roadmaster, Hiram Gailey, and when I walked in he recognized me at once. I was glad he did not make me talk about the army, but he knew about my induction because it had been published in the company bulletin. When I told him I was discharged, he asked about my work plans. I told him I was going to Tucson to start work there, and he had his secretary write me a pass from Yuma to Tucson.

I was riding eastbound passenger train number forty-four, and I told the conductor to let me off in front of Pascua. I got off and walked to the village. Fernando had learned of my coming by letter, and he was home when I arrived. I was in civilian dress, and Fernando was very happy to see me back.

It was May and the heat was starting to feel good. Nothing was discussed about work, since work is all we hear. I had no intention of grabbing an easy job, but being back home, I wanted to feel at home and go as before. I had worked at the University of Arizona with anthropologists as an informant on Yaqui ceremonies at Pascua, so I went to the campus to see some professors and students. When I became an informant again, I went as required, by appointment. Those with whom I was collaborating regularly were professors.

6. PERSEVERANCE

The World of Letters

Here I sit in solemn reminiscence
Contemplating the evening fall.
Majestic clouds float in magnificence,
The setting sun a golden ball.
Clouds change to roses in the scene,
Blur the mountains like purple walls.
　　　　　　　　　—Refugio Savala

My daily work was as a common laborer in section twenty-four of the Tucson section yard; however, I kept my appointments on the campus while working in the gang. Dr. Spicer and Mrs. Painter were still working with me.

I read that the university was going to put on a radio program.* The paper announced, "Yaqui Is Going to Talk." Seeing this, I was anxious to hear this Yaqui. The same evening Dr. Spicer, with anthropologist John Wielde, came to me to tell me who the Yaqui was—a section laborer who produced belles lettres, whatever that is. They explained the program to me as if I were to perform it. Well, more clearly a rooster cannot crow—I was to talk, in English. Dr. Spicer told

---

*In this closing chapter of his narrative, Savala telescopes the span of time from the mid-forties to the late fifties, relating only major events. The radio broadcast actually occurred on October 26, 1941, before his stint in the armed services.

[117]

me he would come the next day to take me at eleven o'clock. The next day I did not go to gandy dance. Spicer came for me and we went to the studio. Harry Behn, radio operator for the University of Arizona station, was announcing. He said, "This morning our guest is Ray... Ray..." until he could say "Refugio." I was supposed to talk, and I hate to talk about myself, but at noon the program went on, and my script was my own story about duck hunting without a gun. I told them: "I went to the lake with bunches of heavy cord. The ducks were on top of the water, so I took my strings and swam under the water to tie their legs. I burst out of the water as the ducks flew up, taking me entangled in the strings. They flew up so high, I could not see anything when I looked down. To come down, I had to let them go one by one. Those that brought me down to earth, I bagged to take home." I was asked if the story was true, and I said, "It's like TV, tell-lie-vision."

After the radio ordeal, I went to work. My buddies congratulated me, telling me they would buy me a glass of beer next payday. That's duck hunting without a gun.

That evening I dropped by the commissary, and the manager's wife asked, "Were you scared?" I said no, having no fear of radio.

In 1943, after I had returned from being a good soldier, I was living with my brother Fernando and his family. Days came and months went, and I was transferred from section laborer to coach cleaner at the depot on the night shift. I was also put to icing Pullman bunkers on evening westbound trains. More work, but with work goes faith. They called us banqueros—bankers—for bunker ice men. Each ice block that went on each train was checked by one man. There was a shanty where we had lockers to keep tools.

I was working as a coach cleaner in August of 1943 when wages were raised, and I worked the year through. But in December the gang was reduced, and I was on the list of those dismissed.

I had worked for a lady, Mrs. Wilson, wife of a World War I veteran, Thomas Wilson, before going into the army. She had had a large poultry yard in a neighborhood north of town. I lived with her then, in her place, and in this family

"...They called us banqueros—bankers—for bunker ice men...."

they all called me Joe. Now being idle, I went to see her. She was planning to build a new house, and she hired me to take down the old poultry shed first thing. When I started, she gave me a room and bed in her big house. It was winter, so she put me inside where it was warm. When I had the ground cleared where the chicken house had been, I started digging the trenches to pour the foundation in. I had enough house building experience, and on this Mom Wilson depended. On my own plan, I squared up the corners for a rectangular wall. This would be the same as the scrap-lumber house my father first built. His plan had been for a two-room house, making partitions inside when the walls went up. The foundation was leveled and the ground tamped down. Two layers came to lay the blocks, and I was plaster mixer for them. The rafters for the roof were built in as the walls were going up. When that was done, I got the ground wet and tamped it for the floor, and the ready-mix cement was poured in through the windows. The block layers did the finishing job on the floor, and the plumbing went under it to drain into a septic tank.

I had made a septic tank before, alone, so this tank job I took for myself. I dug the six-by-six hole and built the forms inside for a six-foot concrete wall. When they were up, we sent for a man who had a mixer, and he came with two helpers and poured the cement. When the concrete was set, I took down the forms and had it inspected. The drainage from the house was connected by a trench. For drainage from the tank, I made a five-foot deep trench extending fifty feet. I filled up one foot with river sand and gravel and on top of that laid the tile for water to flow through.

Captain Wilson had been put in the hospital while I was in the service, and Stanley, his son, was back on discharge from the navy. As I was putting the tile in the trench, Stanley came to me and said, "Joe, Dad died last night in the hospital." This was unexpected. My instantaneous prayer was, "May the soul of the faithful departed, through the mercy of God, rest in peace, amen." The hospital took charge of the funeral, but we three of the family had to go to the burial the next day. Honors for a veteran officer were given—the sound of taps by a bugle.

After the burial, I continued working on my tank to complete it. When I had the tile all laid in the drainage trench, the plumber, testing his pipe connection inside, ran water into the tank. The water that came into the tank drained out the tile drain, and the sewer system job was completed.

When all the sewer system was ready for service, I started putting the ceiling up. This was tile that came in pieces to be put together. It was a porous kind of ceilng that was full of small holes like dots. It took me one week to put it all up. When that was finished I went on my own to do what was there to be done. The building had a wide carport at the back end. It seemed to me to be time to move four oleanders in line with the carport. I thought to work instead of taking it easy.

Mom was slightly sick and would be in bed most of the time. One day she braced herself to go across town to see little Betty. Betty was her foster child whom she loved. We all three went—Mom, Stanley, and I. I told them to stop at the depot, where I walked to the coach cleaners' shanty. There I was told that back paychecks were in the office. As God provides, my back paycheck was ninety-one dollars. I took part to my sister-in-law, the widow of Encarnación. Part of it went to Fernando for his family. Money went as fast as the manzanita brush in one forest fire I saw.

Now there was one more thing to be done at the Wilson's new house, the painting. I painted the windows, doors, and the back porch. The color Mom chose was emerald green. It was a good color for a Pascola ramada, the carport being on the sunrise side.

Mrs. Wilson got very sick with cancer. I was keeping the yard as if it were my own, but one day I told her that I was going to my home with my brother. She gave me thanks for helping her.

I told her not to put anyone on to keep her yard because I was going to keep it. I went to live with Fernando, but I came back to see to the yard regularly.

There was an ancient tamarisk with roots which were growing under the house, cracking the wall. This was one thing I could not overlook, so I took one good day to work on it. The only solution I could find was to cut the roots going under the wall. To do this was to kill the tree, but there was no other way. We had a timber cross-cut saw, and with this I cut the top branches off first. The trunk holding to the roots was leaning to one side, and that one I cut lumberjack style. Then I went down to the roots and cut the leaning part in two. The roots were heavy because they held the soil. I took a pick and dug off all the soil and left some roots sticking out. Holding the long roots, I could roll out the rest of the tree from the hole. I was doing this in front of Mrs. Wilson's bedroom window, and she saw it all. She told me that she had been curious about what I would end up doing and was glad to see the result.

By this time I had everything well prepared, and Mrs. Wilson wanted to move to the finished house. We moved her to the room in the middle, next to the kitchen with the water heater, sink, stove, and cupboard. In her room we placed an oil heater. I made a stout table and placed on it a fifty-gallon oil tank. This was the fuel for the heater by the window. In her room were a wardrobe room and shower room.

Mom Wilson was already very sick in bed, and it was not very long after this that she had a room annexed to the big house. When the new room was finished, we moved her in. She told us that this would be her permanent room. At this time the new house was rented by a couple.

In her room, Mrs. Wilson was very sick. Her doctor made her take oxygen, so the green oxygen tank was placed there and changed regularly.

I was still living at my house by my brother's place but coming to work in Mom Wilson's yard. The pile of dirt which came out when I dug the septic tank I spread on the yard and leveled it smooth, raking the rocks out. With it, I also covered the hole where the old tree had come out.

After I had the yard all in shape, I wondered what would come next. I had kept in touch with the SP shop foreman for possible jobs, and I was assigned to a bridge gang at Ligurta in the Yuma district. I took the regular evening passenger train number forty-three. I arrived in Ligurta at three-thirty in the morning with my bedroll under my arm. I went into a bunk car and got a cot to sleep on until morning. The bell to rise rang at five o'clock.

It was in September when I started working in the bridge camp. The job was very close to the camp, which was in Ligurta section five. We started by digging trenches under the old bridge that was to be renewed. The section gang had dug out the old gravel on top of the bridge. By using a light, one-man scraper, we dragged out all loose sand and gravel and cleared it to solid ground. To keep the track up, a timber block twenty-four by twenty-four inches thick was laid on solid ground, then round wooden piles were cut. It was wonderful how a man named Jimmie could cut the round piles to match length and angles. The center pile was cut square at the bottom, and the two on each side, which were to lean toward the center pile, were cut to fit level. The center pillar was wide at the bottom and narrow on top. Then the forms for the concrete columns were built. There was a double-capacity concrete mixer in camp. Then one carload of gravel and one of sand were unloaded at the bridge end, and we took the mixer by hand on top of the ties on the track. A water deposit tank was filled from one water tank car, and runways were made on the bridge. The mixer was started, and we took the cement in wheelbarrows to the forms. The forms were all filled that day. Finishing required only tamping to set the cement. After the cement work in the center forms was poured on each side, the side wings to hold the dirt banks were filled from the top.

When the cement work was set and well dried, the wood work started. To do this, heavy timber rafters were first laid the length from the center to bulkheads. When these rafters had been placed and bolted to the platform of the bridge, heavy two by twenty-four inch creosoted twenty-five foot long boards were placed on each side and braced with iron braces, with these braces bolted to platform boards. With all the lumber on the bridge nailed and bolted, creosoted ties were laid and the rails gaged and spiked. When this work was in progress a flagman held the trains. This work was done with temporary wooden pilings holding it; however, the new wood was on solid cement columns throughout. The wood pilings were then taken down and put on each side of the track, and one whole car of slag gravel was dumped on the bridge. The section gang raised the track and tamped the ties so the trains could go on an open free line. I saw this bridge completed without mishap, my first bridge.

We moved the mixer to camp by motor car, for there was another bridge to work on in Ligurta section. On this next bridge the work was started as on the first. All the soft sand and dirt were carried out from under the old bridge. The trenches for the new footings were made, and the forms were built. The mixer had heavy duty balloon tires, so we could take it to the job. A platform of old lumber was made for the mixer and water tank, and the material for the cement was dumped by the trackside on a subgrade.

After the mixer started, we loaded and started pouring cement into the first form, which was wet from a recent rain, so the right wing of the bridge had to be barricaded with long poles. One track was buried deep in granite to hold the bracing poles stuck against the form. Despite this precaution, the form could not hold the enormous weight of the wet concrete going into it, and it broke to spill all the cement.

After this nasty spill, we kept to the edges and were more careful. The waste of material, labor, and time was a grief to us all. Truly, it did not happen again to us; we were experts now. On other jobs, we placed a footing of timber block on each side of each form.

There was a big job on Dome section west of the Ligurta section, and the two gangs also worked on this fifteen foot high bridge. A bulldozer scraped the soft ground under the bridge down to hard soil. Then the trenches for the footing and forms were made ready. The forms were built with great precaution to insure safety. The four side wing forms were securely barricaded to staked timber blocks. All precaution was taken because this bridge was very high.

Five wheelbarrows were loading the mixer with gravel and sand, and three wheelbarrows were pouring in the forms. One man worked at the bottom, spreading the concrete.

There was, nearby, a place of beehives. These bees came in swarms to water, and these honeybees were not so sweet to us working on top. They got on our faces as if we had the nectar. Their stings hurt, and for some reason, the bees took more after some persons than others. I was lucky, being one of those who had nothing that the bees were after. However, I was not exempt; I got the taste of their unsweetened sting. I broke two branches from a bush and with these I kept the bees away from my face, but they got around to my neck. The bee man gave us a pail of honey to take to camp, and the next morning we had pancakes with that honey. Eating the sweet hot cakes, we forgot about the bee stings quickly.

When this big bridge was finished and ready for service in Dome, both gangs were moved to another bridge job to work together. We rode to the job, where there was a load of rock unloaded near the bridge. This was to be used on the job. When all was ready on this bridge, we started hauling. To load it, we packed it in empty cement sacks and put these sacks on the truck to take them to the bridge, where the mixer was all prepared to start mixing. As we unloaded the sacks of rock, we poured them into the batch. The forms being ready, we started wheeling and pouring the cement in. After lunch the forms were taken off, and the deck was built on solid cement. Then a carload of gravel was dumped on the new bridge, the track raised, the ties tamped, and the line opened for service. We were just leveling the ground under the bridge when the foreman shouted at me. He was telling me to fill up the footing, which was an old trench. When I didn't understand, he got mad, and so sent me to camp.

I started walking the six miles to camp, but the truck driver followed me and picked me up. At camp I went into my bunk car to prepare to wait for the gangs to come in from work. It was after five o'clock when they returned. I went to our gang foreman, but he told me he could not over-rule what the other foreman did. He could only give an identity for checks, so I could collect my pay. It was Saturday, and we always went to Tucson on Saturday, so I prepared to leave. But this time I would not be returning.

The passenger train that went on the Phoenix line from Wellton came to Ligurta. To get the passenger train that went on the Phoenix line, we rode first on the truck to Wellton. This was my last truck ride to Wellton with the gang. While we were waiting for the train, the boys had a crap game, and they really had them rolling by the time the train came. We arrived in Phoenix at midnight, and I got one quart of wine there. I was traveling with a first-class Mexican carpenter who had been my work partner. This man lived across the street from us in Pascua. He had been raised in Tierras Flojas before he came to Tucson.

It was daytime when we arrived in Tucson. I had a big bedroll, so I took a taxi and came home to Fernando. We got together to wait for the wine stores to open, it being Sunday, so my quart was soon emptied. I told my brother that I got fired. "Fired?" he questioned.

"Yes, it's the son of a gun in me," I answered.

I took the same house to live in as before. The next day—Monday, May 18—I went to see Mom Wilson. She was tickled to death, as you say, but I say she was awfully glad to see me. She called me a gandy dancer, but I told her I had been a bridge gangster of late. I went around the yard to see about work. The hedge needed trimming, the grass needed mowing, and the trees needed pruning.

Mom said to her son, "Don't you know Joe?"

He answered, "Yes, and I know he eats."

When he asked me, I said, "I'm not on KP so lead me to it."

When I got the yard in shape, Mom was delighted to see it. I called it my boy scout deed for the day and went home. I went around and did work for other man-shortage stricken people too.

Pat Lester, the owner and operator of a paint and body workshop, hired me to lay a floor in the shop. He first put me to preparing the ground and tamping it with a heavy plate tamper. When that was done, the cement mixer came and poured the cement. When the men to lay the floor came, I went with their boss to help spread the cement. We raked it level and the finisher finished it, so the floor was a first-class job. We could dance on it, but not Pascola dances. Those need no floor.

Lester asked me if I could continue working for him because he was going to build a house on one end of the lot. I liked that. One dollar an hour I liked also.

Lester had an idea like that of hunting ducks without a gun. He started hauling those heavy ammunition boxes from the air base. When he had enough, we made a cement foundation to lay them on. On this he laid heavy two by twenty-four inch planks onto which we nailed the first layer of boxes. From there on all the boxes were nailed together layer on layer until the house went up. Doors and windows were properly placed in the walls. When the walls were up, we used a small cement mixer to lay the floors. When all the plumbing was made for the kitchen and bathroom, we started covering the walls in and out with chicken wire for the plaster, and a plasterer came to do the work. First he plastered with the trowel inside and outside. When the trowel plaster was on, the top layer was applied by splashing it on. That was the last coat of plaster given the outside walls. I was only an amateur, but I served the purpose cheaply.

This much I know was accomplished; then I got sick with a mental disorder. This mental sickness was caused by drinking too much wine. This craziness, I took as my high-pitched imagination. I was conscious, but I came to discern that I was actually insane when I told about seeing the devil.

There was a Papago woman *hitebi* who had cured other wine craziness, and Fernando as my guardian took me to her. On the way back, we stopped at the home of my brother Fernando, and his wife went to my other sister-in-law, the widow of Encarnación, who was also a hitebi. The Papago hitebi had told me that I was in need of sleep. Now my sister-in-law knew I had the same need. She did night watch for me. This was in February. In the daytime it was stormy and windy and at night it rained heavily.

This strange matter had started one night in my room. In bed I started hearing the voice of a person whom I knew very well. He and his wife were talking and he said, "I will go in and kill him."

The wife said, "Don't do that. He will kill you."

I had my door securely latched with a bolt in the loop of a padlock, but presently I saw a hand in the dark stick out through the wooden door. It slowly pulled out the bolt in the padlock and opened the door. I saw the person standing in

[127]

front of it. He gestured to me to look at the wall, and I looked and saw all the trees outside. The wall was not there. The figure, moving like it was dancing, pulled out a bottle. It walked to my water basin and poured a liquid from the bottle into it. At this, I got up and took a small hatchet and tried to hit the figure. The person looked like a figure in a silent motion picture. When I lighted a match, it disappeared, then appeared again and sat on my bed. Pedro, my nephew, was in the next room, and he heard the noise and came to ask me about it. I told him it was a nightmare that had made me get up. In the morning at breakfast, I related to my folks the crazy details. It was then decided that I was wine crazy and should see a hitebi.

So now my sister hitebi, doing night watch, was in the next room. She had the wood-burning heater going full blast. She laid a mattress on the floor, and I lay on it but could not sleep. On a table near me, I saw something like a serpent, but it was also like a fish with a beak like a parrot. This I tried to grab and toss off the table. When I stood up, my sister quoted these words from Matthew 26:38, "Tarry ye here and watch with me." I was conscious, so I took to fighting my sickness by Divine help.

When I got up, I sat down near a table, hearing a group of drunken people cursing and singing. I was not to answer any remarks or arguments or to act. By this, I knew I was not crazy at all, and they disappeared. My sister then applied powdered herb medicine on my neck and temples. Applying it on my breast, she said, "*Dios enchi yole'ene*" (God will deliver you). I lay down again under a dim light, and my sister told me to meditate. This I did and went to sleep. When I woke up, I was cured.

I stayed and continued catching more sleep in the morning after breakfast. My sister-in-law told me that I should stay at least one week with her. When my brother came that day, I told him this, and he went home while I stayed with my sister-in-law.

During my week away from my home, Pat Lester came to inquire about hiring me, but not for himself. It was for another man who had a wheel alignment shop. His name was

Maxwell, and he was starting to build a house where he took me to work. He had all the plans laid out for digging the foundations, and Lester had told him I was as good at digging as a loose badger. First I dug every trench marked for the plumbing. The cement mixer came and filled up the foundations; then I prepared the ground for the floor. Next came the cement, and the floor was made by the same cement workers as at the body shop.

The Maxwell house was built with a driveway in front and lawns in back and front. A ramada was built on the back property line. Then we set up a patio wall around the backyard. A layer of cement was to go on top of the blocks, a job I did by dragging the molder along the top of the wall to make it oval.

Maxwell wanted the wall to be white, which I did with white Bondex, dabbing it all around the wall with a big lime brush. When the wall was all Bondexed and white, we laid a floor in the ramada, and a barbeque pit was built of hewn stone. Now this residence was a most attractive one.

When all was complete, I was not yet dismissed but kept coming back to work for whatever pay I got. My job was to keep the yard free of weeds. I rode the bus to and from the Maxwell house until I got sick with a case of varicose veins.

My doctor wanted to treat me, but he could not do it in his clinic. I could not get admission to the veterans hospital, having tried many times, so my doctor sent me to the county hospital. This was during the time I was working on the Pascua Easter ceremony for Mrs. Painter at her home, and she knew of my sickness.

Having the papers from my doctor, I went on Friday to the county hospital. I was not admitted right away, but the nurses were deeply sorry for me, seeing my condition. They made a call to a certain doctor in town and informed me joyfully of my admission. In my room I was dressed. The first treatment was medicated water, hung on a support so that it dripped down my legs, which were wrapped in cotton pads to absorb the water. I passed the night in sleep, and when I awoke, Psalm 23 came into my mind.

It was Saturday morning, and I saw a Pascua man who

[129]

was a car-wreck victim with broken shoulders and breast. He also was a veteran, but with a dishonorable discharge. There was another patient, a Pascua man acting as a nurses' aid, who later learned the barber trade.

The next Monday after breakfast, the nurses found my papers, and when it became known that I was a veteran, my transfer was arranged. In the afternoon I was put in a wheelchair and taken to the door, where an ambulance was waiting. I was placed in front with the driver, and he took me to the veterans hospital and pushed me into the office in the lobby. When the receptionist had my papers arranged for admission, she took me in the elevator to the third floor, where ward three/four was called Surgery. I was then put in bed to await the operation. This was 1958, my first time in the veterans hospital.

After one week in bed I was able to do everything myself, but I was required to use the wheelchair to move in the hallway. My wheelchair had an extension for my left leg. I had my meals on my bedside table.

I had been in ward three/four for two weeks when the day came to operate on me, and I had no breakfast. They brought the assistant to shave me from waist to toes, and afterwards I was given a shot to put me to sleep. I signed the papers for the operation, and when I was asleep on my bed, they placed me on the litter for surgery. When I was pushed into the operating room, I was awake, so the nurse told the doctor, and they applied another shot. Then they cut inside of the left leg and removed two veins. When the knife struck the skin, I was still awake and feeling the pain. The nurses told the doctor, but he said it was over; the bandages were then applied. When I was put back in bed, I fell asleep, not waking until dinner time.

After the operation I was put in another bed close to the window on the east side of the room. On my left was a young Mexican who was to have his left leg amputated. He was in continuous pain, crying all the time. He was taken away to surgery, and when he was brought back, he only had one leg and was very distressed. He would comfort himself, telling me that the pain had been relieved. When he started using his crutches, he was in very good condition.

Then I was transferred to ward six on the bottom floor. I was brought at night, and in the morning I found myself in a room with a peep hole in the door because this ward was for mental disorder patients.* I was given a set of pajamas and told to take a shower and dress for some tests on my mind. Patients were not to have matches for smoking, so the aides had to light our cigarettes. I was in room fifty-one, the first room from the lobby. I was given medicines to apply on skin eruptions on my legs after showers. This was reasonable because I could do everything myself. I made my own bed also. Then I started going to the mess hall at mealtime, walking, using both hands for support. I was not yet paralyzed then.

The doctor in this ward was a kindly person of pleasant personality. He would come often to my room to check on my skin disease. After I was four months in this ward, he said I could go home. I told him that if it was safe, I would, and he arranged it. But he said I would have to take occupational therapy once a week. I was also to report to him in a week for a brain test.

The release said that I was available to work out of the hospital. When I came with Fernando, the first person I saw was Maxwell. He saw my release and, considering it, gave me another chance as his yard man. Max said that the pretty nurses in the hospital had been my cure. I told him that therapy had been my cure. Being out of the hospital, it seemed that fresh air and the sun cured me. Above all Divine help is my salvation forevermore, amen.

Besides Max's yard, I was also doing Mom Wilson's yard. By this time she had become very sick and bed-ridden. When she saw me, she braced up with apparent courage. She knew I had been in the hospital but did not mention it, and I wouldn't annoy her by telling her. When it came to the subject of money, I told her not to think of it. I told her I was

---

*Savala's description of his confinement to a mental ward implies his ongoing battle with the problem of alcoholism.

keeping the yard because it was my yard, too. As she always put it, "What do you need for your yard?" Truly, I took it as my own duty to do it, as she was delighted to see it.

I also always had time to go see Mrs. Painter and Dr. Spicer to give them information. Dr. Spicer arranged for me to have interviews with students from his class. This was the time when I became acquainted with John and Lynne, both students of linguistics learning Yaqui vocabulary. Lynne had an apartment, and they took me there.

These two good persons came for me in the morning and brought me back. Our first study was picture illustration with matchstick figures. In this study, I told what each figure was doing to show the use of nouns and verbs. Pronouns I explained in grammar terms. These students were highly intelligent, easy to teach. They learned vocabulary fast. Even though I am not a trained teacher, I discerned their desire to learn. I love to teach people who have a desire to learn because I have been in that same situation.

At that time all Indians were called to participate in a presentation in the high school auditorium. Mrs. Painter took us Yaquis with her. She also took us to her home to have a party. This was very interesting. In the living room we lighted the candles in the candelabra. A fire was started in the big fireplace, above which was the figure of Guadalupe. Mrs. Painter had a Matachini music record, and she played it. It was the "Santa Lucía." I danced the piece with other Yaqui boys who were good at it. Not me.

Afterwards, I worked with Lynne again in her home. We then began to use tape recording for our study. I told her of cradle lullabies, and she desired to have them recorded. "The White Pack Rat" was one, and "The Little Grey Wren" was another. The white rat walks on tiptoes to steal cantaloupe and pumpkin seeds, which it uses for shoes that make a hissing noise when the white rat is walking. The little grey wren sits in the sun and sleeps, sleeps, sleeps. I sang these lullabies for the tape recorder, and then Lynne sang.

Another pretty one was recorded, written, and translated—"*Malonim pahko chikulim yemu, chikulim pahko malonim yemu*" (Gophers make fiesta, the mice eat; mice make fiesta, the gophers eat). When these studies gave satisfactory results, Lynne and I separated casually.

I continued with Mrs. Painter as interpreter or translating Yaqui literature. As part of this work we had interviews about meanings and performances and sermons. Ignacio Alvarez, Ramón Duarte, Pancho Alvarez, and Juan Martínez all helped. Juan Maso and Frank Acuña helped with the Deer Dance. Jesús Garcia was informant about the Chapayeka performance.

It was cotton-picking time, and I went on rides to nearby fields to slowpoke pick. One day at sundown, as we were unloading wood from a car at the Alvarez home, they told me I shouted and fell down. I did not know it, but it happened to me. Seeing this, the boys took me home to Fernando's in a car. I knew I had need of hospitalization, so I reported to the hospital. When I arrived, I was conscious but the fever was terrific. After reception, I was put in ward five on the second floor. I was informed that I had had a paralyzing stroke and that I also had double pneumonia. In my delirium, I was silent until questioned. I could sit up in bed to eat my meals, but at breakfast the bed was lifted so I could eat more easily. Fernando came the first morning to see me at breakfast time. He was told that I was in critical condition and that he could visit me any time, so he came during the day the first week.

I was very sick, sick enough to die. But I was entirely without fear of death. Why are we born? We are born destined to die, to pass away. I was then not in fear of death.

When I was to take physical therapy, I was escorted in a wheelchair. I was placed on a table and strapped down with heavy bands around my legs and breast. Then they raised the table to stand-up position to rest my body on my feet. This was the first day I had stood on my feet since I came. The bands were so tight I could not bend my knees. Then I was taken off. This same thing was done to me every day for a long time. Next I was put on a bed and my arm was moved up and down to open and close my hand. My leg was raised up and down too. A helper had to do all these movements. This was done for many days. Two helpers made me walk a few steps at a time to learn to use my legs. Every morning I walked on the parallel board with two wooden bars on each side to walk between. I had the use of only one hand to hold the right side bar. When I learned to walk across the board forward and back, I was taught to ride on the wheelchair by myself. This I learned well enough at the therapy section, so that I was able to go from the ward and to treatments.

Ann Parten was therapy director, and she taught me to use the cane and gave me practice walking daily. She brought the wheelchair along for my relief until I could make the distance required.

When it was time for lunch, I would go to mess hall, rolling myself. After lunch, I would go back to therapy to do arm exercises. I was also given an aluminum splint to wear on the left arm. When the splint was taken away, my arm was put in a cloth sling. But therapy ordered that I wear the aluminum splint at night in bed. It was put on at bedtime, and I would take it off close to morning to relieve the pain. When I sat up after breakfast, I rolled the bandage which held the splint in place.

During this time my niece was frequently visiting me. A social worker was acquainted with my niece and visited her at her home. My niece Yzabel told her of her desire to have me at her home. The social worker told her to have a room prepared for me within a week.

At this time Mrs. Painter came to see me. A few days later Lynne came with her husband to introduce me to him. I took them to the patio, where they told me about being married.

Soon after this, my doctor came to my room, telling me that I could get a release. This was in September 1960. I told the doctor that I was yet very sick and my pension meager. He explained how it had already been arranged that I was to go to my niece's home. The doctor said that I would take a new wheelchair of my own. Fernando came to take me. He pushed me out to the ramp. The car was there, and I gave the address. My niece Yzabel was waiting and I had supper at my home again after four years. After supper we talked about how close I had been to the land of the dead, the *aniya*. Then I went to bed as usual at home, wearing store pajamas.

I was getting only sixty-six dollars in pension checks. My

niece and her granddaughter gave me the service of a nursing home, and we used all our pension money for household expenses. I had always been considered a hard patient in the hospital. Now my niece was patient with me. She did my laundry, giving me clean change of clothes weekly. She also made flour tortillas to eat with meals that would surpass any tortilla factory's or bread. We managed with my small compensation until Christmas.

My niece was, like my mother, a devout Christmas celebrant. She made the Christmas tamales without which it would not be Christmas. She decorated her Christmas tree in the living room, a white people's tradition. It is customary at Christmas that the oldest of the family tell a story. This story is usually the legend of conception, the rose in the river whirlpool. In this home all knew our Immaculate Conception story. I told the story of the Nativity from Luke. So we had a joyful Christmas all together.

New Year's Day 1961, we had *buñuelos*. These are pancakes fried in lard to make bubbles. They go with syrup or jelly. The children, not knowing the English name for them, were asking me. I told them from bun, jelly buns, came the name buñuelos. In the daytime one of the boys was playing the accordion in the sunny backyard. His mother and his young brother were dancing the schottische to a pretty Mexican selection.

Fernando had been with us Christmas evening. He came on New Year's Day. Later he continued coming on weekends. *Pasi yaloa* is Yaqui for visiting, so he came to pasi yaloa.

In February, I perceived that my niece was very tired of me. I told Fernando that if I went to live with him, it would be a great relief for her. Fernando, seeing the work she was doing to keep me, agreed. When he had prepared a place for me, he took me to live there. He, being my own brother, took good care of me day and night. Fernando's boys were well pleased to have me at home and helped me. During the daytime they took charge, to help me eat. My brother arranged a solarium in our backyard for the daytime, and during nights he was with me in my room.

I was always suffering pain in my left arm and leg. I had

[135]

no pain tablets or any other medicine for pain relief, and one night in March, the pain became so severe that I could not do anything about it. The fever was very high in the morning, and Fernando took me to the hospital. The first week after I came home I was in bed; then I began to ride the wheelchair, and often I went out to take sun in the yard.

Every morning I was made ready to go to therapy with many others. The ambulance came for me. I started to take my own wheelchair but was not allowed to, because they brought wheelchairs for the five of us to go. A Red Cross gray lady was the driver, and one male aide was the escort.

I was started on a bicycle for leg movement. Then I used the Elgin table, sitting against a backrest and pushing a heavy lever with my legs. The weight was measured—heavy or light—by as many round plates as needed. After this I practiced walking and had lunch. The instructors in corrective therapy were both rough. The social worker I knew at the hospital was Anita Stark, a Spanish lady, a Chilean. This lady told me that I would go to a nursing home. I came to the nursing home at suppertime and was given a Mexican roommate. This was in September of 1961.

Mrs. Stark kept coming to see me to find out how I was behaving, and she very often came just to take me for a ride on Sundays. She was always asking if I desired to move to another place, but I told her I was well pleased where she had placed me. Still on her next trip, she took me to two other nursing homes to see if I liked them.

I did not move, but stayed in the first home. I was only moved to another room, where I remained until Christmas week. From there I was moved to the cottage, a separate rooming place. I passed the days in a wheelchair in the living room, looking at the mountain. From the cottage I was placed in the men's ward for a week. My bed was very high, and one evening while getting into it, I fell down. I struck my head on a table corner brace and got a nasty cut a little behind the left ear. A doctor came, and the cut was given ten stiches, dressed, and bandaged.

Christmas evening my brother came, but I could not go with him until the bandages were taken off. He said he would come for me New Year's evening, but a nurse objected, and I didn't go.

It always happens in September since I went to the army. Again this September I was told that I would have to go to the hospital for a checkup. In the hospital a doctor prescribed some red pills. Then an operation started on my urinary system. Soon I was recovering. I was then put in an ambulance and taken to another nursing home. I had visited this place before, so the nun in charge, Madre María, knew me. She called me Don Refugio or Señor Savala. I was just Ray before that. The sisters in this Catholic institution all spoke Spanish. I had opportunity to learn *Kasteyano*, Castillian Spanish.

Again Christmastime came, and decoration started in the big living room. It was December 24, 1962, and I was very much in need of shoes, so I went to a store where I bought gray work clothes, a pair of dress shoes, and a hat. Fernando and his son Pedro were with me. Christmas morning, I was all dressed in new clothing, head to toes. So Christmas was merry for me this year, thanks to Divine help.

In the spring I told Madre María that I wanted to go home to attend Yaqui devotions in Pascua. She agreed, knowing the Yaqui Easter ceremonies herself. Holy Week would be in May, and I told my brother to come to take me. It was Monday before Palm Sunday when Fernando took me home. On Palm Sunday I was in the backyard and children brought palm leaves to me. When they heard Jesus was coming to Jerusalem, the people took branches of palm trees to meet Him. So you read in Gospel of Saint John. Yaquis commemorate it in Pascua.

My nephew Pedro, a participant in the Easter ceremonies, got sick and died in the veterans hospital. This was *kulupti weme*, unexpected, and I felt urgent about it. I did not know where they had taken the body, but I went to South Tucson to inform his relatives. Coming back, I stopped at Mrs. Painter's home to ask her. She called Mrs. Stark, the social worker, and was told where the body was, and I went to mortuary. The undertaker told me to bring one hundred dollars and to send Pedro's clothing the next day. I went to the bank, took the money, and brought the clothing. They gave me the receipt and told me the funeral would be the next day at four o'clock. This gave me time to prepare the Pontal, the night service for the soul departed. I had seventy-five dollars tucked in my arm sling and provided food to serve. So was the night ceremony attended by Kohtumbre Ya'ura and Matachinis. Pedro was my nephew, so to do this for him, I sought all ceremonial groups' help, and his *bato ayewam* [godparents'] and relatives'.

I was informed by the undertaker that the hearse would come at one o'clock in the afternoon. After the night vigilia, we talked about our lutu patko next year. Then the hearse came and all Pascua went to the funeral and burial. The V.A. honored him with the American flag over his coffin. He was put in the soldier's lot with the white crosses.

After the death and burial of my nephew, I remained with Fernando. Then summer came, and I could not stay comfortable, so in June, I moved in with my niece Yzabel again. The afternoon I arrived, notice came to us of the death of a distant relative. For this I was no more prepared than for my nephew's death a while back. My niece only asked for five dollars to help the *bato ayewam*.

Soon after this Yzabel said she was going to Guadalupe near Tempe for one week. When Fernando came, he decided at once to take me back home. I went with him to stay July, August, September, and October, but then I got sick and went to the county hospital.

My brother was working, and I had the need of nursing home. The only available home was a lodge located in the foothills. I was given an examination for entry, and on Tuesday, October 9, 1963, I arrived in the lodge office. Soon I discovered I had been put in the crazy people's section. These people were continuously shouting and pounding on tables until silenced. The nurses were much in distress all the time. Truly it was hard on them. I knew two men who had been in the first home with me. They were mental problems. I was not crazy, or was I?

I informed the lodge that I would be going home the first week in March. I asked my brother to come to take me. It was Friday, March 3, when he came and I went, having my check.

My personal business was the Yaqui death anniversary ceremony for my nephew. My first day home was Saturday, *Tako Pahko* [Palm Fiesta]. On Palm Sunday I received Easter greetings from Mrs. Stark and other white Yaquis. The greetings reminded me that the night before I had left the lodge a friend of mine had had a heart attack shortly after bedtime and had died at veterans hospital. One person had died when I came home last year, and another died when I went home this year. I continued at home through August and September.

On September 24 I went to yet another nursing home after arrangements had been made for me. A Christian Mexican lady came one day to talk church with us. She had known my roommate Manuel Tepia years back and his relatives in South Tucson. Manuel was called Pancho by the nurses. He was very hard of hearing, so the church lady talked with him in a loud voice. From that day on, the porch became Sunday church meeting place. The white church ladies brought music to sing—gospel songs—very *uhyoli,* very beautiful. A Mexican lady took us to church service and dinner at her home. Her church was the First Assembly of God. The ladies came every Sunday to our room.* Manuel, my roommate, was crippled—paralyzed on his right side and confined to a wheelchair. And it so happens that I'm paralyzed on my left side, but we could not coordinate. Manuel was an old Tucsonan. We talked about our times at Silver Lake Dam and El Ojito de Agua, and the days we spent going up the Santa Cruz River to El Mesquital Los Reales. I would tell of events which happened, and in this way we coordinated nicely to pass time. We both could not kill a fly but this way we killed time.

In November Fernando told me of our property being confiscated. This was the first time he had made it known to me. However, he said he would negotiate the money necessary to reclaim the land through a commercial loan. But the

---

*As a result of these encounters at the nursing home, Savala became converted to the Church of the Assembly of God in May 1967. Immediately thereafter he began to translate the Old Testament into Yaqui.

[139]

loan was not granted him, and Christmastime came. Church people came more often to sing the carols; presents started coming. The nursing home was decorated with lights of Christmas colors, like the tree. I had Christmas at the nursing home and enjoyed it greatly. Mrs. Painter came with some anthropologists.* She also gave me a present, a green checkered flannel shirt, which I needed. Christmas dinner was traditional, turkey with all the trimmings and belly-filling.

I told my brother that I would put to work my *koba muela* [head skull] to find a way to keep the house. The court wanted payment made in full—cash, no terms. I was like King Cricket against King Lion. I would not see my home taken without putting up a fight. I had no air force, but my help was a force beyond the skies—Divine help. I waited for my check seeing the paper asked for $216. Then on Friday, April 7, my first day at home, I went to town with my brother to try for a loan, but that failed also. At length I came to my bank, and they gave me their own check for the amount. I went to the courthouse and fixed my business.

King Cricket said, "This is one war where no killing was done as I desired it to be." I say, "This is one time I was not licked, thanks Divine help, amen." For it was not my koba muela that worked but the help beyond the skies, amen.

Now I was in need of a nursing home again, which I had already prepared to receive me. I say with David: "The Lord is my shepherd; I shall not want."

I thank Mrs. Painter and Dr. Edward Spicer of the Arizona State Museum in Tucson. The university faculty and staff people I also thank heartily. The characters most notable in my life story are in the first part: my sister Agustina, by turn named Názarra, who is now dead, the oldest of us three children; my mother, Tomasa Flores, who by Divine help came out of jail in Magdalena; my father, Martín Savala, who

---

*Throughout the early 1960s, Savala was continuing his work on this autobiography and other Yaqui projects with Mrs. Painter. His series of moves back and forth between his relatives' houses and various Tucson nursing homes only briefly interrupted these literary efforts.

in search of peace and freedom came to Arizona. In Tucson, most notable is my brother Fernando, who has been always my guardian even to these present days. God preserved him; I have so often lived with him as an invalid. God has justified me; with judgment he gave me a Providence, so I can go disabled having every means that I should have need of: resistance, self-consciousness, satisfaction, and happiness, amen.

My story closes in the Yaqui manner of closing a sermon: *Senyoresim achalim malam inie beleki enchim mampo tawak into Diosta nampo tawak Dios enchim hiokoe ute'eia.* [Gentlemen, fathers, ladies, this much in your hand remains, also in God's hand remains, God forgive ye strongly.]

BACKGROUND AND INTERPRETATIONS

by

Kathleen M. Sands

1. RELOCATION

The Search for Freedom and Security (1904–1911)

Refugio Savala was born into a time of uncertainty and turmoil for the Yaqui Indians of Sonora, Mexico, and the United States. His name signifies not only his own flight as an infant, but the refugee status of thousands of Yaquis who fled the repressive measures of the Mexican government from the late 1880s until 1911.

During this period, the Mexican military occupied the eight pueblos of the Yaqui people which stretch east along the Rio Yaqui from near Guaymas. The occupation led most families to leave their native villages, because they would not accept domination by the Mexicans.

Some Yaquis became guerilla warriors in the Bacatete Mountains, while others sought refuge by blending in with the peon population on haciendas throughout Sonora. Yaquis who were caught by federal troops were deported to the sugarcane fields of Oaxaca or the brutal henequen plantations of Yucatán. As Refugio points out, Mexican peons were often rounded up with the Yaquis and shared their fate.

The Savala family fully experienced the crisis of the Yaqui

[145]

people. Refugio's father Martín, who had spent his boyhood on the Río Yaqui in the villages of Torim and Cocorit, fled with other young men to the Bacatete Mountains after federal occupation, living off the wild countryside and dodging Mexican troops. At the age of forty, he abandoned the mountain stronghold to escape capture and deportation. Drifting north, he spent a short period near Magdalena, then set out for the United States with his wife, Tomasa Flores, a native of Potam, another of the eight Yaqui pueblos, and their three children, Agustín, Agustina, and Encarnación, Martín's son by a previous marriage (Spicer 1936: fieldnotes). In Arizona, Martín Savala, like many Yaqui refugees before him, found work with the railroad, laboring as a section hand between Nogales and Benson.

Like so many of their fellow refugees, the Savalas had a deep hatred for the Mexican government, and, as unofficial immigrants into the United States, an enduring fear of deportation back to persecution in Mexico. Despite the danger, when Refugio's mother became pregnant, she determined to return to her relatives in Magdalena to bear the child. Thus Refugio was born in Mexico at the height of Yaqui persecution and suffering under Yzábal, whose reputation as a brutal hacienda owner was well known to Yaquis long before he was placed in the governorship by the Torres family. He accelerated the deportation and annihilation of Yaquis to a peak from 1904–1907. The risk of his mother's return to Mexico for Refugio's birth nearly made her a victim of the fearful Yzábal policy, for as Savala explains, his mother was rounded up with other Yaquis for deportation to Yucatán when he was only a few months old. She had gone to the plaza to sell tortillas to raise money to get back to Arizona where her husband was working as a section hand at Patagonia when she was caught with hundreds of other Yaquis. As family legend has it, her personal charm and plea of recent motherhood gained her release. There is no written record of the event, but Savala's mother's reputation for piety and charm throughout her life gives substance to the motive for the jailer's unusual compassion.

Years later Refugio preserved his knowledge and feelings about this crisis in the history of his family and his people in the autobiographical poem that precedes his narrative in the beginning of this book.

Refugio's poetry captures the fear and terror of the upheaval of life experienced in the great dispersal of the Yaqui people. The line "The wolf was on every trace," portrays the government troops as predators, stalking the helpless Indians. The image is more personal as he speaks of his own father's departure as made in "desperate frenzy." He sees his people as "forsaken" in a land where they once enjoyed fulfilling lives. Images of desperation are juxtaposed with symbols of faith and hope, as in the line "Out of the hand of Yzábal, through miracles of St. Francis." Throughout the poem the basic elements of faith, family, and perseverance create a sense of dignity yet preserve the feelings of outrage. The poet does not forget that his people still "Bear the scars of their master's whip." Though the meter and rhyme are sometimes forced or faulty, the condensed images contrasting brutality and innocence, terror and hope, penetrate to the center of the conflict.

It was a year after the incident in Magdalena before Martín Savala was able to find and join his wife and family in Mexico. In 1905, they made their way north in a burro cart to the section house at Patagonia, where Martín was working for a dollar a day (Spicer, Ms. 1:4).

For the hundreds of Yaqui families that made their way into Arizona during the great dispersal from the Río Yaqui Valley, two major means of livelihood were open. Many went to work on farms and ranches as far north as Phoenix. Others were employed by the railroad. As far back as 1882, Yaquis had been brought into Arizona to labor on the construction of the rail network. In that year, 100 Yaquis were hired by the New Mexico and Arizona Railroad for the completion of the branch extending from Benson south to Nogales (Myrick 1975:269–277). The pay was fair and accommodations were adequate; thus the reputation of the railroad as a good employer began.

As disturbances and hazards in Mexico increased and the flow of refugees grew with it, the numerous railroads of Arizona provided work and sustenance to many Yaqui people. While Savala singles out the Southern Pacific, there were other rail companies operating in southern Arizona at the time which offered jobs to the Yaquis. The New Mexico and Arizona, the Twin Buttes Railroad, the El Paso and Southwestern, and the Tucson-Nogales railroads also employed Yaqui refugees (Myrick 1975: 269). However, all of these lines were eventually absorbed by the Southern Pacific.

Refugio's father was an extra gang section hand, so he and his family lived in rail cars, moving from area to area as construction and maintenance of the line required. A permanent gang of three laborers was usually assigned to each ten-mile section of track and accommodated in small permanent buildings constructed of concrete block, but major jobs required gangs of from fifteen to thirty men (McKissick, Nov. 17, 1975: interview). The laborers lived with their families in cars equipped with stoves and sleeping space and were accompanied by a commissary car and a water tank. Although such practices have been discontinued by the Southern Pacific and other railroads in the United States, at the time of this writing mobile rail camps could still be observed in Mexico, where extra gangs lived with their families in cars and traveled from job to job as they were needed, a uniquely self-contained unit of society.

Benson, Arizona, was a major junction for the several railroads then operating in the state. From there operations branched out to Patagonia, Sahuarita, and Nogales to the south; north to Tucson; and east to Deming, New Mexico (McKissick, Nov. 17, 1975: interview). Families moved on the lines as jobs demanded and stayed until the work was completed, making acquaintance with other workers on the rails. Foremen were usually Anglos, but many Mexicans as well as Yaquis were employed on the crews. While the Savala family abhorred massacres of Yaquis in Mexico and hated the executors of this policy, this hostility did not extend to the Mexican people in general, as Refugio's friendship with the two Mexican section laborers attests.

The move to Tucson meant a more permanent home for the Savala family. They traveled north on the Twin Buttes Railroad originally built to service the rapidly developing copper mines south of Tucson. The fare from Sahuarita to Tucson was $1.60. The line north from the mines passed within a mile of the San Xavier Mission on the Papago Indian Reservation ten miles south of the city, where young Refugio was impressed with the mountains and undoubtedly viewed the stark white towers of the church.

The Tucson Refugio entered that day was an active community of 13,000 people. In a desert valley surrounded by four ranges of mountains, the city had been an Indian village before the Coronado expedition and had served as a Spanish presidio before the United States annexation of the Gadsden Purchase in 1853. On March 20, 1880, the Southern Pacific Railroad connected Tucson to the rest of the nation, beginning an era of rapid growth (*Arizona Daily Star* 1975: 23). With the hardships of desert travel eased by the railroad, businesses flourished and population increased rapidly, drawn by a healthful climate and a prosperous economy.

Although Tucson had been incorporated as a city since 1877, and streets were laid out on a grid pattern above the flood plain of the river with regular subdivision of property, allocation by "squatters' rights" was not uncommon even after the turn of the century (Donovan, Nov. 18, 1975: interview). Thus, the Savala family assumed their location on the outskirts of the Yaqui community of Barrio Libre simply by building on the site. Like most families in Tucson, they dug their own well.

The house was built with an attached ramada, a structure roofed with branches and open on three or four sides, which was for outdoor cooking and living. The home was similar to those the Savalas had inhabited in the pueblos of the Río Yaqui in Sonora. Although Yaqui dwellings are traditionally built of woven cane, wattle, and daub, the scrap lumber used by Martín Savala was highly practical in view of the subsequent removal of the house to another location. The house probably had a dirt floor and may have been surrounded by a fence. In the yard was a simple wooden cross, the tevat kus.

[149]

St. Joseph's Academy was located in the St. Augustine Cathedral plaza seven blocks north of this Savala home. The first school in the territory, it had been opened by the Sisters of St. Joseph of Carondolet in 1870. A staff of fifteen sisters served 450 children of all denominations. The poor attended without tuition charges (*Arizona Daily Star* 1975: 23). The school was closed years ago, but it is clear from Savala's recollections of his days there that young children were given especially tender consideration. The primary teacher not only taught her young pupils but cared for them individually, giving Refugio, who was probably four or five, a snack and lullaby daily.

The Savala family attended mass at the nearby Cathedral of St. Augustine, but they also held their own Yaqui services around the houseyard cross. This practice becomes especially clear in Refugio's description of the baptismal ritual held shortly after their arrival. Every Yaqui child is formally baptized by a Catholic priest, but the ensuing ceremonies in the home are equally important, for they formalize personal relationships which are essential to the extended kinship and godparent-compadre basis of the Yaqui community.

Shortly after a baby's birth, the parents carefully select sponsors, who then become the compadres of the parents and godparents of the child. It is their duty to take the child to the church for the ritual performed by the priest. From this time on a bond exists between the child and godparents, which entails serious obligations and privileges. The child regards his padrinos with much respect, greeting them in formal terms. He also turns to them for advice or for necessities, such as food or money. The padrinos are responsible for spiritual assistance and guidance. Furthermore, in the event of the godchild's death, they are responsible for all funeral arrangements (Spicer, 1940: 95, 96, 101–103).

Following the baptismal ritual at the church, the parents of the child provide a feast for the godparents, which formally establishes the obligations of the padrinos to the child. An important part of the feast is the participation of a Pascola dancer, an essentially secular figure in Yaqui ceremonies who acts as host at public ceremonies and frequently entertains with clowning. At the baptismal ceremonies he participates in everyday dress except for rattles made from cocoons and pebbles wrapped around his legs, dancing to the traditional music of violin and harp.

Essential to the home-centered portion of the baptism is the hand-touching ceremony which follows the feast. Before the houseyard cross, parents and godparents formalize the relationship between child and padrinos and between the compadres, accompanying the touching of hands with appropriate speeches and giving of the baptismal certificate to the parents. Fireworks, often a part of Yaqui ceremonies, are included in the ritual which Savala describes.

While Refugio's life as a young child was obviously home-centered, he was an enthusiastic observer and participant in activities in the community. The Ojito de Agua he describes, though it turned out to be merely a broken water main, was greeted with enthusiasm for good reason, because until 1900, a natural spring, long called Ojo de Agua, had existed not far from the downtown area near the later location of the Tucson Community Center.

Until the water table began to recede, the area just southwest of the city had provided water for both practical and leisure use. The Silver Lake region was the location of two major recreational centers until floods in the Santa Cruz river washed away dams in 1900. Even after the disastrous flood which engulfed the Elysian Groves amusement center and Warner's Bath Houses, a dam created a lake for picnicking and swimming where the tall cottonwood trees shaded West Silver Lake Road (later West 29th Street), which Refugio calls El Callejón. Another popular swimming site used by youngsters was the acequia, a large irrigation ditch which ran from springs at the base of the Tucson Mountains directly west of the city, turning north on the east side of the river and paralleling the main street when it reached the city itself (Donovan, Nov. 18, 1975: interview).

It is somewhat puzzling that when the Savalas were forced to leave their original Tucson homesite they did not move into a Yaqui village. Several did exist. The largest at the time was Barrio Libre, very near the site chosen by the

[151]

Savalas. Yaquis, Mexicans, and Papago Indians settled together in this small area. Barrio Anita and a ranch called Tierras Flojas were Yaqui settlements north of the city. The other communities Refugio mentions—Mesquital and Mesquitalito—no longer exist.

Before 1909 none of the Yaqui communities in Tucson had revived traditional community ceremonial life, most importantly the Easter ceremony, which they had been forced to discontinue in Sonora for fear of being identified and deported. The refugees were not yet secure enough in their acceptance by the United States government to call attention to themselves by public practice of their religious ceremonies (Spicer 1940: 5, 21).

Squatting on land outside the confines of an established Yaqui village created hardship for the Savalas, for they were soon forced to move by city officials. The storm that accompanied the move places the event during the late summer rainy season, when giant thunderclouds appear, dumping torrents of rain on the desert, causing normally dry arroyos to roar with floodwaters.

Once settled, Refugio's mother took the children to San Xavier Mission to glean in the wheat fields. In the early 1900s Tucson was at the center of a thriving agricultural area, and the nearby San Xavier Papago Indian Reservation to the south on the river contributed significantly to the agricultural economy.

On the reservation harvesting was unmechanized. Bundles of wheat were cut in the fields, then looped with a length of rope which allowed the cutter to bundle it for tossing into a horse- or mule-drawn wagon. Each family harvested its own fields, aided by relatives or hired help. The hand operation in the fields left some wheat behind, which might be harvested later by such families as the Savalas (Ríos, June 22, 1974: interview).

The harvest of saguaro fruit can be traced far back into Papago history, and Yaquis soon shared in the enterprise, as Refugio notes. The red fruits grow at the highest tips of the giant saguaro cactus, renowned for its treelike arms and extraordinary heights. The fruit of this cactus can be eaten raw, but it is most often boiled down to a syrupy consistency to make a sweet drink or a jam.

The gleaning expedition, Refugio's gathering of mesquite beans to feed Alfredo Durazo's pigs, the selling of menudo soup in the early mornings, the saguaro harvest, and the gathering of vegetables from nearby farmers all give indication of the hardship of life among the refugees, especially with the father absent. The Yaquis however, were not strangers to hard work, for in their life in the eight pueblos in Sonora, a susbistence economy had been the rule.

The return of Martín Savala to his family was a time of great personal joy for Refugio, because it was from his father that he first acquired his great love of Yaqui lore and music. The traditional ceremonial life of the Yaquis is impossible without the music that accompanies the dances. Craftsmen make the violins, flutes, and harps used for both the sacred and secular portions of each major ritual in the ceremonial year, and the musicians hold a responsible and honored position in the community hierarchy. As Martín Savala explained on the evening of their arrival in Tucson when he so delighted Refugio with his impromptu music, the tonal classifications of Yaqui music fall into three separate melody types. Each is reserved for the appropriate period of the all-night ceremonies—evening, midnight, and dawn—and each accompanies particular dance patterns. Refugio's reverence for both his father and Yaqui music is captured in the following story he wrote:*

A HARPER'S LEGEND

That evening in the village there was a very pleasant sunset. A tall slim man was a harper, and a beautiful harp of most exquisite art was upon his lap. He sat with his back against the clay plastered wall of the hut that was his home. He began to tune the instrument with such skill that the sound was very beautiful. A little boy of rare brown complexion, clothed

---

*All of the Savala works quoted in this book are on file in the Arizona State Museum Archive in Tucson.

[153]

poorly and shabbily, with a wide straw hat worn by time, was on the ground sitting cross-legged watching with great enthusiasm.

The young harper was registering the taut cords of the harp with his magic hand. The little idealistic boy was admiring with great pleasure. To him everything was graceful: the color of the harp, the strings the harper who was about to show the little boy the great art. Now the man had the instrument tuned as if he were going to play something. The little boy was very happy and was waiting anxiously. He smiled broadly at the man every time he by chance looked at him. But as the things most beloved are so dear in this world, it happened that when the harper tuned his harp, he put it aside and rolled some tobacco in a corn bark (husk) and lighted it to enjoy a smoke. With a wide cloth he covered the harp and took it into the house. His little neighbor who had come with such stirring emotion and thought to hear the music of the harp was staring at the harper almost pleadingly, but he could not tell him to play for him. He was already too weak, and when the man had gone, the little boy wept bitterly. Then he knelt on the ground and with tears in his eyes prayed in this manner: "The pride of this man is too great, but Thou art, Oh, God, very compassionate." Within himself he thought, "I shall someday play the harp too, but there will be no pride in me, and then this man will be naught."

Strange as it may seem, this little boy was a harper of great skill at the age of twelve. He became very well known among his people, and as curses are, the other man had become utterly disabled.

When the little boy wept, no one saw him, but he told me not long ago, and now at the age of seventy, he loved exceedingly to play the harp for little children. Unfortunately he died at the age of eighty-six, December 31, 1934. Over this I also grieve because he was my father.

With Martín Savala's second departure for Yuma, the unity of the Savala family was permanently broken. They would never again reside together in one home. But the bonds of affection and love were not severed and, as with many sons, the model of the father's life was to become repeated in the son's love of beauty, legend, ceremony, music, and even in the work he was to pursue.

2. GROWTH

Merging of Labor and Love (1912–1923)

With the coming of his stepfather, José Morillo, life became easier and more stable for Refugio and other members of his family. Morillo was a sober man, who, by Yaqui standards of the time, made a good living at making sun-dried adobes, one of the traditional Yaqui skills.

With the growth of Tucson, demand for adobes for construction provided steady work. A crew of Yaquis mixed mud and straw and poured the mixture into forms. The bricks were then allowed to harden, removed from the forms, and laid out on the ground to dry in the sun.

Ranch work was another of the traditional areas of labor for Yaquis in Arizona, and Savala's memory of the weeks spent at the Rancho Samaniego are among the most pleasant of his recollections. The family headed north from the city toward the Santa Catalina Mountains, crossing the dry bed of the Rillito River, where water ran only during the rainy season. After a climb they passed through Oracle Junction and turned east onto a broad plain covered with cholla cactus. Here the cattle grazed on the tender new pads and succulent fruit of the cactus, collecting spines in their muzzles. The ranch Refugio's stepfather pointed out at Toro Cañada had been a stop on the Tucson, Oracle, and Mammoth Stage line, which still had been in existence as late as 1899 (*Arizona Daily Citizen* 1899:3).

As Savala notes, ore trains pulled by mules were a common sight in Tucson in his youth. The city was surrounded by both large and small mines, and although large operations such as the Anaconda copper mine south of the city were serviced by rail, small companies relied on mule trains to convey ore to smelters.

Life at the Samaniego Ranch amounted to a kind of vacation for Refugio and his brother after their varied and demanding work in Tucson. Though they were responsible for herding cows for milking, the job cannot have been arduous, since only the cows that had calved in the spring were suitable for milking, and even cheese-making required only a few milk cows.

Usually bounded by city life and responsibilities, Savala's appreciation of nature was reinforced by the ranch's desert environment. From his stepfather he gained both an understanding of the wilderness around him and its significance in relation to Yaqui belief. Years later, these lessons were reflected in his poem commemorating his weeks spent on the ranch:

> *It was to my eyes unknown,*
> *The place were nature took pride.*
> *The sunbeam on the mountainside*
> *Seems to match the breeze that's blown*
> *From the silentious forest's frown,*
> *When through the forest it humming strides.*
>
> *When the scented evening falls,*
> *The birds retiring to their nests*
> *Quiet their voices and lay to rest,*
> *The canyon within its walls,*
> *The hurrying stream that below rolls*
> *Curling itself through the forest.*

[156]

When the early lights of dawn
Touch the tall uppermost pine,
The beauty there seems to me Divine.
My mind dares to follow the dawn,
The beauty that the mountain crowns
Until I see it faint in broad sunshine.

Again, when the evening purples
The earth, mountains, and sky,
There in my soul is something shy,
For like dead going down to the sepulcher
Majestic "Catalina" in shade crepuscular,
Its mountain beauty to me denies.

The intimacy with nature that Savala gained in those weeks on the ranch was to grow consistently as opportunities for observation increased.

In the fall of the same year, the male members of the Savala family left their home in Tucson to engage in another form of ranch work. Cotton picking was a seasonal job in which frequently the whole family was employed. Almost every Yaqui family used to participate in such work, since the whole family working together might make as much as thirty dollars a week. The irrigation work and irrigation ditch cleaning that Savala mentions were the usual employment of Yaquis on ranches outside cotton harvest time (Spicer 1940:30).

When this job ended and the Savalas returned to Tucson, they moved into a district at the northwest edge of Tucson named after the Blue Moon Dance Hall, a place of entertainment called El Puente (The Bridge) by Spanish-speaking Tucsonans. From here the family set off to work in still another of the traditional Yaqui jobs—woodcutting. The wood they cut, mesquite, is known in the Southwest for its intense heat and clean, long-burning fire.

With the coming of World War I, Refugio followed the vocation of his father Martín, working as a section hand for the Southern Pacific. The youth approached his new job with the same enthusiasm as he had approached school, seeing it as a new kind of education. As a narrator, he approaches his first experiences as a gandy dancer in terms of language, savouring the colorful names of the tools and equipment and enjoying the teasing he took as a new "student."

The maintenance work gang number ten did ranged as far as Maricopa, over one hundred miles northwest of the Tucson home base. While there were permanent section crews working out of each of the stops he mentions, the extra gang furnished labor for large maintenance jobs and construction, and for emergency work such as the wreck of the fruit express. Fortunately for the section hands, this wreck took place next to a siding, so that a crane car could be brought in to right the cars. The tanker was returned to the track by placing switching rails under its wheels so that it could be pulled along them to where they merged with the main track and the tanker again placed on the rails.

Savala's first stint with the Southern Pacific was relatively brief, but it was exciting and memorable and was soon to be followed by years of service for the railroad.

For him and his family 1917 was a year of many excursions, ranching, cotton picking, woodcutting, and quarrying. In each working situation there is a sense of the enjoyment in personal endeavor, and particularly in Refugio's enterprises the sense of independence and overwhelming delight in his adventures and in the desert terrain through which he passed on his way to and from Tucson. He is not fearful when he is warned that he may encounter a specter but anticipates it with interest. And, again, an excursion beyond the city provides both time and more suitable setting for the transmission of traditional Yaqui literature from stepfather to son. Savala subtly draws together the tale of the lion and cricket in the wilderness and his stepfather's admonition against fear with his personal experience of confidence and success on his journey through the desert west of Tucson. The moral is not made explicit, but the appropriateness of his stepfather's selection of the tale is discernible.

A period of growth and expansion for Savala, 1917 was

also a year of importance to the Yaqui communities of Arizona. An event occurred late in that year which precipitated the formation of an organized Yaqui group in Tucson, leading to the eventual formation of Pascua Village.

Late in 1917, a band of eleven men set out with arms for Sonora, believing that the fighting going on there was an uprising of the Yaqui people against the Mexican government. They were stopped by a detachment of U.S. Cavalry from Fort Huachuca and brought back to Tucson to face charges of violating the neutrality of the United States by attempting to carry arms into Mexico. This incident caused much agitation and concern among Tucson Yaquis and a man named Juan Pistola (Juan Muñoz) acted as their spokesman several times during the trial in February of 1918. The men were later freed, and they and their families regarded Pistola as a leader in Yaqui relations with the Anglo community in Tucson.

Pistola gathered around him a number of subordinates, and the group set itself up as a council to administer the affairs of Yaquis in Tucson and other parts of the State (Spicer, Ms. 2: 2–4). In October of 1918, they issued a proclamation advising all Yaquis entering the United States from Sonora to report to them on arrival and keep them advised of their whereabouts. The proclamation, a classic example of garbled legalese, was published on October 9, 1918, in the *Arizona Daily Star:*

> The colony of the Yaqui tribe, residents of the city of Tucson in Pima County, Arizona, hereby give notice to the authorities, civil and military, local and federal, and to whomever it may concern, that Juan Pistola is their captain, general commander, representative and adviser in general, and whatever transaction affecting one, either or all of their colony of alien friendly Yaqui tribe now residing throughout Arizona or who may come into this country in future from the state of Sonora, Mexico, so that authorities may advise their said general and captain of any newcomers and thus enabling their said captain and general commander to keep them under peace, law, and order while in this country.

Pistola also warned Yaquis against contact with Sonoran Yaquis engaged in armed conflict with the Mexican government and arranged to secure jobs for Tucson Yaquis. Since no elections were held to place Pistola in his leadership position, many Yaquis refused him allegiance or support, causing dissention within the community in Tucson, particularly on the issue of aid to Yaquis in Sonora.

The friction was intensified when, in the spring of 1919, a youth from Mesquital Village was killed during a fiesta at which a rather loosely organized and unofficial "police" force formed by Pistola was in charge of keeping order. Pistola was exonerated in court of any responsibility for the killing, but he lost his following in the southern Tucson communities. However, he still continued to have strong influence among Yaquis in northwest Tucson, where Savala lived (Spicer, Ms. 2:3).

In 1918, Refugio's brother Fernando was married in a traditional Yaqui ceremony. Prior to the ceremony which Savala describes, the couple would have gone in the early morning to a Catholic church to be married in the orthodox manner. The bride and the groom are traditionally each accompanied by a ceremonial sponsor during both the church ceremony and the Yaqui celebration, but, as can be seen from the description, neither the couple nor the sponsors are very much in evidence.

The center of attention is the antics of the two Pascola dancers, who parody the bride and groom by comic impersonation and exaggeration of marriage customs. The important ceremony consists of an exchange of feasts, one at each of the marriage partners' houses, an exchange of food gifts, and finally a ritual capturing of the bride by the groom's relatives and ceremonial sponsor. The groom then takes his new spouse to his home (Spicer 1940: 73–76). In this rather unusual instance, the couple went almost immediately to live in a railroad camp.

Savala's encounter with Sonoran Yaqui laborers at the camp in Kim, where he joined his newly married brother, was a source of further education in Yaqui tradition. Not only did he remember these experiences in detail, but later, when he began writing, he preserved the old Yaqui attitudes toward witchcraft in the following short essay:

Witchcraft was greatly exercised long ago and it was thought to be the nature of a person to have powers to hurt another through willpower. The person who knew how to do this usually harmed another while in a profound dream. It came to pass that the subject dreamed that he was tormented and, usually, in his dream, he saw that a wolf, dog, hog, or other fanged animal had bitten him. In that same moment, the person awakened with an irresistible pain where he was bitten, and, if not saved in a few hours, the person surely died. But there is another person who, also by nature, has the power to cure the stricken person. The good wizard and the bad one are always in great combat to gain control over one another. The good wizard knows every intention of the bad witch. People who are not used to the wilderness are subject to many ailments due to the bewitching by animals such as the deer, coyote, fox, and rabbit, and snake, even though they are not bitten by them. So people assert that the human witches exercise the nature of these animals. Likewise, the curer has the power to cure any of these blows, if the bad witch does not have more power. If he does, it will kill his opponent even from a long distance. This evil does not have any power over people who do not have Indian blood, but the curer can use his power for both Indians and others. In some cases though, he will frankly tell the trouble and explain his inability to treat it.

Witchcraft has vanished through great efforts of good witches. When one was discovered, it was reported to the Indian council and they required that all people who exercised this bad art be burned alive.

A great pile of green wood was made into a crib, so it would burn quickly and make great heat, so that people could not come near it. The person to die usually gave plenty of proof of guilt. When questioned, he usually burst into cursing everyone present and in no way showed the slightest fear. He would want to fight if he was turned loose, up to the very moment he was thrown into the fire. The body was usually burned twice to make sure of complete death. Sometimes reptiles came out of the fire, and they were thrown into the fire again and made great explosions.

All the people witnessed the persecution, so any person learning the art would give up his cruel ambition.

There are also people who have it by nature, who rejoice upon seeing people weep over their dead, and if they do not use their power often, they are greatly tormented by their evil spirits, which oblige them to eat up human beings.

This awful art is long ended and only a few are still practicing and are not very powerful as they once were, so the good witch is also disappearing.

The burning of witches was never a part of Arizona Yaqui life, but it lingered in the memory of the Yaquis from Sonora. The seriousness of the offense and its punishment casts some light on the risk taken by the man with the black stone and the choni, since they are ritual objects of witchcraft.

Savala contrasts this portrait of evil with his version of a traditional story of Yaqui origin, ways, and beliefs. His version of "The Singing Tree," first published in 1945 in the *Arizona Quarterly,* is literary in nature. He creates a dramatic framework for the essential part of the tale, focusing on the elders gathered in confusion at the opening, and, at the ending, gathered in assent and response. The imaginative characterization of the young heroine and the description of her exploits and powers is much amplified and lyricized in the Savala version of the singing tree myth. This is not simply matter-of-fact reporting of an old Yaqui story, but rather the dramatic recreation of an event that is central to all Yaqui belief and identity. The climax, the revelation of the singing tree, is carefully approached and speedily concluded so the core meaning of the story is heightened.

When Refugio returned from working with the Río Yaqui hands on the railroad just east of Yuma, his original sympathy with Juan Pistola's endeavors led to a direct relationship with the leader, who was living with the Savala family at the time. Pistola was a Mayo Indian from Sonora just south of the Río Yaqui area. Having worked in mines in Sonora, he had drifted into the United States around 1900. As Savala points out, he was uneducated, a lack he must have felt keenly in his position as spokesman for Tucson Yaquis. Perhaps that is why he encouraged Savala to continue his schooling.

Pistola's impact on the Tucson Yaqui community is most evident in this same year, 1921, because, as well as receiving support from Tucsonans who hoped to consolidate all Yaquis in one location to aid in controlling their migration into the U.S., he conceived and developed the idea of a Yaqui village called Pascua, northwest of Tucson. Anglo hopes that the village would become the center of a "Yaqui Nation" in Arizona were not realized. Those families already established in the South Tucson villages of Libre and Mesquital did not respond to the plan, and the breach between Pistola's followers and opponents widened. However, the village did draw many Yaquis, some of whom were already squatting on the site, and before Pistola's death in 1922, it had become a well-established ceremonial center.

At sixteen, Refugio began attending night school in an adult education course in English grammar for Spanish-speaking people. Though he did not attend regularly, he studied the Spanish-to-English grammar books and fulfilled assignments by writing short, first-person essays. His night school teacher, impressed with his command of English, told him he was a writer and encouraged him to continue studying and writing on his own.

Savala took her advice and began producing essays and poems, mainly in English. He wrote very little in Yaqui, and most of those works have been lost in his rather continuous moving. The Yaqui Easter ceremony materials and some translations of Yaqui traditional lore are exceptions. Savala's only Spanish work consists of songs which he did not record in writing. He seems to find English compatible to his desire to transmit knowledge of Yaqui life and lore to a white audience. He also shows an intense interest in the English language itself. In a 1977 interview Savala explained that he learned most of what he knows of literary forms and techniques from reading Spanish literature but has vague recollection of having read some English literature too. The fact that Miss Richey and earlier teachers who influenced and encouraged him were English speakers undoubtedly strongly affected his preference for English as his literary language.

At this point in his narrative, Savala begins telescoping his writing career, relating events of the 1930s and early 1940s as if they had occurred in the context of the 1920s. The article in the June 29, 1941, *Arizona Daily Star* was actually headlined, "Yaqui Poet Produces Belles Lettres Here." The following is an excerpt from that lengthy article by Bernice Cosulich, reporter and Tucson historian:

Refugio Savala is a Yaqui of Pascua village and a section hand on the Southern Pacific Railroad system. For all his aristocratic manner and cultivated speech, one would not suspect that this quiet man of 38 years is a literary giant among his tribesmen.

One may say of him what Nathaniel Hawthorne said of himself more than a hundred years ago: "I am the obscurest man of letters in America." Obscure he has been, for not a line by Refugio Savala has been published until this day. His poems, essays, plays, short stories, songs and compilations of Yaqui history and myths have been read by few.

If all his writings were brought together in a book, the publishers could write an interesting "blurb" for the jacket. They could tell of his life as a section hand, roaming about throughout the Southwest, seeing life with the eyes of a poet. They could recite the dramatic incidents of his parents' lives, which so compactly tell the history of the Yaqui people for the past 75 years. They could speak of Refugio Savala as a language teacher for none other than a Guggenheim fellowship holder and University of Arizona instructor, Dr. Edward H. Spicer.

But Refugio Savala hasn't had a book published and probably does not think of himself as a man of letters. In spare time from his duties as a section hand he writes with almost equal fluidity in Yaqui, Spanish and English, makes his own translations from any of the three. Sometimes this self-educated man lets drop a Latin word or phrase. In whatever language he writes, however, his prose or poetry sings, has power and beauty.

His friends of Pascua village or Barrio Libre, south of

Tucson, are unaware that Refugio is a literary chap with an intuitive ability for literary forms. They know he plays the guitar and sings, that he's written one song of his own.

"He could have been a maestro," they say of him, remembering his neglect of Yaqui ceremonial dances and rituals in which he might have been their leader and teacher. "He is a wanderer," they add, recalling his travels with section gangs throughout the Southwest and out of work. They, no more than Walt Whitman's family when the author first finished *Leaves of Grass*, would think it worthwhile reading Refugio's manuscripts....

The manuscripts which so impressed the *Star* reporter had been strongly influenced by Savala's maternal uncle, Loreto Hiama, who spent a year with the family in Tucson. Strangely, Savala quickly glosses over the arrival and stay of this important visitor. Loreto Hiama was a source of traditional Yaqui literature and information during that year, and his influence inspired the work Savala was soon to undertake with great energy and seriousness. In a conversation with Dr. Edward Spicer in 1941, Savala recalls the importance of his uncle:

He used to tell me so many things, I couldn't get it all. I used to ask him questions. By God, I would make a lot of questions, because it was hard for me to understand. I was just a kid, and you know how hard it was to understand. He told me many things. There was so much for me to get in one year. He came up from the Yaqui River when I was about thirteen [actually, he was seventeen]. He walked all the way up from the Yaqui River to Tucson.... He was a great warrior down there, and by God, he used to tell us everything, everything about down there.... So I listened to old Loreto all the time and then, I used to go out and tell the kids those stories. I would be playing ball or something in the evening and I would say, "Come on boys, I bet I can tell you a story you won't understand." They would listen to me and I would tell them. They used to like it and sometimes they would ask me to tell it the next night, and I wouldn't mind, because I wanted to get it in my head (Spicer, Ms. 2:268).

[165]

Savala's parents had been country people and had had little contact with ceremonial life in the eight pueblos of the Río Yaqui. The unrest and persecution in their early adulthood had also disrupted their contact with traditional Yaqui life. While they knew and told Refugio the myth of Seahamoot and some other stories little touched by Christianity, they knew little of the Yaqui version of Bible stories.

Hiama on the other hand was deeply involved in the Christian tradition that went with Yaqui ritual and conveyed these stories to his nephew, awakening a deep interest in Refugio that would later influence his writing of stories. This influence is particularly evident in his longest and most complex poem, "Jesus, Mary and Joseph," the Yaqui version of the marriage of Mary and Joseph and the Immaculate Conception of Jesus through Mary's contact with a rose. His uncle obviously influenced his later writing of prose versions of Bible stories, such as the one of Jesus and Peter:

Peter was Jesus' most beloved disciple. Wherever He went He took him along. Peter was always asking questions which the Lord answered, and if he did not understand, He told it by parable or action. One day Peter and Jesus were going from one village to the other when, just out of the village, they saw two lovers under a tree. Jesus blessed these lovers and proceeded. Peter did not like it very well because they did not observe the day God had made holy, but he did not question the Master. Going far up the river, they came where a woman was washing clothes. Jesus did not give this woman the blessing. Peter was again thoughtful and found it necessary to ask the Master, "Thou hast blessed the two lovers under the tree, but this woman Thou dost not bless?" Jesus did not answer this question but went on till they found a nest of hornets. He broke the limb whereon the nest was hanging and gave it to Peter to carry along. They were not going very far when Peter began to make complaints about the hornets stinging him. Jesus told him then, "The woman washing in the river is hurting my Father also that much. The flirtation of the lovers is blessed, for it is natural since the beginning." By and by they came to the next town, and Peter had an urgent desire to eat lamb's kidney. He was just thinking about it when the Master told him, "Peter, go into the city and buy a lamb and bring it out here and prepare it, so we can eat roast lamb here." By the

[166]

time Peter returned, the Master was sound asleep. Peter, without disturbing Him, slew the lamb, kindled a fire, and the first he got out was the kidney. This he roasted and ate before the Master had gotten up. When the lamb was about done, the Master arose and told him, "Peter, roast the kidney separately. I will eat that." Peter could not find any excuse for this moment. He told Him, "Master, this lamb had none. I searched for it and found it not." The Master smiled meekly and said, "Peter, these things are also weaving a crown of thorns for Me." Peter was sad over this and could not answer the Master. But the Master told him not to be sad, and they ate and went in the city, and there were many people who received the Lord, and He stayed all day with them teaching.

At evening He was leaving. Outside the city was a big house, where they stopped to ask for water to drink, and when the people in the house saw them coming, they hid themselves in a room and told a servant to give the beggars food and bid them depart. This they said because Peter and Jesus were poorly dressed, and their hands were bruised and feet ulcerated. The servant did give them water and food, and when Jesus was leaving, he told the servant, "Open thou thy master's door." The servant obeyed and a flock of hogs came out, rushing toward a pond of water, and presently they were digging in the mud and rubbish with their noses.

The content, setting, and details of Refugio's version of a parable are uniquely Yaqui, but the parable form and literary style are consciously preserved. Whereas the events are condensed, the concerns—breaking the Sabbath, Peter's lie, and the swine—are all recognizable motifs from authorized versions of the New Testament. Christ and Peter are drawn with attention to character, speech, and appearance that is distinctly Savala's own method of recreating traditional stories.

Refugio's uncle's visit also marked a new phase in Yaqui history. The Mexican government decreed that Yaquis could return safely to their eight pueblos on the Río Yaqui. Shortly after Loreto Hiama's return to Sonora, Savala's mother set out by wagon and rail for her home village of Potam and was warmly welcomed by her uncle with a feast. But it was only a visit; the Savala family was well settled in Pascua. They had become an Arizona Yaqui family and did not desire permanent return to Sonora. So, after one year of separation, the family was reunited at the fiesta of St. Francis held in Magdalena, the place of Refugio's birth.

Upon returning home, Savala again set out with his original section gang, number ten, for work south of Phoenix, and while there became the victim of an attack by a witch whose evil power incapacitated him. Leaving the train at Maricopa, he completed his trip to Tucson on a doodlebug, a small car run by a gas motor used by section laborers.

As she had earlier received presentiment of her first husband's return from Yuma, Savala's mother had premonitions of her son's suffering. The next day she brought a curer to exorcise the evil. When a Yaqui adult or child is seriously ill, his family often promises him to a ceremonial society if he is cured. In this case, no such vow was made, although during a serious physical illness in Savala's youth, he was promised to the Matachin dance society for three years, an obligation which he did fulfill but only for the duration of the promise.

Intense or continuous participation in Yaqui ceremonial life would have been quite contradictory to Savala's natural bent toward observation and reflection. Even in his youth he seems to have recognized that his role among his people was to be one of recorder and literary recreator rather than actor in the drama of his people's revitalization of traditional culture in Arizona. He attended ceremonies regularly and seems to have felt quite comfortable and accepted in his passive role. Actually though, he was, if not physically active, intellectually and artistically active, unswervingly committed to the transmission of Yaqui culture by a means that he was uniquely able to pursue—words.

Work with words was Savala's special skill, but manual labor was necessary for his survival. One week after his return to Tucson, his physical and spiritual endurance reestablished, he was back on the job for the railroad, this time in New Mexico.

Savala's late childhood and early youth were times of relative stability and increasing confidence for him as well as for his people in Arizona. As the Yaqui communities of Arizona revitalized their ceremonial life and brought it back to public performance, he became more firmly grounded in his knowledge of traditional Yaqui literature and acquired the necessary linguistic skills for his own recreations of traditional materials. With his personal and communal identity strong and his preparation for both his livelihood on the railroad and his vocation as a writer undertaken, Savala was on the threshold of expression as a creative artist.

3. EXTENSION

Protecting and Providing
(1924–1928)

As Refugio entered adulthood, he settled into regular work on the railroad. But even then there was always time for Yaqui ceremonies, as his interest in the Easter celebration in Yuma attests. Although the town on the Colorado had only a small population of Yaquis, the influx of railroad workers provided the local group with enough participants for the complex rituals of Easter week, a cooperation made possible by the approval of the section gang's foreman.

As usual, Savala was not a participant in the fiesta, but his reverence for and pleasure in the rituals, particularly the sermon, is evident. He shared intimately in the "spirit of Lent" that pervaded the section camp. Lacking the traditional Yaqui church, which is entirely open at the front to allow dancers to approach the altar, the Yaquis held the ceremonies at the home of a Yuma Yaqui and erected the stations of the cross nearby for an essential portion of the Lenten ritual. The home may have been that of Refugio's Uncle Félix Esperanza, with whom the Savala family had stayed upon their initial arrival in Tucson.

The Yaqui Easter ceremonies are organized and supervised by a society of men called the Kohtumbre, comprised of the Fariseos and the Horsemen, or Caballeros. Among the participants are the Pascolas as ceremonial hosts and dancers, and the sacred Matachin Dancers.

Culminating the intense ceremonial activities of Holy Week is a farewell sermon by the Maestro of the village. In this case, the Maestro reviewed the role of the Fariseo soldiers and the masked Chapayekas, who, during the Holy Saturday ceremonies, make a ritual attack on the chapel but are finally overcome by the forces of good, who shower them with flowers and bring them to surrender before the altar. The complete ceremony, which takes place from Ash Wednesday through the last week of Lent, is in many ways similar to a medieval mystery play, but with elements also of the morality play. Some of the participants represent evil beings engaged in the persecution of Jesus, culminating in the surrender of Pilate's irreverent and mocking soldiers, the Chapayekas, and the burning of a Judas effigy which pops and whistles with the explosion of fireworks stuffed into the straw.

With the completion of the ceremonial season, the men again went to work on the completion of the new rail yard in Yuma. As always, Savala found satisfaction in the efficiency of railroading methods, as in his enthusiasm for the U-turn which allowed trains to enter and leave the hard without having to back into the "Y" in order to turn around.

The PFE ice plant Savala mentions in conjunction with the location of his accident was a servicing point for the Pacific Fruit Express refrigerator car line owned by the Southern Pacific and Union Pacific. The development of a system for icing cars allowed coast to coast shipment of fresh produce without spoilage. Such plants were placed at intervals along SP tracks in order to insure that fruits and vegetables would remain chilled. Huge blocks of ice were prodded down chutes and into spaces along the top of each car, with the ice being replenished as needed.

Refugio was fortunate not to have lost a leg when he fell under the wheel of the platform water car. The accident temporarily interrupted his work, and when he returned to Tucson, he fulfilled the vow his sister had made for his recovery, walking the twelve miles from Pascua to the mission of San Xavier del Bac on the Papago Indian Reservation south of Tucson.

Well enough for baseball, he was able to return to his work, this time for the El Paso and Southwestern Railroad. The 1925 Polvo branch project Savala worked on changed the route of the EPSW track heading out of Tucson from due east to south, then east again. The track, originally laid in 1880, headed directly east toward El Paso, passing the later site of Davis Monthan Air Force Base. On this project, the track changed course just east of the PFE yard at a section stop called Polvo, running southeast to the south yard of the EPSW railroad and then parallel to the original track (Myrick, 1975: 230).

Although track-laying machinery was in use by 1925, this project was completed with manual labor (Myrick, Dec. 29, 1975: interview). The frog Savala describes was a portion of the switching equipment. Weighing about 2,000 pounds, it was used to join the south leg of the track to the existing rails. Because not all rails were of the same weight or size, the frog was laid to allow the train to pass from rails of one size to the new ninety-pound rails without jumping the track. Once ties and rails were laid, waste rock from nearby mines was used to fill in the spaces between the ties, allowing for smooth passage of the cars over the line and preventing weed growth along the tracks (Wright, Feb. 11, 1976: interview).

During the work on the Polvo branch, Savala was able to remain at home, commuting to the nearby job each day. By the Lenten season of 1926, his brother Encarnación's illness had reached a terminal stage. As captain of the Caballeros, Encarnación Savala requested the presence of the heads of the society at his deathbed.

The dying man foresaw his brother Refugio's efforts to record and preserve the beauty of the Easter fiesta and encouraged him to take great care in his descriptions. What influence this request had on Refugio's later participation in the transcription and translation of the Yaqui Easter sermon under the direction of Muriel Painter is impossible to know. However, the influence of his brother's advice is suggested in the painstaking work of translation from the Yaqui which he carried out in conjunction with the Maestro who delivered the original sermon. Refugio worked long hours on not only the translation but also on interpretive notes, to which he gave his own characteristic literary flavor. The work was published nearly thirty years after this brother's deathbed prophecy.

Encarnación's death was the first of many family losses that Refugio was to suffer. These losses would compel him to poetic expression of his pain and sorrow during the prolific period of his late twenties. At this time, however, he was not ready to express himself poetically, and the religious and economic aspects of the death occupied him.

At the time of the death, Savala's brother was taken to the mortuary, prepared for burial, and then returned to the family for the velación, the Yaqui funeral rite. In this ceremony, the body is removed from the coffin. A burial garment is placed over the clothing, rosaries are laid on the body, prayers are sung by the Maestro and women singers, dancing is performed by the Matachinis, and a final leave-taking is made by the family members. After the last rites at a Catholic church, the body is taken the next morning for burial.

Aside from his ritual duties to his brother, Refugio became the representative of his heirs in a rather confused episode about insurance benefits. The insurance delay was quickly straightened out, however, when Refugio referred the matter to his job foreman. Although paternalism was not a policy of the railroad, the foreman's action was not inappropriate, since foremen were often called upon to aid their crews in personal matters and were usually willing to attempt to ease the problems of their men.

When Savala again returned to railroad work, this time north of Tucson in the Phoenix area, he was again summoned to what was apparently another death and more legal and economic harrassment. Fernando's injury fortunately was not fatal, and Refugio's wit and innovation settled the harrassment problems permanently.

With the close of the formal period of mourning at the lutupahko, the death anniversary ritual and fiesta a year after Encarnación's death, Refugio was free to follow his work as a section hand wherever it would take him. When he was offered the opportunity to work in northern California, he departed with his mother's blessing and encouragement. The pursuit of work and adventure were not his only motive in accepting the Shasta Division assignment, however, for during these years of his early twenties, Refugio had fallen in love with a young girl from Pascua Village. In the evenings he would meet her in the cottonwood grove north of the village, and after two years of romantic rendezvous, Refugio built a small house in the village. The young woman, pregnant with his child, came to live with him there, but when the baby died almost immediately after birth, the girl refused to stay with him any longer. So Refugio's departure was not only a search for new experiences but a retreat from the sorrow and memory of the death of the child and failure of a relationship which affected him deeply.

Savala's failure to include any mention of this love affair in his narrative, despite its obvious impact on his life, stems neither from vain privacy nor anguished remorse. Rather, the nature of the concerns of the autobiography preclude detailed analysis of such an episode, for Savala is seldom occupied in his prose writing with the intricacies of personal relationships outside the kin circle, and he never dwells on death, sorrow, or failure. The analysis and protrayal of emotion is reserved for his other writing, where it is refined and molded carefully and informed always by images from nature and a passionate trust in the benevolence of Divine protection.

Such a transformation of both the joy and grief of personal love can be seen in the following selection of his fictional prose. In this tale, Savala translates passionate human emotion into a dramatic format employing fantasy and witchcraft. The tale has no direct relationship to his own personal life, but it illustrates his talent for objectifying realistic human emotions into fictional form.

This tale of witchcraft and tragedy, of the merging of love and evil, is far removed from realism, yet this very quality of the fantastic allows Savala to dramatize the conflict of human passions and the frailty of the human condition. It is only in the literary context that Savala engages in such description of emotion as he does in dramatizing Pacisco's intense and blinding love for the dangerous Marita. And even here the love motif serves only as a framework for the dominant theme of witchcraft and transformation. The natural world provides the central rationale for the story, with the tale of love operating primarily as a motive for the ensuing action in the forest. Only in the final sentence is the ironic outcome of the destruction of an evil love power revealed.

A young Indian cowboy went far into the Mayo Indian country where he, as it is always the case, was in love with a fair Indian maiden. Her name was Marita, which means Mary in Mayo; the young man was a Yaqui Indian; therefore his name was Pacisco, which means Frank in Yaqui. This man did not know the Mayos very well, but he loved Marita just the same. So he married her and lived with her at her home where her parents had a ranch in the wilderness of "Río Mayo." The Yaqui boy was a very clever cowboy so he could get along nicely with this people. After a year with his wife, he noticed that this young woman was very expert in all sorts of witchcraft; she usually went out at night and came home early in the morning. One day Pacisco was overwhelmed over this and decided to find out all about his wife. He questioned her but she refused to tell him. But in turn, she said that if he was willing to learn her art, she would reveal it to him. The boy could not answer. Now Pacisco was greatly angry and disappointed. He left her one night but failed to travel in the forest because there were too many beasts in the jungle, so he had to come back again; he had attempted this escape several times without success. And Marita knew everything he was doing, so she decided to reveal her secrets to him.

One night she was going out and took Pacisco along; they traveled that evening into the wilderness. When they were a considerable distance away from their ranch, they hitched their *remuda* and walked the way afoot.

When they came where a big ant hill was (an ant hill is always bare of weeds), she made him take off all his clothes till he was completely naked; she did likewise so both were naked. Now she bade him to tumble over the ant hill, and it came to pass that when he had done this, he was transfigured into a ferocious leopard. When this was done, she did the same and was a female leopard. Pacisco was in a very ugly condition to consider, a human being under the skin of a beast from which he could not escape. He could use his claws on his paws, and he could also grunt like the beasts.

Marita had advised him to be unafraid even among the other real animals. They would not be discovered, and in case of a fight, all they had to do was to stay away from it till it ended. Now evidently this was a big party for the beasts and Marita wanted to be there. When they both were leopardized, she began to howl like the beasts; when she was so doing, beasts began to arrive and soon a great number were gathered and the party was on. After they had enough, they went into a place where they could find prey. Now Pacisco could not climb for he could not use his claws, so he sat under the trunk of a big tree. Presently one of the beasts caught a handsome steer which all the other beasts attacked. Now Pacisco, in order to make the beast believe that he was a real one, also made an attack biting the steer on one leg.

And the dying animal kicked him so hard that he was knocked unconscious for a few moments. When he recovered consciousness, he found that the beasts had devoured their prey. Now he could not get along with the beasts, so he thought to escape. He was not far when some cowboys came and chased the animals away. They had some hunting dogs which, while chasing the beasts, found Pacisco the leopard. He ran but the dogs were using their legs which Pacisco could not. When he was far away, he began to talk to the dogs. These were trained so they were astonished and were afraid of Pacisco the leopard. He escaped easily but he was alone and he came to where the cowboys had their horses. The horses were afraid of the fierce appearance of Pacisco. The trained horse that he mounted recognized his voice and stood calm. Now he was trying to mount the horse but his body was not shaped for it. After he failed in his intentions, he went back to where the scene began; he rolled his body over the ant hill, but he was not the person to restore the body. He was unsuccessful; he was very sad and was sitting on the ant hill when a ferocious beast appeared in the bushes; he attempted to run away but remembered he was also a powerful beast. While the other advanced toward him, he was in position to charge upon it; he was determined now.

He had entirely forgotten that Marita was also a leopard. She said that she had lost him and thought he was caught in the raid. Now that she found him, she was glad and promptly went to restoring their human bodies. She made him roll upon the ant hill and he was again Pacisco himself, and she did the same and was Marita again, and she had a great bulk of the best meat. When they dressed, they roasted the meat and ate, and soon they were on their way home. Pacisco was glad, and how much more glad he was to have his body again. He was very much disappointed; he had tried to escape on several occasions, but he was always surrounded by all the beasts of the jungle which threatened to devour him, and the only manner of escape was to go back to Marita. In this manner Pacisco went to many jungle beast parties but never did like them, and he was always endeavoring to run away.

As a cowboy, he also had friends in the other ranches, also cowboys. Among them was an old man who was a good medical man, for almost any case of trouble was brought to him and he cured it. Now this man did not trust Pacisco for the reason that his wife was a dangerous witch. Now, in order to win the confidence of this man, he had to tell him his case and how he longed to escape and go into the native land where he would enjoy freedom. The old man listened, pitiful, and finally decided to help him out, but first he told the young man to find every secret that he believed Marita to exercise.

Pasciso could do this easily because he had learned many things. He almost could do the things she had always tried to teach him, if he only had the will. When the old man knew this, he could provide the right thing for it. They prepared for a certain day, and when the day came, he rolled tobacco in a corn bark which served as cigarette paper. With this rustic cigarette, they could know every movement that Marita was doing and Pasciso was provided with three of these cigarettes, and the most important of all was the "choni" scalp of an old Indian with long hairs woven into a pigtail with a chamois ribbon at the end. He also had a good bow and arrows.

When Pasicso was ready to go, they smoked and the boy was bade farewell. At nightfall, the scalp kept the brutes of the forest from devouring Pacisco. The virtue it had was that it could easily tie the beasts' necks and choke them to death at once. In this manner, it kept them far and killed those that were too close to Pacisco. All night the young man rode his steed which was greatly excited and traveled faster than it usually did. It was almost daylight and all the beasts had ceased to follow, or rather the "choni" had killed them all but one which was following close and grunting furiously, but in the old man's advice he was entirely unafraid of the last beast, and he let it come close, and it came to the feet of Pacisco and fell dead. He pulled his knife and cut the huge beast's wrist and discovered the bracelet on the human arm of his wife.

Although his own tragic liaison is conspicuously absent from his narrative, it is not without impact on his fiction and his poetry. At the time of the romantic meetings, Refugio composed nature lyrics in Spanish, and after the parting, when he was so grief stricken, he told friends in Pascua he "wished to die." He wrote a poem which begins:

> There was a night of deadly melancholy
> And I could see only that one called Death.
> She was there and looked like an angel
> And I was going to follow along with her.
>
> (Spicer, Ms. 2:269)

Years later, he was able to express his attitudes about women and love much more objectively, if less intensely, when he said:

> To love a woman is the same as to love God. When you love a woman you go to her and tell her everything. You admit all your mistakes to her. This is just the same as you do when you confess to God. But loving a woman is different from loving a man. A woman has a hold on you that is different and once you have been with her, she will always have this hold because you will get to thinking of her and will go to her. She doesn't have to do anything at all to make you come back to her.
>
> (Spicer, Ms. 2:269)

[179]

The verse is a lyric of innocence as well as grief. The prose statement is personal commentary, informed by experience and maturity and a barely disguised sense of irony.

Refugio's pensive moment as the train pulled out of Tucson passing Pascua village, was quickly dismissed, and he enjoyed the trip beyond the limits of his previous journeys. The track over the Mohave Summit was of special interest to him, since he could look down into the cuts in the mountainside where the track the train had just passed over was in clear view. New towns and cities read like a timetable, and the scenery of northern California, particularly the lakes and springs, impressed him with his distance from his native desert.

Savala's description of his participation in fire fighting at Black Buttes is among the most precise and detailed of all his autobiographical writing. The story became a favorite with him and was subsequently published in a newspaper article (Cosulich, 1941).

The depiction of camp life needs no interpretation—work hazards, drinking, violence, and jail were all a part of gandy dancing. Though guilty only of common sense and compassion during the fight episode, Savala took his arrest in stride, mildly amused, holding no grudge.

From the description of the work of taking up the branch line, one gets the impression of cooperation and camaraderie on the job. As he describes the men breaking by hand the bolts that join the rails and loading the rails on a flatcar to be used on sidings where second hand rails are acceptable, Savala makes heavy work seem light. In reality each rail weighed ninety pounds per foot (Myrick, Dec. 29, 1975: interview).

Even after his traveling companions from Tucson departed for home, Refugio determined to stay on, moving farther north to Mistletoe, Oregon. Here he stayed, sharing his boxcar with the mice for more than six months. The volatile nature of the section labor camp is again illustrated in the Sunday afternoon fight. The real concern of the story, however, seems not so much the actions of the participants as the significance of names and an implicit moral lesson. The scene is simultaneously comic and brutal, and it illustrates Savala's willingness to risk his own safety to prevent serious consequences.

The track in the area of Mistletoe was extremely steep and winding, requiring booster engines to push the cars to the top of the grade. When Savala walked the Siskiyou Tunnel each night—all 3,108 feet of it—he could be sure of catching a ride on a booster engine as it returned to the bottom of the grade for another line of cars (Myrick, Dec. 29, 1975: interview).

Isolated in Mistletoe, far from his Yaqui community during the 1925 Christmas season, Refugio brought to the holiday a traditional Yaqui interpretation of Christ's birth. This story is severely condensed from his much longer version of the same legend, which is on file with Savala's other works in the Arizona State Museum Archive. The longer version offers a more complete portrait of the crisis caused by Mary's conception of Jesus, and it also develops the reconciliation of Joseph to his role of father to the Divine Child, as can be seen in the following excerpt:

> Mary began to talk to her husband caressingly: "God answered my prayers, for I found grace in His presence. It happened that when thou had left me, I exclaimed with tears in my eyes to Him who selected thee from the great multitude of men and made thee my husband. He heard my voice and brought thee back to me. What the rose I found in the stream signified was unknown to us, and the Creator revealed it to me. A child is conceived within me in the form of the rose. This I am to bear, a great miracle that God will send to the people of the world. Already thou hast seen this, Joseph; through Him, God will make Himself visible to humanity. Those who have abided in darkness all their lives will see the light. Those who were bound since childhood shall be freed. Whosoever has lost his home shall be given a new mansion to dwell in. Those in lamentation shall be comforted. People will rejoice upon His birth in generations to come, and the wonderful conception of the Child will make manifest the great power of the Creator. And it is a sin of neither I nor thee." These things did Mary say to her husband and Joseph saw these great events and believed his wife and remained with her, being the most tender loving husband thereafter.

The passage is also different in tone from that told in Mistletoe, for the prophecy of the blessings to mankind which the Child will confer has the quality of a chant or litany. The emphasis on Mary as speaking "caressingly" to Joseph juxtaposes the intimate relationship of the husband and wife caught in a marital crisis with the awesome significance of the events they have been chosen by their Creator to share in. Savala has enhanced this significance by employing a heightened style in the quoted portion of the passage, where Mary describes the revelation made to her by God. This style contrasts sharply with the colloquial quality of the introductory and concluding passages describing the marital relationship.

The same biblical episode is also the subject of the first section of Savala's religious epic, "Jesus, Mary and Joseph," which he had begun before leaving his village a year and a half before. Though marred by a preoccupation with versification, the following stanzas from the epic are much more detailed than the version delivered at Mistletoe and convey a more intense vitality because of the dramatic use of dialogue and the injection of emotion. Savala describes Mary dipping her cantara into the pool where the rose whirls round and clasping the flower to her breast. Then he writes:

She inhaled the sweet fragrance.
Into her loose robe she dropped
The flower in a merry trance.
Her husband she sought to show it,
"This will please Joseph in abundance
When the rose in his hands I deposit."

Joseph was too singing merrily
Upon the labor of the day,
When Mary shouting so happily
In her manner pleasant did say,
"I brought something, and it's for thee,
The most beautiful rose of May.
To me it's the star of the East."

And Joseph in so great a stupor bound
Was not expectant in the least
For so great a surprise around.
She searched the flower in her breast,
But the rose was never found.

Because Mary never before
Was known to tell her husband a lie,
She was so sad and wept therefore.
Her husband gave a tender sigh,
Caressing her forevermore.

The personalization of the biblical characters is vivid, and the contrast of Mary's joy and her sad weeping is keenly caught in the poetic form of this story, as is Joseph's patient tenderness as he sighs and caresses her. The immediacy of the moment is captured in two ways. Savala compresses time, as Joseph's forgiveness follows immediately upon his wife's weeping. He also contrasts Mary's truthfulness with the notion of Joseph's doubt that motivates her tears. All that is explained in the prose version is suggested in Mary's sadness, creating a more intense experience for the reader than the brief prose version told that Christmas day in the snowy mountains. The three versions of the same episode also serve to define the versatility and sensitivity of the young writer, for though each work is essentially the same in content, the style of each is in a different genre, which determines the selection.

Christmas 1928 marked the end of the period in Savala's life which was a prelude to his most intense and prolific writing. The cycle of death, love, and life that began with the death of his brother and ended in the death of his newborn child motivated his journey to the mountains of the north. The loss of those dear to him and the gains in experience through travel would soon be transformed into the substance of his poetry, prose, and song as the Depression of the thirties curtailed his work on the railroad and offered him the opportunity to express the experience and knowledge he had gained.

4. RETURN

Mining, Writing, Gandy Dancing (1929–1934)

In his adulthood, Savala could not bring himself to stay in Pascua. He was a kind of tramp, never remaining in one place for very long. But wherever he might be during the Lenten season, "the spirit began to urge" him to return home for the sacred ceremonies. For two years the Yaqui had been absent from his home, and the excitement and anticipation of the return is evident in the pace of his narrative as he describes the trip down from the mountains and into San Francisco.

He had hardly returned when he set off again with his sister's family, this time to work in a mining town. He was young, unattached, restless, so the opportunity to go to Hayden, north of Tucson, was welcome. He was soon employed at the concentrator, where the ore from the nearby copper mines was milled and refined.

Considering his education (he had completed the first two years of high school), his talents, and his ability to adjust to Anglo culture, it may seem strange that he found manual labor acceptable and was willing to take odd jobs at the Hayden smelter. But his restlessness and that urging of the spirit that periodically drew him homeward were so deeply

[185]

characteristic of his cultural and personal identity that he apparently never really considered abandoning his seasonal returns and cultural concerns for economic or social advancement. Talking with a professor in 1936, he said, "I am only a laborer and will never be anything else" (Spicer 1936: fieldnotes).

But Savala was much more; he was also a poet. And despite the distractions of work and the responsibilities for the welfare and comfort of his mother and family, his intense creative urge was about to carry him into a period of prolific writing. What he had already produced, he turned over to Dr. Provinse of the University of Arizona Anthropology Department. Of those early works he said, "What I wrote in that time, I do not like to think about now. I wish to—what do you say?—ignore it" (Spicer 1936: fieldnotes). He felt he hadn't known enough then to write, especially that he didn't understand enough about God. These early writings, given to Bernice Cosulich, later became part of the material for the lengthy article on Savala as a poet, which he knew nothing about until his friends informed him. He later recalled:

> Some fellows began talking about me, saying I had been in the daily papers. I didn't know what they were talking about. It was my name day, and a great bunch of them came around, and Torres, who is an English-speaking boy, told me he wanted to congratulate me. He said, "How did you make it? There was a very long story in the *Daily Star* about you."
>
> I said I didn't know about it, and I was afraid there was something wrong in it. You know how drunken fellows are. They get rough and they like to kid you. Well, I didn't see the paper because I didn't ever read the papers, and they kept talking, and I got worried that maybe there was something said bad about the people, and I didn't like it. Then we went in town and they asked me about the story there. I guess they wanted to congratulate me. Then there was the reporter from *El Tucsonense,* and he wanted to talk to me, and I didn't know anything about it. They kept coming around. My brother said he liked it all; it was nice to have me around because people came to his house.
>
> But the story was all right. There was nothing bad in it, and it made me feel good (Spicer 1936: fieldnotes).

Though exact dates are somewhat confused in this portion of the narrative, the essential chronology is accurate. It was Miss Richey, the teacher at the Pascua school, who encouraged Refugio in his literary efforts and arranged for him to meet Dr. Provinse. Through Dr. Provinse and his association with Dr. Spicer, the contact with Mrs. Painter came about and the work on *A Yaqui Easter Sermon* began, with Refugio and Maestro Ignacio Alvarez from Pascua Village serving as informants and translators. The final manuscript, published in 1955, contained the literal as well as the free translation given in Savala's narrative. The following excerpt is the same portion of the sermon in Yaqui with literal interlinear translation:

gobusan semanapo a'a santo libro a iba'anamaka tewekau
seven week in his holy book it embracing heaven to

bichaka oraroak a netanek waka inile benak sewata
toward prayed for it begged that this like flower

ahta ke inie beki ta'apo waka santo kumplimientota a
until at this many day in that holy fulfillment it

yak hunumu'u enchim santo templo kateka'apo
made there right your holy temple sits where

Itom Ya'uchiwa Die -su Kristota presensia kari
Our Leader God Jesus Christ presence house

ya'aripo waka tachiriata ko'om yuma'apo tua au
made His in that light down comes where truly him to

ko'om yumak wa'a oraroaka'u tewekau bicha a'a
down came the prayer done heaven to toward he

netaneka'u wa'a santo sewa
asked for that the holy flower

Besides the literal and free translations, Savala contributed to notes which interpret each line of the text. For instance, he explains the phrase *"aet yeu sikamta"* by saying it "means one who comes out right on it without mistakes. Fundamental mistakes, not ones made through ignorance. Mistakes made by his own will knowing it is wrong. Suppose he is a 'maestro' and didn't bring his book. Or a Matachini and didn't

[187]

bring his crown. Those would be mistakes. Whoever did not make his mistakes with his own conscience he is supposed to get the reward from heaven. If a person doesn't come out right on it, he will be in someone else's hands—he will be in hell" (Painter, Savala, Alvarez 1955: 21–25).

A work of scholarly importance, the sermon was also of value to the Yaqui community, as the Maestro himself demonstrated the year following its publication, when he read from the very book he had helped to compose.

Savala's description of the Deer Dance is also of importance to a more comprehensive understanding of the Yaqui Easter Ceremony, of which it is an important part. Besides the description he gave to Mrs. Painter, he offered a lengthy and complex analysis of the Deer Dance in a later discussion of the subject with an anthropologist. The following is a portion of that explanation:

> At first the Deer Songs were for hunting. Then they added the dance so it could be held at a fiesta with the Deer Songs. The dance started when a man who lived in the country—one who probably made his living by hunting and was much in the wilds—saw the deer, mostly young ones, having a fiesta of their own in the woods. They were dancing and gamboling in the woods. This man studied their dancing and was able to interpret it and do it himself. He taught others. The deer were seen to be dancing and playing around a "lake" in the woods, so that is why water is brought into the deer dance now. The deer is always said to be *awam hiluki,* rubbing its antlers. The *hirukiam* [rasp] was produced to make the sound like a deer rubbing its antlers....
>
> The Deer Dance is very difficult and taxing for the performer. It tires him to dance. The movements are hard, for he must dance constantly on his toes. He can't just shuffle along when he gets tired as does the Pascola. He has to outdance three Pascolas. The movements of his arms are very tiring. He also has to move his hips to shake the *rijutiam* [hoof waist jinglers] and that is hard work....
>
> Singing the deer songs is like praying because there are no bad words used. It is like prayer because the songs are in-

spired. They come from the wilds—just like when you dream. When you dream, you go to a place in nature. Nature is the source of inspiration and prayer. The songs are about nature and were inspired by natural objects. Therefore the songs are like prayers.

At the same time Savala was contributing this information for study, he was preserving related material from traditional Yaqui stories, among them brief portraits of the characteristics and qualities of various members of the traditional Yaqui community: the fireworks maker, the honey gatherer, and the fisherman. One of these is a brief portrait of the deer hunter, a man of the wilderness, one who might have first brought the deer dance to the Yaqui people.

THE DEER HUNTER
Part One

The deer hunter has a very peculiar method of working out the plan of the hunt. Since this method is not performed with a gun, the hunter goes into the forest and sets the traps. These traps are the Indian method, a rope of mezcal fibers which is the color of the earth and long enough to reach the top of a big tree. Near the lakes where the path of the deer is visible, there in the middle of the path, a round hole is dug deep enough to bury the rope, and four stakes are driven deep to hold the rope. The one stake that holds the key has a fork where the rope passes, and the rope has a little wooden knob which is hooked to the fork of the stake. The long rod that goes in the center is another key which locks the little knob on the rope from the four stakes. The three other rods lie on top of the key rod so the knot lock of the rope lies loose in a round coil. The stake of the fork holds down with the rope a very strong limb which is bent down, hooked with the rope to the stake. Now when the deer steps on either one of the four center rods, this bent limb throws the lasso on the deer's leg so that sometimes it holds it without touching the ground with the leg where the rope has caught it.

When the deer hunter has all his traps set, in the evening

he and two others begin to sing the song of the deer hunter which is very beautiful in composition. Sometimes the singing lasts all night. The hunter, or rather trapper, leaves at dawn and finds his prey alive in the trap, and he slays it with a knife which he thrusts into the deer's collar. Thus the blood is drained and the meat is good to eat, and in this manner, the skin is not damaged. Now, to carry his game on the shoulder, one of the hind legs is tied on one of deer's horns, because in this way it will not squeeze the carrier's neck or shoulders. If one would try to tie the legs together and carry it on the shoulder, it would squeeze the blood out of it. If one would try to carry it with loose body, it would roll off the shoulder.

Part Two

The deer hunters sometimes use the arch and arrow or gun, when they want the deer just for food, they also sing some hunt songs before they go, and they bathe early in the morning or evening previous to the hunt. When they leave, they burn some weeds and cover them with a blanket to perfume their bodies so the deer cannot scent them within a close distance. The deer has a very keen perception for humans; for this reason a deer hunter must be clean. The trapper also uses the same method for the hunt when he goes to set the trap. He also bathes and fumes his body, and above all, everything that the trap is made of is carefully rubbed with some green weeds and tree leaves so that no trace of human odor is left where the trap is.

The deer trapper also makes a living out of his trade. He tans all the skins and probably his wife is also a good tanner and may be a good maker of skin jackets which are in demand in the Yaqui country. People who work this art are always making more money because even women wear the deer skin outfit, or at least the trapper sells the tanned skin to those who work it in fancy styles, and when they go into the "Yorim" they sell the skin for a good price. No matter what quantity, Mexican "talabarteros" [saddle and harness makers] usually prefer the Yaqui deer skins.

There are people who stay in the wilderness all the year or part of the year merely trapping and hunting deer; in season of progeny only bucks are slain in order to preserve the game.

Savala, in his careful observation and preservation of the stories his family had passed on to him, has given, in these three separate presentations of the deer hunt, songs, and dance, a comprehensive view of the ongoing importance of the deer ritual in Yaqui culture. Although traditional concerns came first to Savala in his writing, making up the larger portion of his canon, he regarded the everyday world also worthy of his creative attention. The two disparate spheres of his life—Yaqui culture and the railroad—merge in his writing.

As the Yaqui community became caught in the Depression of the early 1930s, Savala began to write, first in Spanish, but more and more in English. Although he picked up odd jobs here and there and created them when there were none to be found, none occupied his time fully, so there was time to consider his experiences, remember the stories he had been told in his youth, and begin to write in earnest. The railroad song he records in the narrative is only a small portion of the twelve-verse ballad, a variant of which he recited during his 1941 radio broadcast:

Early that morning the train pulled out
With all the material on platform cars,
Boxes of bolts and spikes and plugs,
Rail anchors, tie plates, and angle bars.
The falling rails, Oh, they rang like a bell,
For us it was only fun and play,
While some of the fellows who didn't know steel
Got scared of the work and ran away.
The rest of us then laid out the steel,
And over a mile was a long, long run.
The section foreman admired the work
He said the machinery had done.
The burrow crane, it lifted rails,
The adzing machine, it planed the ties,
The screw machine, it tightened bolts,
But still the sweat ran down our eyes.

The final verse concludes:

> *When all the rails are measured right,*
> *And the switch point down on the headblock tight,*
> *And the stock rail bolted right in line,*
> *And the frog in position nice and fine,*
> *The foreman then begins to name*
> *All the aces of number one.*
> *It takes good maulers to run a gauge,*
> *And over a mile is a long, long run.*
>
> (Savala, Oct. 26, 1941: interview
> [transcript, pp. 3–4])

The song, first written in Spanish and called "The Rails," was set to music on the guitar. It was appropriate to the Depression and Savala's immersion in railroad work. It conveys his intense pride in his gandy dancing, in his physical toughness and endurance over that "mile long run."

Risk is an aspect of railroad work Savala never stops to analyze, but demonstrates clearly in this part of his narrative. In quick succession he is witness to three serious accidents. When his foreman caught his hand in the disk-type friction clutch of the motor car, Savala, perhaps because of his command of English, served as witness and suggested a new safety procedure. In the second incident, the motor car which was used by the section hands to travel short distances on the track was being lowered from a flatcar by means of a pole ramp. Probably because of uneven distribution of weight, one pole whipped up, catching the workman's ankle. In the third case, the equipment was faulty, and a dangerous compensation was made. The air compressor was defective and the steel belt which was held in place manually with a steel bar that connected it to the drive motor was too long. When it slipped off its pulley, it struck the same foreman who had caught his hand in the clutch.

During this period with the railroad Savala held the position of flagman for a time. His job was to stop trains while work on a section of the track was completed. Crews usually attempted to complete maintenance between scheduled trains. In this case, however, the compressor used to push gravel under ties to raise the track to the standard level was directly on the track, moving with the work and necessitating redirection of freight and passenger trains. While acting as flagman, a job he obviously took very seriously, Savala formed a case for his railroad watch from a metal box used to hold the engine number on a train. Each train had such a box which enclosed a light. Cutouts of various numbers could be inserted into the front of the box so that the light in back shone through the numbers to identify each train.

At that time, all regularly scheduled trains heading east were given even numbers. All westbound scheduled trains, freight and passenger, had numbers preceded by an "X." Local trains, those both beginning and ending their run in Tucson, were simply identified by the regular engine number. Such short runs went to Nogales, Douglas, and served the mines in Hayden, carrying freight within about 150 miles of the Tucson yard. The system was later changed, with all eastbound trains having even numbers; all westbound, odd numbers; and trains not regularly scheduled having numbers preceded by a "Z."

Savala also noted that in the northern divisions of the Southern Pacific, as in the Shasta division where he spent eighteen months, trains were numbered according to northern and southerly directions. The system, however, was not determined by division, but rather by the relationship of each train to the city of San Francisco. The Southern Pacific operated on the basis of only two directions. All trains moving away from San Francisco were considered eastbound, whatever direction they may have been moving in; all moving toward San Francisco were westbound, and westbound trains normally had right-of-way over eastbounds (Wright, Feb. 11, 1976: interview).

Much of the work done during this period of Savala's employment with the Southern Pacific was renewing worn rails, particularly those rails on the outside of a curve, where the train wheels wore most heavily on the inner, gage side of the rail. Such track could either be completely replaced, or, as Savala describes, transposed—traded with the rail from the inside of the curve to allow even wear.

With the heat of the desert summer, the rails also expanded severely, requiring emergency maintenance, since such expansion set the tracks running, or moving, often so severely that the gage, or the width between the inner sides of the rails, was distorted, endangering trains by derailment. Despite rail anchors meant to prevent any downhill movement, the pressure of expansion and a downhill grade sometimes led to the track's—rails, ties, anchor plates and all— shifting, or as Savala puts it, "running" downhill (Wright, Feb. 11, 1976: interview).

In 1934, Savala again gave up his nomadic life as a section hand to return to Tucson. This time he took WPA work building a road up to Mount Lemmon, the highest peak in the Santa Catalina Mountains north of Tucson.

His decision undoubtedly had been influenced by the fast failing health of his eighty-four-year-old father Martín. The aging Yaqui had been living at Barrio Libre and participating actively in ceremonial life there for some time. Despite the long separation between them, the relationship between father and son remained warm and strong. So Refugio moved in with his brother Fernando to comfort Martín in his last days, placing his cot beside that of his father, then commenting on the Yaqui ability to meet death calmly, "taking things as they come."

As had Refugio's brother Encarnación, his father also requested the presence of the leaders of the ceremonial societies at his deathbed and died at the close of their ministrations. The death brought a brief reunion of the complete family when Refugio's mother and sister joined in the all-night death vigil and ceremonies.

After his father's death, Refugio again returned to his wanderings, but despite restless movement during 1929–1934, this was a period of intense creative growth and recognition. He had refined his poetic style, producing the major portion of his biblical epic, "Jesus, Mary and Joseph." He had drafted carefully structured dramatic versions of traditional Yaqui myths, written well over twenty vivid prose sketches of Yaqui character, composed railroad folk songs, and made a vital contribution to the rich translation of the Easter sermon, all in four years, despite the interruptions demanded by economic and personal responsibilities.

Sadly and early in Pascua rang the bell
That in my notice caused sharp pain.
Instantly, I saw her lifeless remains.
What I did after, I am not prompt to tell.

Later, as if a long journey in my way befell,
My eyes incessantly tears did drain.
I wandered as never before, in vain,
So bitter was the spot wherein I fell.

The angel of comfort in the event came:
"Take her, O God, she is no longer mine."
My despair was then enjoined by God's name.

She was reclaimed by the Master Divine
And the justice of God forever the same
In my darkest moment His light did shine.

5. ACCEPTANCE

Cycles of Grief and Joy
(1935–1943)

Savala's return to the railroad was a short one, since the death of his mother was imminent. Her final illness was neither sudden nor unexpected, but it was nonetheless devastating, because she was the center of love and stability for her son. Tomasa Flores was a woman of such great charm that Yaqui and Mexican women came daily to her home to chat. She had told Refugio many of the stories he later wrote, primarily in Yaqui, though she spoke some Spanish (Spicer, Ms. 2: 267). For Refugio, her actions and values represented the ideal of Yaqui womanhood, and at her death he felt a "great loss," described in a poem on the facing page.

The death occurred on May 3, the feast of Santa Cruz, in 1935, and the burial vigil went on simultaneously with the devotions in observance of the holy day. This celebration is sponsored by the owners of the image of "Santa Cruz," a special form of the Holy Cross representing the Virgin. Mary is patroness of the Matachin Society, and the Matachinis were dancing to honor her as well as Savala's mother. This double function is probably the reason for their refusal to dance the

Escape Dance, which ends with their disappearance into the night. Such a disappearance would not have been appropriate at a time when the Matachinis had sacred duties to the Virgin.

If Savala's dates are accurate, and they appear to be, a full year is left unaccounted for in this chapter, a year during which he traveled extensively, burying his grief in section work throughout the western states. Upon his return to the village in Tucson, he entered into an informal marriage, partly in response to economic convenience, but also in fulfillment of what he saw as the inevitable.

With work in Tucson still scarce, the couple decided to pick cotton, but Savala did return to Tucson for the feast of All Souls' Day on November 2, 1936. A year later, during his work with Dr. John Provinse at the University of Arizona, he recorded his description of the Yaqui observance of this holy day:

ANIMAN

The second day of November you will see some food served on tables at every home under the tevat kus. This, in the Indian credence, is the day when all the souls are given one day to come into the world to taste the food which their relatives serve early in the morning. It is said that the animan [souls of the dead] inhale the fragrance of the food rising in the vapor when it is hot. The person who prepares this usually serves the foods the dead relatives used to eat most. For example, for dead children, candy and fruit are on the table. For grown-ups, there is some original Indian food. At about nine o'clock, the Indian priest whom we call "Maestro" goes from table to table. He performs the "responsos," the mass for the dead, and the "vigilia" when requested by the person serving the food for the dead. It is very much believed that the responsos, vigilia, and mass for the dead are a great relief for the departed souls. The Maestro gets some money for either the vigilia or mass, and the food that is served on the table also goes to him and the women who assist him in the ceremonial hymns. There are several Maestros, but sometimes the rites are not finished until after nightfall.

The next day, all these things are done in the cemetery. The people's requests for their dead relatives are performed at the foot of the tombs.

Savala again returned to Tucson for the early December fiesta in honor of St. Francis, celebrated at the Papago Indian mission of San Xavier south of the city. A year later, a professor talked to Refugio about attending the San Xavier celebration and asked if he were Catholic. Savala replied that he "could not deny it, because his family had always been Catholic." But he had seen many other religions and "really had no religion." He said that, despite this ambivalence, he always went to a Catholic church when he came to a new town, noting that there are certain things which must be done if you are a Catholic. However, he felt that if they were not done, life was just the same and nothing happened (Spicer 1936: fieldnotes).

At the San Xavier fiesta, Refugio's sister Agustina delayed his return, asking his help in the arrangements for his niece's wedding. Angelita's wedding was performed in the village of Guadalupe near Phoenix, the largest Yaqui settlement in Arizona at that time. Immediately following the wedding was a lutupahko, the ceremony which closes the formal period of one year of mourning for a deceased relative. For the first twenty-four hours of the ceremony the mourners, who wear black cords around their necks, refrain from work and engage in prayers. The second day there is a fiesta with feasting and dancers, after the cords have been burned in clay bowls. The ceremony is usually held around the date of the first anniversary of the death, but, in this case, eighteen months had elapsed.

At about this time, Savala began his association with Dr. Edward Spicer, who was doing anthropological fieldwork at Pascua Village. It was a period of severe depression for Refugio, who had begun to drink. In December 1936, during his first intimate conversation with Dr. Spicer, Savala admitted that he often wished to die and that his father before him had had the same desire (Spicer, Ms. 2:1). He had also told Miss Richey, his Pascua school teacher, that he thought he might throw himself under a freight train, as a comrade of his apparently had done (Spicer 1936: fieldnotes). Through study of his narrative, his creative work, and descriptions about him by associates, it is clear that talk of suicide was not just self-indulgence or the manifestation of a temporary black mood.

The conflicts and contradictions which he faced in living a marginal existence on the fringes of two cultures pressured him dangerously, so that he found life not quite bearable.

There were enduring consolations—his intense feeling for Yaqui culture, his pride in his work, his love of nature, and his writing—but the depression and despair would not pass, and for a time, when it was most severe, he even abandoned writing. The jubilant spirit of the following poem, written almost ten years before, was never recaptured. Its tone of youthful expectation and resiliency contrasts sharply with the solemnity of the poem on his mother's death:

> *How things are natural in the wild*
> *When the flowers, streams, and the light*
> *And the trees offer the shade so mild,*
> *And protect the feeble bird aflight*
> *Like the mother's tender love for a child,*
> *Add to pleasure the most sensual delight.*
>
> *Lie on the sand beneath a cottonwood,*
> *The shade so pleasant and the sky.*
> *Either for pleasure or livelihood,*
> *Watch the fowls, how they fly.*
> *The Creator to them and all is good,*
> *And with good so vastly, all supplies.*
>
> *Let time be as useless as can be.*
> *Far away I go at evening*
> *Where the beauty I love, I see,*
> *Where happiness abides enlivening,*
> *Describing this loveliness to me;*
> *There sorrow changes its meaning.*
>
> *Here I sit in solemn reminiscence*
> *Contemplating the evening fall.*
> *Majestic clouds float in magnificence,*
> *The setting sun a golden ball.*
> *Clouds change to roses in the scene,*
> *Blur the mountains like purple walls.*

Nature's cries come to my ears,
When restless people its beauty destroy.
And the birds flee where men appear.
Humanity perverse! Enjoy!
Wrecking this loveliness so dear,
In which the perceptive senses rejoice.

Mortals of the trodden ground
Now want roads on mountains.
Perhaps God will their speech confound
As he did at Babel, bringing pain,
Making speech a confusing sound,
So naught of its power did remain.

Characteristic of Savala's mature writing is the following tale, a tragedy of cruelty, death, and revenge. While the content and theme have no direct relation to the events of his life, and the story itself is his version of a known tale, the sense of anguish and hopelessness pervading it parallels the sense of alienation and bleakness experienced by Savala in this period of his life. Even the introduction of the story attests the frequency of tragedy in Yaqui existence:

THE SON OF NOTHING

Things like this so frequently happen among the Yaqui Indian race, very little notice is taken. This event happened in Cumuripa, Sonora, Mexico.

Maria was an orphan girl, cared for in the home of foster parents. This girl, in spite of being the subject of all inclemency, grew up to be a beautiful maiden. Her foster mother strictly opposed her getting married, not because she loved her, but because without her, she would have to do all the housework.

One day a young man, Dionisio, of Mayo Indian and Mexican mix, arrived in Cumuripa. As he was a clever young man, he soon won Maria's friendship without her parents knowing the least of it. They kept the secret for some time until it was discovered at the girl's home that she was guilty of maternity.

Her foster mother threatened and questioned the girl, but she denied her lover, and her mother began to suspect her own husband. After she had punished Maria severely, she sent her away. The girl was very glad to escape alive from the angry woman. She went to her lover and told him about her condition. A few weeks later, Maria was with Nicho, and her life was even worse than before. Nicho treated her cruelly, and when the child was about to be born, he went away and left her to the mercy of her own fate.

In the neighborhood lived an old couple who took Maria into their home and took care of her in the worst of her situation. The child was born and the mother died. The good old woman took the baby. It was a very precious thing to her, and she took care of it in the manner of a mother.

Gregorio was the name of the boy after they christened him. In the home of these good people, he was growing under their good care, with not even the slightest idea that he was an orphan. Through relationships among the village children, he learned that he was not the son of the two good old souls whom he dearly called father and mother, so one day the boy cautiously questioned his parents about this matter. They were very much disappointed, but they loved the child so much and knew that someday he would know the truth and that to tell him a lie would be illicit. They took him inside and carefully told him about the misfortune of his mother and the cruelty of his father with her. The story made the boy somewhat sorrowful, but he felt the love of his foster parents so tenderly stimulated that he soon forgot all about it because he loved and respected them exceedingly.

After twelve years, Nicho was seen once more in Cumuripa. He had come to the village just for old time's sake. Nicho was a handsome young man, neatly dressed in the fancy style of a Mexican "Don." Rego saw him and knew that this man was his father, but he did not try to see or speak to him, for which his foster parents were thankful. Finally Nicho disappeared and was never seen again in Cumuripa.

Rego was living happily with his parents and was very proud to have them. Without them life seemed impossible. But as anybody knows, good things in this world don't last for a lifetime. In the midst of his blissful young life, one of the good old souls had to part with him forever. He was fifteen years old when the old man called him to his side. He was very sick, but he told the boy these things: "Our children did fail to live for us and thus we came into old age. But in the extremity of our lives, God saw our grief and sent thee to make our days of old age very happy. Likewise, I am very pleased that in all, God did answer my prayers. Not a feeble child do I leave thee in the world, for thou art a man prepared to meet all the difficulties that life will present to you." In this manner he spoke and died.

Rego considered this the first difficulty to meet and go through. From his foster father he had received all the benefits that a poor man could offer. He was taught to read and write Spanish and cipher a little. And as for manual work, he was good in almost any kind of work, so he remained and was duly supporting his old mother.

Three more years made Rego eighteen years old, and the last and most precious thing he had in the world also had to leave him. Now, this was another enormous blow, and with no one to share his grief with him, he was the most miserable man in the world. Cumuripa, the village where he was born, and the places that he loved about as much as he did love his foster parents, all had to be abandoned. He was going away from Cumuripa for the first time in his life. Just like his father, Rego disappeared and was never seen again in Cumuripa.

Two years later in Tucson, Arizona, in the northwestern part of the city, Rego was going along the road. He saw a man approach him. With his keen perception, he recognized him. In a moment the man came close to Rego, who then shouted: "Thou art the man I have long searched for. I have found thee! Now prepare to defend thyself. Thou art going to get plenty of a licking." The other man, in surprise, could not even speak and the young man stared at him. Finally the man said, "There seems to be no reason that we should fight."

"Thou never doest reason," Rego said and rushed upon him. The other man, being a fighter of great capacity in self-defense, matched him in the battle. For about thirty minutes, they fought desperately; in the finish, Gregorio came out victorious.

The defeated said, "That thou art a good fighter, I do not deny, and that thou hast beaten me is also all right, but who thou art, I know not."

Rego said, tembling with rage, "I am the son ... of nothing that was born when my mother died in Cumuripa ... you"—And he almost struck him again, but Nicho was saved by another man and Rego was taken away.

[203]

This dramatization of loss and grief is related to Savala's own grief. Further, there is the need for both Rego and Savala to abandon the place of suffering. Though the two sets of events are not parallel, the themes of man's mortality and frail happiness are linked to Savala's own feelings of frustration and anger and grief. The protagonist in the tale can act these feelings out, but Savala turns his emotions upon himself in quiet desperation.

Not that all of life was bleak and humorless for Savala in his maturity, for he retained his sharp perception of the comic, as his discussion of memorizing his social security number indicates. But even in that there is a touch of irony.

The sense of isolation is acute when Savala writes of returning to Pascua to live alone in a hut on his brother's property without Catalina. When he left Pascua to work in Globe, a series of events began which would keep him from participation in Yaqui life even longer than his stint in the Southern Pacific Shasta division had. In September of 1941, Savala reported for draft induction. Though he was not a citizen of the United States, his narrative reflects patriotism and appreciation of his life in the U.S. These feelings led him to enter the service despite being past the draft age limit.

His adjustment to the structured system of military life is remarkably smooth, considering his cultural background, but years of service with the railroad, responding to the orders of foremen and living in almost military section-hand quarters, made the transition easier. His account of his military career is marked by extremes in style. Much of the text is a rather flat reportorial prose, meticulous in detail. This unembellished writing, however, is broken periodically by dramatization of particularly memorable events, as when orders are "barked out," catching the abruptness of the military way. The mystery of the recruits' destination is intensified by the shouts of the experienced troops from the darkness, "You'll be sorry." An occasional bit of wry humor also breaks the text. "Oh, the sergeants!" and "You start to like where you are, and you have to move," are the universal complaints of service men. But in Refugio's tone, they are musings rather than grievances. He takes his orders and performs his duties seriously, but also with goodwill and humor.

Having more than fulfilled his obligation to his adopted nation, Refugio again felt the urge to return to his family and people. With assurance that the Southern Pacific would employ him, he showed no reluctance to leave the army and considerable pleasure in retracing those familiar SP tracks. Once Savala reaches San Francisco, however, a sense of regret enters the narrative as the isolation from his army buddies and the loss of his rank confront him and apparently motivate the drinking spree which follows.

On his trip south, the encounter with the woman on the train illustrates Savala's sense of alienation, as does the brief encounter with an old railroad worker in Los Angeles. But when he crosses into Arizona and is reunited with his family in Yuma, his vitality and good spirits reassert themselves. His warm relations with his family seem to restore his spirit, and, with his welcome in Tucson by Fernando, his long and often lonely journey is completed.

The years from 1935 to 1943 mark a distinct change in the character and narrative of Refugio Savala. Loss pervades his life, and the emptiness is filled with a sense of isolation so oppressive that his depression often borders on despair and the lure of suicide haunts him. Yet he does not give up on life, turning instead to the elements in life which have always brought him consolation: his work, his family, his love of nature and his country, and an enduring trust in Divine help. Still, the grief of his mature years will not admit the restoration of the unified sense of affirmation of life that pervades the earlier portion of his narrative. No longer can he write of the joys of life as he did ten years earlier when he composed this poem:

> It's springtime again in Pascua.
> We are all together again.
> Happiness crowns the little village.
> Laughter replaces the thought of pain.
>
> Yonder the tiny bell is rung.
> Its rhythm is symbol to rejoice.
> The vespers of evening are sung
> In rhythmic contrast of voice.

Palm, gourd, and crown, dress the Monarch.
In time as the music's reply,
The dancers jubilantly march,
Rockets like meteors adorn the sky.

Heedless of time, hard toil, and need,
The pastor Maestro sings the Psalms.
This is grown and children's creed,
And God all pains tenderly calms.

To praise God all the humble kneel
In the Altar of the Temple,
Thanksgiving and praise of goodwill
In all respects the others resemble.

Pascua was chosen by my people
When Saint John the Baptist
Sought for water with his feeble
Credence to celebrate a feast.

Now we live happy in our village.
We love, laugh, sing, dance, and weep.
Style, food, and the other language,
Unchanged our custom will keep.

The music of the violin and harp
Is beautiful in this style.
Those people who learned it as art
Also tackle trouble with a smile.

Though it was springtime in Pascua when Refugio returned, the Savalas could never all be together again, and the laughter he describes has been overwhelmed by pain and "thought of pain." Yet the rituals he pictures endure, the spirit of the people goes on, and like them Refugio himself determines to "tackle trouble with a smile." Though he can no longer "celebrate" or remain "unchanged," he wills to go on, despite the trouble and the pain, "heedless of time, hard toil, and need."

6. PERSEVERANCE

The World of Letters
(1944–1969)

With Savala's return to Tucson, he resumed his work for the railroad and also continued to act as a collaborator with professors in the University of Arizona anthropology department. In the first material collected by Dr. John Provinse in 1935 are several prose sketches of crafts and other traditional Yaqui occupations in Mexico. In a short essay, Savala briefly describes the roles of several different craftsmen:

THE CHANDLER

The man who makes the candles for the churches in the villages prepares the good wax from the bees and other cheap material from the fat of the deer. He works similarly to the Mexican chandler, and the soap maker also does the work in the same manner.

All these things that the Indian used to work at are almost lost to us: the saddle makers, shoemakers, blacksmiths, silver, and goldsmiths. Among those remaining, we only find the bricklayer, plasterer, and carpenter.

When the Indian had wool in great quantity, there were some expert weavers in the villages who made some blankets of high grade. These same men made the tincture to color the blankets and woolen bands used as belts in the Mexican style. The color never faded.

The hat maker works the palm leaves in the most exquisite way to make the rough work hat. This same person makes the palm *petate*, which is used as a rug or as a bed to save the blanket from the dust.

The *batellero* is the man who makes the *bateas*, which are used for kneading the dough for the tortillas and the long wooden spoon. These things are very useful for the women. This same man also makes the canoes from the big cotton-wood logs. These are used in the rivers.

The cowboys are all good rope makers—bristle or leather. In the Indian country the majority of the men are good horse riders. When the Indians came into the United States, they gave up all the things they had learned.

More fully developed character sketches are "The Fisherman" and "The Mescalero." In the first, Savala implies the danger of the contract between a female sea deity and the Yaqui fisherman, who must supply an innocent to satisfy the old lady of the sea:

THE FISHERMAN

The men in this business are said to have taken their art from the old lady of the sea, whom they call grandmother. It is said that by enchantment they can go into the mansion of the old lady, and she gives them a handful of popcorn and lets them go. This popcorn is the bait which the fishermen use, thereby getting a large catch even in a poor place. The mansion of the old lady is said to exist under the mountain called Tacal-Lime [The Fork] in the Yaqui coast toward the sunset. The person receiving the benefit, the fisherman, is required to take another person to the old woman, and if he fails to do so, he is taken himself into the depths. The person taken by the fisherman is usually one who does not know anything about the sea.

The fisherman works by net or by the Indian method of fishing when tide ebbs and the sea goes far out of its bed. A wall is built before it returns again. Wooden stakes are driven separately in the sand to fence the returning water in this net fence. Only big fishes are caught, for the space of the net allows small fish to escape and return with the tide. The man working on the wall usually works early in the morning before sunrise. He begins to select the good fish and throw the bad ones back into the water. In this manner he loads up his mules and departs with them into the village, where he surely sells and trades all his load.

This man is also making a living out of his work, for there are people who don't fish but do other works which the fisherman does not. So in trading with these workers, the fisherman gets along very well.

The mescalero, under no threat of danger, expresses a reverence for nature as he chooses his plants carefully and speaks apologetically before striking with his hatchet:

MESCALERO

There is another man who makes his living by carrying edible mescal from the mountains. This man gets it high in the mountains and carries it on his back to where he has a mule or burro. When the load is finished, it is sometimes taken into the village unprepared; otherwise, the mescalero prepares it at his camp in the forest. A large hole is dug in the ground, and it is filled with dry massive wood. The fire is made in the afternoon, and when the wood has all burned out, some big hard stones are cast upon the live coals, till they cover the bottom. Then the mescal is placed upon the hot stones, the bottom up. When the hole is filled to the rim, the mescal is covered with earth. It is left in all night, and in the morning it is uncovered and dug out, thoroughly cooked and ready to eat. But if you eat the hot mescal you know that it is a good laxative. The mescalero brings the prepared mescal into the village and soon sells or trades it for the things he needs. The man doing this work has a sure market for his goods, because the mescal is preferred in large quantities and is obtained through great difficulty up in the mountains.

A man who makes his living by this trade usually has a herd of burros to carry the mescal into the village.

This man addresses the young mescal in this manner. "This one is now whistling. I shall not take it." When he finds a ripe one, he talks to it also: "Thou art deaf. I must take thee to the village and thou mayest be as food for my people." Then he throws the hatchet upon it and cuts it and throws it upon his shoulders and carries it down the mountain singing the song of the Mescaleros.

Each of the brief essays above is a portrait of the Sonoran Yaqui life which was lost by those who came to the United States; yet its lore is preserved and kept vital through Savala's enduring interest in all aspects of his culture and his willingness to preserve and convey that information in the form of literature.

Savala, however, was not particularly willing to perform publicly, as can be seen in his obvious lack of enthusiasm about being scheduled to participate in the radio program he describes. His annoyance, however, seems not at the actual program but derives from the manner in which he was informed of his part in it after arrangements had already been made and announced. Once involved, Refugio's characteristic enthusiasm and good humor emerge. The script of the program provides a record of many of the aspects of Refugio Savala the Yaqui writer and student of Yaqui culture already seen in various portions of his autobiography. For instance, he summarized the origins and history of the Yaquis in Arizona briefly in the following portion of the radio script:

No one knows how long my people lived beside the great Yaqui River, farming the land. When the Spanish padres came, the peaceful Yaquis carried them upon their shoulders with a great multitude who trudged along to all the villages. There was some strife, but not very serious.

As time passed the Mexicans took some of the land from Yaquis and gave it to Mexicans. Then there was trouble to a miserable point.

My father knew those terrible days. Many Yaquis were sent to Yucatán and killed. But my father escaped and worked on the railroad from Benson to Nogales. My mother stayed in Magdalena, Mexico. I was born at one of those times of trouble for the Yaquis in Magdalena. My mother was put in prison, with many others. She was the only one to escape. She had spirit. At last my father brought all of us and our few possessions and our burros to Arizona.

In Arizona we Yaquis are very grateful, always endeavoring to maintain ourselves unstained, to respect laws, to educate our children, and to work hard.

(Savala, Oct. 26, 1941:
interview [transcript, pp. 2–3])

During the course of the half-hour broadcast, Savala also read from several of his poems, sang a portion of his railroad ballad, "Steel Stew," and retold part of the "Singing Tree" legend. The program, entitled "A Yaqui Troubadour;" succeeded in displaying the range and versatility of his writing talent. Refugio modestly accepted the praise of his fellow workers and acquaintances and immediately returned to the more prosaic events of his life, which at this time included loading ice into refrigerator cars conveying western produce to eastern markets. Ice blocks were prodded down a trough onto the tops of the Pacific Fruit Express cars and then pushed into upper compartments of the cars to chill the produce inside. This was heavy work, since the blocks were massive in size.

Dismissed from this job, Savala took up landscaping and building trades again. By September of 1943 he had again acquired regular employment with the Southern Pacific, for the first time working on a bridge gang rather than regular section maintenance. His description of the process of building the two bridges in the Ligurta section, east of Yuma, is noteworthy for its detail. Less clear is Savala's narration of the event which caused his dismissal from the crew. The cause of the conflict is obscure, especially considering Savala's previous respect for foremen and his lack of aggressive behavior throughout the narrative. The outcome of the incident is not clearly stated, although he implies that he was fired. Actually he was relieved only temporarily and after a short layoff returned to work under his own foreman (Savala, April 1976: interview). Work with the number five bridge crew was, however, the last full-time position Refugio held with the railroad. Temporary work and odd jobs are the pattern in his subsequent employment, with drinking bouts which eventually affected his health.

The seriousness of Refugio's drinking problem becomes apparent as he relates his nightmare hallucinations. It was so serious, in fact, that two curers were summoned, one Papago and one Yaqui. His visions were ominous and violent, yet Savala, true to his previous behavior in risky situations, confronted the forces that threatened him, and in doing so overcame them. In contrast to the grim images of the dreams are the ministrations of the curers, who gently encourage meditation and sleep and invoke herbs and scripture to cure Refugio's alcohol madness. As in the curing of his bewitched body in his youth, the same methods are observed in healing his disturbed mind, faith being a key factor in the success of the process.

Restored to health, Savala returned to construction work but also continued to collaborate with Mrs. Painter in recording information about Yaqui culture. Having already given considerable account of the role of the Deer Dancer in Yaqui ceremonies to the University of Arizona anthropology department, he gave further information on the origins and significance of the Pascola Dancers to Mrs. Painter, describing in detail their performance. The following essay discusses both the origin and the functions of these ceremonial figures:

THE PASCOLA, SON OF THE DEVIL

A young maiden was wandering in a deep forest and met a handsome young man. She mated with him and conceived and bore a boy who was very ugly. The young man who deceived the maiden was truly the Devil. The boy, as he grew, was conscious of his father being the Devil. This was apparent in that the boy was fiercely ugly in appearance, and his mother was continuously being tormented by the Devil. To save his mother, the boy sought Divine help. He was instructed what he should do by the spirit of God in a dream. He made three skyrockets of high dimension and placed a tevat kus on the eastside patio. During the night watch to *alba* [dawn], he walked to the cross and stood in front of it facing the sunrise. Saying, "San Miguel Arcángel," he lit the three rockets to explode in the air. The Devil is very sensitive and hearing this explosion drove him away to darkness. The boy's face, which is the present Pascola mask, became a human face again, and he walked back triumphantly, shouting and dancing, a natural boy. For his performance, his father taught him with a satyr's piper and drummer. Now this Pascola dance is seen in every ceremonial fiesta. Also, after the boy was on God's side, his mother was saved from the Devil.

The Pascola came into practical use for ceremonies for departed baby souls. His outfit to dance in is blanket pants

[212]

wrapped on his legs to the waist. The pants are held in place by a leather girdle that goes over them. On that girdle hang a number of brass chimes, jingle-bell fashion. The largest of these bells hangs from the middle of the belt in front. He also wears the *teneboim, buichia karim* ["worm houses" in Yaqui slang]. These are bags in which larvae have been hatched out. They are sewn on a long chamois string to be wound on the legs below the knees. With these rattles on his legs, he dances to the music of violin and harp. To dance to the flute and drums, he wears the goat-face mask, for the piper in the forest was a goat from waist down to feet. The goat-face is carved out of a solid block of light wood; the long white whiskers are of cow tail and eyebrow bristles. In the ceremony for a dead baby, one Pascola serves the night performance. At evening, the Pascola is brought into the dance ramada by the *moro*. He comes in like a very old man, wearing the mask. At this time the violin and harp play *canario,* the opening music. The moro leading him leans the stick on the harp and leaves him, and the Pascola starts asking help of his own saints: *"Santo Koarepa empo ba'ap hiapsane neania ian tukapo"* (Saint Bullfrog, you who sit living in the water, help me tonight). *"Santo Motcho'okol itom aye walupeta venak konak neania"* (Saint Hornytoad as our Lady of Guadalupe, as it is your crown, help me, thou). *"Santo Rey Ki'chul empo hekapo sontaokame neania"* (Saint King Cricket, thou in air, who has soldiers, help me, thou). Then to limber up, he does a few dancing steps; holding the cane under his left arm, he turns to the flute and drum music. Then the moro walks him to the altar in front of the cross. He lights the three skyrockets, and they both go to the altar and kneel down to say the Lord's Prayer and Ave María a Gloria. When he comes to his dancing area, he dances the canario and stops the music. At this moment the flute and drum burst into a rapid sound of music. To this he dances, howling. This exciting joy is to enact what the boy did after he sent the Devil away.

After he stops the flute and drum music, he starts the salutation. He stands facing the sunrise and makes the sign of the cross with the cane saying, *"Liohta achai, Liohta u'usi, Liohpitu Santo hibau amen"* (God the Father, God the Son, God Spirit Holy, always forever, amen.) He moves, facing north, and does the same performance and words. These four performances are all done as the Pascola stands in the center. He starts greeting men by their trades: *"Emesu masorom Dios e'emchaniabu"* (All you deer hunters, God aid you), *"Emesu*

[213]

kowileom Dios e'emchaniabu" (And all you wild boar hunters, God aid you), *"Emesu baiteom Dios e'emchaniabu"* (And you miners, God aid you). This is in the dead baby ceremony, at evening. The baby is in an altar with angelical decorations, attended by the godparents.

To do the *caminaroa* is a trip to the distant altar cross. The flute and drum player goes. He ties a loop around his neck, beating with his right hand, playing the flute with his left hand, walking. The holy figures are carried by the godparents who go in one group ahead of the procession. In the second group comes the baby and the Maestro who sings the *alabado* [hymn]. The Pascola with the mask on his face and the hand timbrel goes between the two groups. He is howling at intervals as in the beginning. At the end of each alabado a *kueto* [rocket] is lit and goes up and explodes high overhead in the dark. From a distance, they look like meteors. When the procession comes to the altar, the Pascola comes to his place [under the ramada] for the night.

The Pascola stands in the middle facing the crowd and greets all together. He asks if anyone stepped on a thorn, *"Kahabesosak bo'opo?"* (No one got a thorn stuck on the road?). The reason for this question is that all visitors are to accompany in the procession. The journey is done early in the evening for the dead baby ceremony. From then on, violin and harp music go by different frequencies [with different names]: at evening, *campania;* midnight, *una vahti;* dawn, *vakothia weye.* The moro, as manager, has nothing to do about these frequencies in music. The tampaleo has to follow these: *chiham yoawa* (wild animals); *wukitu lobo* (prairie wolf); *konisa'akame* (crow rattle snake). After *vakothia weye* [the music] changes again to campanilla at sunrise for the contradanza. Contradanza is borrowed music, and anyone can borrow [volunteer] and dance the piece he borrows. The tampaleo plays *Yori numukia* (drunken Mexican), and the Pascola dances and imitates a drunken Yori's talk. After that, the morning canario is tremulously played by violin and harp. The Pascola, with the mask on, apologizes to the visitors for his bad behavior and talk. He asks forgiveness and gives them thanks, turns around, dances the canario and stops. This is how the dead baby ceremony is ended.

Only in the baby ceremonies is there one Pascola. In [all others] ... there are two or more. At baptisms and weddings they wear civilian clothes and hat, the chime girdle, and leg

[214]

rattles and dance the music of contradanza. Only his shoes, he takes off. Borrowers dance with shoes on. The Pascola takes for granted constitutional freedom of speech. He answers all questions harshly and comically with mocking humor. For that, he apologizes and asks forgiveness from all visitors. He also delivers a closing sermon.

Of particular interest in this piece is Savala's integration of a traditional tale concerning the source of the Pascola dance with its application to contemporary practice. The tale purports to explain the inclusion of the Pascolas' clowning in the religious ceremonies of the Yaquis; the young boy, in gaining the restoration of his human form, legitimized his role by choosing to be on "God's side."

As Savala's narrative draws toward its close, he accounts for his days and months, and even years, less completely, telescoping the span of time from the mid-forties to the late fifties to relate only major events, such as his hospitalization for surgery and his recovery. Although constantly fighting the problem of alcoholism, Refugio remains active. Neither his physical nor mental state can overcome his determination to continue useful work both landscaping and collaborating with Mrs. Painter, a project that required long hours of translation and discussion. With his release from the hospital, he took on still another project, contributing his skill in the Yaqui language to a study in linguistics. In Lynne Scoggins Crumrine's monograph *The Phonology of Arizona Yaqui,* published in 1961, she describes in detail the methods she employed in eliciting material from Refugio and also from his brother Fernando. She states:

Four eliciting techniques were employed in order to get materials to be recorded. The Indiana University Archives of the Languages of the World eliciting drawings were presented to the informant. These evoked long and complex utterances.

Next, short English utterances were presented for translation.

The third type of eliciting was directed toward obtaining

[215]

directional and relational material of use for future morpho-
logical study as well as for phonological study. A three-
dimensional model of a Yaqui house and yard, with ramada
and other typical items, was placed before the informant.
Matchstick figures of a man, dog, horse, bird, and housefly
were manipulated into different positions with respect to the
other elements of the model. An effort was made to cause the
stick figures to represent actions that the animals they sym-
bolized would normally perform. The pantomime was done
largely without English, except to identify each matchstick
figure to the informant.

Savala specifically recalls the use of the stick figures in his
narrative. In her book, Crumrine records in Yaqui, gives literal translation, and provides free translation of Refugio's
descriptions of the stick figures, as in the following example
from her text:

1. *nim hamanak*   *boo bo'oka* + 2. *niika*   + *huyata*
   here where-some road lies   of-this   tree

bahi   tatakalaim awaka'apo   ne wa'am siika   ne 'au   waate
three forks   points-at   I   by   went I   to-it remember

#3. *hunae bo'owi*   #4. '*intok* + *nii   huya hunuk* + *kaa inien*
    that   road-on   and   this tree   then   not like-this

sialiakan   ian   intok uhuyoisi   + sawak
green-was now and   beautifully   leaves-with

1. There's a road going through here somewhere. 2. This
tree with the three forks, I remember when I went by it. 3.
on this road. 4. This tree was so green and now it's beautiful
with leaves (Crumrine 1961:13).

This study in which Refugio cooperated with enthusiasm,
like his work on the Yaqui Easter ceremony, has become a
standard reference for the study of the Yaqui language and
has aided in establishing the written form of the language for
both Yaquis and others.

Savala's continuing work with Muriel Painter on the Easter sermon was progressing, and by this time she had also
encouraged him to write his personal narrative, segments of
which he regularly turned over to her. But unexpectedly his

work was curtailed as a result of the paralyzing stroke he suffered which brought him very near to death. Rigorous therapy aided him in regaining partial use of his left leg and enabled him to walk with a cane. His arm, however, remained paralyzed, a disability he later blamed on the constant use of the splint or sling (Savala, April 27, 1976: interview). Yet despite his handicaps, he regained strength and continued to work on his personal narrative and on Yaqui material for Mrs. Painter, only briefly interrupted by the series of moves from his niece's home to various nursing homes in the early 1960s. His interest in Yaqui ceremonies was still lively, and he returned to his brother's house in Pascua Village to participate in them. During this visit there in the spring of 1963 to view the Easter ceremony, the death of his nephew demanded his reinvolvement in family and ceremonial affairs. He not only took charge of the civil arrangements but organized and financed the greater part of the death ceremony in the village, revealing a patriarchal role. This role is further indicated during the following year when he succeeded in rescuing the family property from confiscation when Fernando was unable to obtain necessary funds.

During these years of brief visits to his family and long months in nursing homes, Refugio became more and more influenced by the women who visited him to discuss religion and conduct services.

During the years from 1963 to 1967 his growing interest in the message of the women from the Assembly of God Church developed, and in May of 1967, he announced his conversion at their chapel in Pascua Village. He rose before the congregation and said, "It has been revealed to me that the Yaquis are in darkness and that the translation of the Bible into Yaqui will bring them to understanding" (Savala, May 3, 1976: interview). Members of the congregation agreed with his decision to begin translation of the Old Testament, and he began the following day, May 3, 1967. In an interview he explained his translation work, saying that he felt it had been God's plan for him and the reason that he had been saved from the perils of the Mexican persecutions as an infant. He

[217]

viewed his work with people from the university as preparation for the task of translation, work which he vowed would go on as long as he lived. Three years later, in 1979, he was still keeping his vow, working with vigor and dedication on his Old Testament project several hours each day.

After his move to the Tucson veterans hospital in 1969, Savala ceased to attend ceremonies at Pascua Village. However, he continued to discuss them and other historical and cultural aspects of Yaqui life with his friends and family.

Refugio's character and life have been perhaps best summarized by Edward H. Spicer, a professor with whom the Yaqui began work in 1936:

> His conflicts are not cultural ones, but those of a sensitive man frustrated by the ordinary events of living, such as death, disappointment in love, and the difficulties of making a living. He has never been interested in social status, but remains entirely outside the world of status either in his own or any other society. His devotion to Yaqui culture is to be explained only in terms of the devotion of any man to what he has been brought up to and knows something about. He is the creative man who loves whatever is before him, and for its own sake (Spicer, Ms. 2: 274).

In one sense Refugio Savala has always been a man living on the margin, caught between Mexican and American nationalities, Yaqui and Anglo cultures, manual labor and artistic endeavor. In another sense, however, he has been a man very much at the center, for his gifts of observation and literary expression have allowed him to penetrate the boundaries of nationality, culture, and occupation to record the unique character of his people, and perhaps more importantly, of himself.

BIBLIOGRAPHY

WORKS BY REFUGIO SAVALA

Published Materials

Painter, Muriel Thayer, Refugio Savala, Ignacio Alvarez
    1955   *A Yaqui Easter Sermon.* University of Arizona Social
           Science Bulletin 26: 1–74.

Savala, Refugio
    1945   "Two Yaqui Legends." *Arizona Quarterly* 1:20–24.

Manuscripts

The following manuscripts all are on file in the Arizona State
Museum Archive in Tucson. They are undated unless otherwise indicated.

    POETRY

    Indian Poetry
    Cañada del Oro
    It's Springtime in Pascua
    Jesus, Mary and Joseph (parts 1–5)
    My Mother (5/2/1935)
    Steel Stew

PROSE

A Harper's Legend (1936)
Animan
History of the Yaqui People
Marita and Pacisco
Mescalero
Otam Kami
Pasco Ohola
Peter and Jesus
Prophecy of Conquest
San Pedro
Sionima
Son of Nothing
Story of the Big Tree
The Bee Hunt
The Chandler
The Conception and Birth of Christ
The Coyote
The Deer
The Deer Hunter
The Fisherman
The Lion
The Origin of Pasco Ohola
The Powderman
The Raccoon
The Rain
The Second Great Event
Witchcraft

WORKS PERTAINING TO REFUGIO SAVALA

Cosulich, Bernice
6/20/41   "Yaqui Poet Produces Belles Lettres Here." *Arizona Daily Star,* 2, 23.

Crumrine, Lynne Scoggins
1961   *The Phonology of Arizona Yaqui.* Anthropological Papers of the University of Arizona, #5. Tucson: University of Arizona Press.

Savala, Refugio
7/1/41 Interview with Carlton Wilder on Yaqui Deer Dancers and Singers, and Pascolas.

10/26/41 Interview entitled "A Yaqui Troubadour," Arizona Broadcasting Company, University of Arizona. Transcript.

1976 Interviews with Kathleen M. Sands verifying autobiography editing, factual information, and poetry influences. April 20, 27; May 3.

Spicer, Edward H.
12/1/1936 Fieldnotes on Spicer's first meeting with Refugio Savala. Pascua Village, Arizona.

7/5/41 Fieldnotes on Refugio Savala's attitudes toward women and religion. Pascua Village, Arizona.

Manuscript 1. A Short History of Pascua. Arizona State Museum Archive.

Manuscript 2. People of Pascua. Arizona State Museum Archive.

Manuscript 3. Refugio Savala, Yaqui Poet. Arizona State Museum Archive.

OTHER REFERENCES

Arizona Daily Citizen
6/1/1899 Stagecoach Advertisement, p. 3.

Arizona Daily Star
9/18/18 News article.

8/24/75 "Tucson's Bicentennial, 1775–1975," p. 23.

Donovan, Judy, *Arizona Daily Star* reporter
11/18/75 .Interview on Tucson history and geography.

McKissick, Charles, Southern Pacific Transportation Company
11/17/75   Interview on railroading terms and practices.

Myrick, David
12/29/75   Interview on railroad terms and practices.

1975   *Railroads of Arizona: The Southern Roads.* Berkeley: Howell North.

Rios, Theodore
6/22/74   Interview on wheat harvesting on San Xavier Papago Reservation.

7/17/74   Interview on saguaro fruit harvesting on Papago Reservation.

Spicer, Edward H.
1940   *Pascua, A Village in Arizona.* Chicago: University of Chicago.

1974   "Highlights of Yaqui History." *The Indian Historian* 7:1–14.

Wilder, Carlton
1963   *A Yaqui Deer Dance.* Anthropological Papers No. 66. Bulletin of Bureau of American Ethnology 186: 1–208.

Wright, Jim, Southern Pacific Transportation Company
2/11/76   Interview on railroad equipment.

2/26/76   Interview on railroad equipment.

INDEX